Arguing Development Policy: Frames and Discourses

edited by

RAYMOND APTHORPE and DES GASPER

FRANK CASS
LONDON • PORTLAND, OR

in association with
The European Association of Development Research
and Training Institutes (EADI), Geneva

EADI

First Published 1996 in Great Britain by
FRANK CASS AND COMPANY LIMITED
Newbury House, 900 Eastern Avenue
London IG2 7HH

and in the United States of America by
FRANK CASS
c/o ISBS
5804 N.E. Hassalo Street, Portland, Oregon 97213-3644

British Library Cataloguing in Publication Data

A catalogue record for this book is available
from the British Library

ISBN 0 7146 4294 0 (pbk)

Library of Congress Cataloging-in-Publication Data

A catalog record for this book is available
from the Library of Congress

This group of studies first appeared in a Special Issue on
'Arguing Development Policy: Frames and Discourses' of the
European Journal of Development Research, Vol.8, No.1, June 1996
published by Frank Cass & Co. Ltd.

Typeset by Frank Cass & Co. Ltd.

Printed by Antony Rowe Ltd., Chippenham, Wilts.

Book —(R)

Contents

Introduction: Discourse Analysis and Policy Discourse

DES GASPER and RAYMOND APTHORPE

Introducing a collection on policy discourses and argumentation in international development, this review clarifies meanings of 'discourse analysis', and emphasises that discourse analysis requires systematic attention to texts as well as contexts. It outlines work in policy discourse analysis, notably on metaphors, framing and policy narratives.

Discourse analysis of policy-stating, -arguing and -justifying provides a rewarding way to consider development policy. While recent work on development discourse has brought many striking and notable insights, there is need now for sifting and clarification, followed by more searching applications of discourse analysis. The work on development policy in particular has been weakly connected to relevant work on policy discourse and methods of analysis. And since 'development policy' (or, as known in the US, international development policy) is many faceted we should be cautious in generalisation. Widely different things are done under its name; and stances to 'leave it to the market' are just as much policy interventions as those advocating control by central planning.

To sustain the empirical and theoretical work required on development policy discourse, one should look at three existing areas: discourse analysis in general, development discourse, and policy discourse. We would like in this introduction to comment on these three background areas, how they link to our foreground area, and to the nature of the papers that follow. We will try to clarify the terms 'discourse' and 'discourse analysis', specify a number of different varieties, including as applied in development studies, and explain why effective discourse analysis requires systematic attention to both text and context, based on serious methods and theories. In the second section we outline a corresponding agenda of work in policy discourse analysis. And in

Raymond Apthorpe, Five Houses International, PO Box K410, Haymarket, Sydney 2000, Australia (fax 61-2-261-1222). Des Gasper, Institute of Social Studies, PO Box 29776, 2502 LT The Hague, The Netherlands (e-mail: gasper@iss.nl). The authors' thanks go to Cristóbal Kay for his encouragement, and to the contributors for their co-operation at all stages. Des Gasper gratefully acknowledges the support of Shanti George.

the final section we introduce the contributions and comment on the collection as a whole.

Discourse analyses of development policy can strive for demolition or look for ways forward. Our main thrust is to increase room for manoeuvre in analysis and reform, not refuse or diminish it. And while the varieties of discourse analysis run from the linguistic-semantic to the ideological-political, our major emphasis will be to analyse development policy discourse as argumentation. Discourse analysis involves 'argumentation analysis' when, through precise readings of text and subtext, it emphasises discursive moves as being moves in logic as well as of style or community.

'DISCOURSE', 'DISCOURSE ANALYSIS' AND 'DEVELOPMENT DISCOURSE'

The term 'development discourse' is used in a variety of ways, for example, to mean talking rather than doing; diversionary and deceptive language; a prescriptive rather than descriptive stance; or as expression of the type of modernisation approach that became derogatorily known as 'developmentalism', originally in Latin America. We mention a few other ways later. This plurality reflects the state of usage of the term 'discourse' more widely. For besides everyday misusages, significant gaps exist between the definitions in different research streams in the social sciences and policy fields. (Van Dijk [*1990*] gives an overview of various streams.)

Some work uses the term to signal awareness of post-structuralist and post-modern theorists. When more than purely fashionable, this first usage is often broadly as follows:

(1) Discourse is here defined as an ensemble of ideas, concepts, and categories through which meaning is given to phenomena. *Discourses frame certain problems; that is to say, they distinguish some aspects of a situation rather than others* [*Hajer, 1993: 45*] (emphasis added).

Such use of 'discourse' to mean an intellectual framework (for example, Corbridge [*1992*]) has given a new name for talking about alternative schools, approaches, 'paradigms', 'disciplinary matrices' and so on. A strength, but also a danger, of some of this type of work is a presumption that intellectual positions are structured like a 'tree', that is, that they are based on a few fundamental and invariable assumptions. In reality, positions can and do support themselves in different (even contradictory) ways, and do evolve. Further, the comprehensive sense of 'paradigm' can be misused in claims that only a small number of 'package deals' are available, with all one's choices flowing from a single choice. People may then label each other 'liberal', 'Marxist', 'populist' or whatever, and neglect the individuality, novelty and

[handwritten note: Look at text + context | misleading to think of discourse as 'package deals' – it evolves!]

overlaps of positions. This is not conc   ntent
and framing of specific arguments.[1] A   xtual
analysis, such work can lack system   el of
supposed paradigms and for precise e   to a
second, older, usage – actual discourse

(2) In Linguistics, a stretch of lan   [is a
    discourse] [*Bullock and Stallybrass, 1977: 175*]; ... any piece of language
    longer (or more complex) than the individual sentence [*Honderich, 1995: 202*].

From the two senses, (1) 'discourse' as an intellectual framework and (2) 'discourse' as an extended stretch of language, comes a hybrid sense: an extended discussion within a particular framework.

Discourse analysis in this second usage means more than the analysis of single terms and of sentences as isolated propositions, namely:

> the study of those linguistic effects – semantic, stylistic, syntactic – whose description needs to take into account sentence sequences as well as sentence structure [*Bullock and Stallybrass, 1977: 175*].

Such analysis requires further tools – methods, concepts, methodology – than those for looking at single terms and propositions. Discourse analysis here draws out what is connoted in what has been denoted. Thus Gastil's [*1992: 469*] review of political discourse covers rhetorical strategies and conversational tactics, not only lexicon and grammar. 'Rhetoric' here can refer to 'all the ways of accomplishing things with language' [*McCloskey, 1988: 14*], not only to persuasion regardless of reason. Modern 'informal logic' and 'new rhetoric' have arisen to study these ways, going of necessity beyond both the classical deductive logic for single propositions and a classical rhetoric of illogical persuasion. (See Gasper on policy arguments, in this collection.)

A third major sense of 'discourse' is (3) conversation, debate, exchange. Language is interchange for communication. Louise White's [*1994*] recent survey of 'Policy Analysis as Discourse' matches this sense. It says little on words, style and argumentation, and considers instead the roles, locations and social structuring of debate and intellectual exchange in policy-making. The work it reviews starts in common from the view that 'there is a plurality of values and arguments available for thinking about any specific policy issue. Analysis, therefore, has to be part of a process in which these several points of view are taken into account or directly included in the analysis' [*White, 1994: 507*].

In a traditional dictionary we find this third sense and a variant of the second: 'discourse' is defined as 'talk, conversation; dissertation, treatise, sermon' (*Concise Oxford,* 1964). Thus to use 'discourse' in the first sense, to mean an intellectual frame, or work within such a frame, moves the word away from earlier meanings which continue in use. Behind the move is a claim: 'a "discourse" is not just a set of words, it is a set of rules about what you can and cannot say' [*Barrett, 1995*], and about what. (See Apthorpe on languages and universes of discourse, in this collection).

Going further in that direction, and further too from original and everyday usage, we find two more usages.

(4) Discourse is '"practice and theory" – material activity which transforms nature and society and the modes of thought that inform this action ... In earlier days the word might have been "praxis"' [*Moore, 1995: 30*];[2] 'a discourse ... an interwoven set of languages and practices ... ' [*Crush, 1995a: xiii*]. Sometimes the term 'discursive practice' is used like this.

And as perhaps one version of (4), 'discourse' is also presented as:

(5) 'a modernist regime [order] of knowledge and disciplinary power' [*loc. cit.*].

A sister term is 'discursive field, a system of power relations which produces what Foucault [*1984*] calls domains of objects and rituals of truth' [*Watts, 1995: 56*].

More ambitious than the first variant (the examination of intellectual frameworks alone), these fourth and fifth versions are adopted in much of the recent work on development discourse [*Escobar, 1995a; 1995b; Sachs, 1992; Watts, 1993*]. One danger in such usages is loss of a distinction between discourses and practices. Thus several authors when referring to development discourse or practice often instead say 'development', as in 'development simultaneously assigns each territory a characteristic morphology' [*Crush, 1995b: 15*]; '[i]nternational development ... depoliticizes this issue' [*Mitchell, 1995: 142*] and so on. 'Development' becomes an actor, protean, potent, all-purpose – as in '[d]evelopment, for all its power to speak and to control the terms of speaking' [*Crush, 1995b: 8*] – but sometimes no longer an aid to clear thinking.[3] Work in this vein has potential for both illumination and confusion. Its ambitions require complementary use of systematic methods.

Discourse analysis is fashionable; many of us now claim to do it. The label impresses, hints at uncommon insights; but to deliver on this promise is less easy. For, as seen in the problematic history of attempts at computer simulation of text understanding, 'producing and understanding discourse requires vast amounts of effectively organized knowledge' [*van Dijk, 1990: 6*]. The journal edited by van Dijk, *Discourse and Society*, aims to bridge the gap between the macro-analysis of social structures and ideologies and the micro-analysis of specific texts and conversations in order to examine 'the complex relationships between structures or strategies of discourse and both the local and the global, social or political context' and 'unravel some of the fundamental processes at work in the modern forms of the reproduction of inequality' [*ibid.: 14, 11*]. Such processes have to be demonstrated, by more than intuition and assertion. This work needs 'a level of multidisciplinary sophistication that is not usually required by traditional, monodisciplinary research or academic journals' [*1990: 13*], because 'both text and context need explicit and systematic analysis, and this analysis must be based on serious methods and theories' [*ibid.: 14*] (emphasis added). Both Fairclough [*1992*] and Backhouse *et al.* [*1993*] have extended this 'argument for systematic textual analysis as a part of discourse analysis' [*Fairclough, 1992: 193*].

'Serious methods and theories' are available from several sources, such as work on informal logic and argument analysis [*Wilson, 1986; Walton, 1989*], the rhetorics of the social sciences [*McCloskey, 1985; 1994; Nelson et al., 1987*], political discourse's terms [*Barry, 1990; Connolly, 1993*] and methods [*Gastil, 1992*], and argumentation in policy analysis and planning [*Gasper, 1991; Fischer and Forester, 1993*]. Such work situates and elucidates texts as typically reflecting social-political world views and contexts but it tries to do this through precise and detailed analyses, not declaration alone.

Not all the literature on development discourse goes this far, the many striking contributions (especially in two major 1995 collections, edited respectively by Jonathan Crush and by David Moore and Gerald Schmitz) notwithstanding. Some of it attempts discourse analysis without procedures for examining texts, or only with apparently fixed formulae and pre-set conclusions. Escobar [*1995a: 62–3*] claims that analysis of rhetorical forms looks at surfaces, whereas his Foucault-derived characterisation of discourse goes much deeper into socio-political roots. Watts makes similar charges against Apthorpe [*1986a*], Roe [*1991*], and others:

> Some recent scholarship self-consciously explores development as a text, or more properly as a series of texts, from a semiotic or rhetorical perspective ... However, Roe's analysis, like those of Apthorpe and McCloskey, generally ignores or does not develop the social basis of ideas, the social and historical context in which such stories are produced and told, and how or why some stories become dominant and others relegated ... [*Watts, 1993: 265*].

But concerns about the influence of arguments' contexts and purposes imply a need for more careful, more sophisticated, examination of the argument contents. Thus we require a disciplined examination of *both* text and context, as complementary. Watts's and Escobar's stance may underestimate what the work on rhetorics in social science and on policy and planning discourses attempts: to probe texts, contexts and their interrelations, using more tools, more system and a more open mind than only providing confirming instances for hypotheses about mentalities, ensembles and essential visions. Corbridge [*1993*] is one example of combination of a paradigms-analysis – remaining aware that the paradigms are ideal-types – and a more detailed and nuanced analysis of actual, nuanced texts and contexts.

POLICY, POLICY-SPEAK AND POLICY ARGUMENTATION ANALYSIS

'Policy' often has the sort of meaning seen in 'policy statement', 'policy release' or 'policy initiative'. Such 'policy' is a kind of gloss on events: typically a position that claims to be exemplary in some way is presented in language chosen mainly to attract and persuade one of this. It normally neither invites nor accepts refutation, especially when it takes a high moral posture; rather, by every trick and trope in the book, its hallmark is nonrefutability.

This received sense of policy, as conception, stands in naive contrast with execution (see Clay and Schaffer [*1984*]; Schaffer coined the term 'policy practice' to transcend the dichotomy). Similarly, policy speech often refers to things which inescapably ought to be done, and which at the same time can and will be done provided only that policy is 'in place'. When 'policy' and its advocacy are uttered in this way as if they were the same thing, policy-talk is too easily written off as 'mere rhetoric'. This implies a clear difference between such 'talk' and something else called 'policy making', supposed to go on as a rational decision-making process. Policy as proposition, statement and style, is indeed not policy as decision-making, interrelated though the two are. Yet one learns from experience that policy-speak is not just rhetorical hype, nor is decision-making just rational search. Crucial in all policy practice is framing, specifically what and who is actually included, and what and who is ignored and excluded. This framing cannot be settled by instrumental rationality, precisely because it frames that.

As is vexedly well-known by those who return and return again to them, typical planning and policy problems are 'wicked': they lack a definitive formulation, clear stopping rules, and an enumerable (or exhaustively describable) set of potential solutions [*Rittel and Webber, 1973*]. Thus policy problems differ from those that science conventionally gives itself to solve. Neither what would conventionally be understood as scientific reasoning nor a classical syllogistic procedure will do. Policy and policy analysis must find their own way.

We must be ready to examine a series of (interlinked) aspects, including the following:

(a) The Formation and Use of Concepts

This area is an obvious one; examples may suggest the non-obvious insights that investigation of 'naming' can yield. Development planning makes repeated use of 'target group' labels such as 'rural poor' or 'peasant' or 'landless' which are at once overdeterminate [*Wood, 1985*] and under-descriptive. Public policy and analysis at large, including development policy and analysis, often seeks to persuade through means of 'polar words' [*Arnold, 1937: 167–79*], 'either/or' [*Nott, 1977: 75–87*], and similar binary couples [*Apthorpe and Krahl, 1987*]. (On inward/outward orientation, see Gore in this collection.) Nothing seems more bold, resolute and brilliant than to put things (sometimes literally) into 'black' and 'white' (for example, 'underdevelopment' and 'development'), and then to proceed wholly on dualism's face values. Modernisation and dependency writing on development is riven by such dualisms [*Marglin and Marglin, 1990*].

(b) The Use of Tropes and Other Stylistic Devices

Tropes are figures of speech, where words are not used in their literal sense; for example, with metaphors we describe something as something else, to imply a similarity. A wealth of recent discussion (triggered especially by McCloskey [*1985*]) highlights metaphors in the literature of economics and economic development [*Porter, 1995*]. Effects and affects are most where the status of a turn of phrase as a discursive artefact escapes attention. Porter suggests we distinguish: metaphors in particular concrete contexts of practice; organising metaphors in a broader practice, such as the idea of constraints-and-their-removal in post-1940s mainstream development planning; and under-lying master metaphors, primarily biological ones in Marxism and mechanical ones in the neo-classical mainstream.

For instance, 'market' is widely used metaphorically to mean 'mechanism'. *Some* processes, such as aspects of 'competitive' pricing, may indeed be described as mechanistic results of the 'forces' (as the metaphor continues) of supply and demand. Yet some other features of markets, including other aspects of pricing even in 'free markets', are not automatic at all but legislated or contingent on other extra-market conditions. Also the operative ideas and rules which make marketing conceivable and intelligible are not mechanisms but matters of history and institutions and non-economic processes. Further features, such as in processes of market entry or exit, reflect both mechanism and institution. So positions which proceed as if 'market' denoted mechanism only are misleading: they make a machine of the ghost. Arguing as if market were institution only, makes a ghost of the machine. These different inclusions and exclusions can bring different studies and different policies (see Apthorpe in this collection).

Discourse analysis of development policy writing should also examine the use and effects of other figures of speech and stylistic device. For example, the status given to nouns as compared with verbs [*Tonkin, 1982: 112*]; the status of many official terms as normative not descriptive statements [*Abel and*

Blaikie, 1986: 736; Apthorpe, 1986b: 351]; use of keywords as banners (on 'informal sector' see Peattie [*1987*]) and as slogans to parade grand strategies such as 'basic needs'. In policy and policy analysis 'basic' means basic to values held or attributed. The scores on policy indicators paraded in this as well as other areas are vindicators more than just descriptors (see Apthorpe in this collection).

(c) Framing

Going beyond the roles of metaphors and other figures of speech in channelling attention, policy discourse analysis must examine the framing of problems to be tackled, and its connections to the generation of answers offered. Such connections often remain implicit, either forgotten or suppressed; only when frames are obtrusive or otherwise out of the ordinary are they likely to be noticed.

The idea of framing is itself of course a metaphor. We used it above as concerning what and whom are included and excluded. Hajer similarly uses 'to frame' as 'to distinguish some aspects of a situation rather than others' [*1993: 45*].[4] The contributions here by Paine on the presentation of Bhutan as beset with physical difficulties, and by Gore, on the focus on differences in national policies as being the key determinants of differences in national economic performance, illustrate this well. The best-known users of the term, Martin Rein and Donald Schön, treat 'frame' somewhat more broadly, equating it to 'paradigm' [*1993: 148*], the matrix of intellectual commitments within which a line of work proceeds. Gasper in his paper on policy argument suggests we use 'frame' in the narrower way, restricting it to more clear-cut matters of inclusion and exclusion, rather than let it cover all aspects of situation definition and conceptualisation, for which there are established and apposite terms available. Whatever the definitions used, the pieces in this collection try to probe in close detail the structures in selected discourses, and so avoid the possible misuse of 'paradigms' analysis that we mentioned earlier.

(d) Stories and Narratives

Evidence and arguments are commonly integrated in narratives, such as causal stories, which wrap up information and messages and convey plausibility. Forester [*1993*] cites the so-called Goldberg Rule: it is better to ask 'what's the story?' than 'what's the problem?'. People are often puzzled, or mistaken, concerning the nature of the problem-situation they face. They more readily think in terms of a story/narrative which combines, implicitly and explicitly, reportage and elements of definitions of others and of self, of problems and values, priorities and constraints.

According to a leader of work on development/policy narratives [*Roe, 1994; 1995*], much development planning, especially if foreign aided, employs a narrative structure comparable to the archetypal folktale [*Roe, 1989*]. A problem (often a 'crisis') is encountered; it will be 'solved', through the epic endeavour of a hero (the project/policy), who faces and overcomes a series of trials (constraints), and then lives happily ever after. Employing this story line near-guarantees disappointment. But, like some religion, it thrives on disappointment: its many versions endure precisely because of widespread felt needs for simply grasped, generalised stories with an inspirational 'message', with which to interpret and respond to situations that can otherwise seem bafflingly complex, variable and 'other' [*Roe, 1991*]. The contributions here by Gore and Moore scrutinise the simple stories about East Asian industriali-sation, and about 'governance' and crisis in Africa, used by the Washington development institutions. Roe argues that the needs for simple general narratives mean that to counter poor narratives requires counter-narratives, in which 'what are conventionally treated as the causes of program failure will now have to be taken as the preconditions for successful new programs' [*Roe, 1995: 1067*].

'Policy narrative' might become another catch-phrase. Sometimes it is one more synonym for 'paradigm' as a way-of-seeing [*Hoben, 1995*], sometimes a synonym for 'scenario'. In contrast, Fortmann [*1995: 1054*] employs 'narrative' as a synonym for 'story' in the everyday sense, but uses 'discourse' in the newer-fangled way: '[s]tories are a vehicle for transmitting and making accessible a framework of meanings, that is a discourse'; in other words, stories are Kuhnian 'exemplars', and can have special power and roles. This she vividly illustrates through the conflicting stories told by villagers and large commercial farmers in Zimbabwe.

(e) The Explicit and Implicit Rules of Validation

All policy writing, considered as text and subtext, is open-able to various interpretations, some of them conflicting. Even where the writing aims to reduce the scope for interpretation as far as possible, validating one interpretation as compared with another is still not verification; we can do the former rather than the latter. Validation and invalidation 'is an argumentative discipline comparable with judicial procedures of legal interpretation having a logic of uncertainty and of qualitative probability' [*Ricoeur, 1979: 90*].

In sum, discourse and argumentation analyses in development policy studies have to draw from areas customarily regarded as far away: semantics, semiology, socio-linguistics, philosophy. Such areas only seemingly have nothing to contribute to the action that the latest 'crisis' is claimed to require urgently; for we should understand the world better – which world? – in order to try to change it.

White's review of American work on policy analysis as discourse – as debate and intellectual exchange in policy-making – discerns three overlapping streams or perspectives. The first she calls analytic discourse: it recognises the limits of any single method or policy frame, calls for recognition of and interchange between multiple approaches, and offers procedures to sift from the different pictures and build a more adequate view for the case or issue concerned. In development research this is often summarised as 'triangulation'. The second stream White calls critical discourse, which 'is more self-consciously philosophical, ... emphasizes that value questions have to be explicitly included in analysis' [*White, 1994: 512*], and identifies structural biases in policy processes, related to unequal power positions. Different approaches must not only be represented but philosophically – and ideologically – examined, for example along the lines suggested by Fischer (see Gasper's study on analysing policy arguments in this collection). The third stream, entitled persuasive discourse, studies the role of ideas in policy change.

> Because preferences are always being interpreted and because they can and do change, [policy] entrepreneurs are not limited to traditional brokering roles, but can and do trade in the currency of ideas and problem solving strategies to build coalitions and promote change. The lesson is that political conflict is less about negotiating clear interests and more about framing policy issues [*White, 1994: 516*].

Much of this applies beyond US politics. Analysts' most important roles are then to introduce new information and generate new frames, rather than offer solutions. White's three streams are reflected, in varying degrees, in each of the six contributions that follow.

THIS COLLECTION

In this collection an interdisciplinary group of authors delineate and apply, for their chosen areas in development policy studies, the discourse analysis ideas and methods they consider important for the task. The emphases on policy and on discourse analysis methodology distinguish our enterprise from most current work on development discourse, where the focus tends to be (for or more usually against) 'developmentalism' in development studies generally or in the work of international donors.

The set starts with two methodological studies and ends with another. In between are three case studies. The methodological studies look respectively at: framing, naming, numbering and coding; argument structures and argument assessment; and essentialism.

In 'Reading development policy and policy analysis ... ', Apthorpe advocates what B.S. Green calls 'emancipatory reading'. He presents the ideas of languages and universes of discourse, and then reviews the discourse analysis of development policy, including by situating and evaluating his own 1986 study which helped to open up this topic. What are generally known as framing and naming are highlighted as core procedures in policy discourse. To these he adds 'numbering': the various forms of use of quantification; and 'coding': the choice of sense-making styles of composition which lie behind, as well as on, the printed page in front of you. Illustrations are given from humanistic and economistic discourses in poverty studies.

In 'Analysing Policy Arguments', Gasper provides an elementary survey of methods for examining policy argumentation. The first set are *general tools* from 'informal logic', including: (1) Toulmin's format for looking at a particular proposition or well-knit set of propositions, which has been widely applied to policy arguments; (2) the more open-ended exploratory methods of Scriven and others for specifying and then assessing the components and structure of extended sets of propositions that make up broad arguments; and (3) compilations of possible fallacies in argument. A second set comprise commentaries on important *components and tactics in policy argumentation in particular*: (4) general lists of component; (5) checklists of elements that deserve special attention in framing and structuring policy arguments – notably ideas about the boundaries of analysis, the burden of proof, the 'without-policy' case, the alternatives and means available, and the relevant constraints; (6) 'pitfall marking' – illustration of tactics and dangers associated with each of these types of component; and, closely related, (7) illustration of particular stylistic devices, for example, those used to exclude some matters from consideration. Style provides, in McCloskey's phrase, 'the details of substance'. Tactics build structures, not only fill in details; and argumentation theory gives us tools for unpacking how various elements are tied together towards conclusions. The final set of methods seek to specify and appraise overall *systems or structures of policy argument*: (8) methods for specification – including by Hambrick, Fischer, and the 'logical framework approach'; and (9) pointers for assessment, together with tactical advice on presentation, such as given by Scriven, Dunn and MacRae.

The three case study papers focus respectively on aspects of geographical, economic growth and governance discourses.

To get closer to the substantive associated with the discursive can be especially difficult when the discourse itself is 'physical' and seen therefore as unarguable. In the case of Bhutan, Adam Pain explores how its environment is described in words which have tended to be interpreted only negatively. Policy then takes the features as intractable constraints or has sought to mitigate them. Yet he argues that there are many positive elements of being mountainous and so on, that could be 're-framed' and harnessed towards broader national objectives.

Charles Gore's contribution dissects 1980s' and 1990s' Washington-style economic growth discourse, notably as seen in major World Bank documents and policies. He shows how poorly it grasps 'the East Asian model', relates this to a discordance between its global normative approach and its nation-state focused explanatory frame, and mounts a sustained critique of the latter. He shows in depth how the neo-liberal Washington growth discourse has sought to accommodate and 'tame' alternative views and the East Asian experience, by a series of discursive devices, including tacit shifts in the meanings of several key terms, such as 'structural adjustment' and 'outward-oriented'.

David Moore in 'Reading Americans on Democracy', argues that 'any study of contemporary development policy must take into account the ... American efforts to create economic, political and ideological hegemony on a global scale in the last fifty years'. Probing behind changes in languages of discourse, from the 1940s to the 1990s, he finds continuities in thought and policy. Official American discourse on governance for Africa remains paternalistic: 'guidance' and periodic physical intervention are necessary to help the African toward democracy as defined in Washington. Unjust in its claimed prerogatives of definition, it is also likely to be ineffective and erratic, resting on liberal theories of democracy which assume market freedom and political freedom are highly compatible. 'When the two do not match in reality American policy makers have to turn either to "order" or to "exit"' (Moore, this collection).

Finally, Gasper warns against conceptual and normative oversimplification through forms of essentialism: in defining terms; in characterising certain policies as having inherent virtues or failings; and in identifying schools of thought (especially those that one disapproves of). 'Proper', 'basically' and 'essentially' should be treated as warning-signs of possible oversimplification.

Early and some more recent treatments of development discourse have been under-differentiated. Once a stimulating new scene has been set, the plot must move forward, the story should gain in breadth and depth, and come to terms with the variety, dis-unity, and lack of clear boundaries of development discourse. We have argued the role for methods of discourse analysis, not only general claims about paradigms or essential discursive commitments. In a field of wide scope and many faces, analysis needs many tools not a few. This collection seeks linkages in particular with broader work on policy analysis, including on policy discourse.

In the absence of methodical approaches to the dimension of discourse in policy, too much is made of it, too little, or both. If too much is made of it, the processes of the stating of policy may not sufficiently have been distinguished from those of its making. If too little, the art and craft of stating may be overlooked. In both cases, the chances of making a serious difference to policy become low.

At its best, discourse analysis in all its varieties has great value. Applied in policy analysis, discourse analysis's appetites are for the ways of other discourses, the customary and new means of legitimation and delegitimation. It can become open to criticism as too voracious, as not knowing where to stop. Some discourse analysis has gained a reputation of being only destructive, a dead end. Discourse and argumentation analysis as pursued in this collection is not nihilistic. Where it finds a theory, policy or advocacy poorly conceptualised or formulated, the aim is to renew, not give up, the struggle. Towards these ends it can enhance established lines of analysis in development studies, and add something new.

NOTES

1. The interconnection of elements in a position would imply just a small number of intellectual 'package-deals' only if, *inter alia*, elements were precisely defined. Instead they can in general be variously formulated, developed and linked up (see Gasper's study on essentialism in this collection).

2. Moore [*1995: 30*] adds that '[d]iscourse remains much closer to the practices of discrete institutions, the struggles within them and their "micro-power", than is ideology'. This assumes that all discourses share a similar degree of generality. Porter [*1995*], referred to in the subsection on metaphor in this introduction, suggests we instead think of three levels of generality. This might still oversimplify.

3. The usage is of course deliberate. For Escobar [*1995b: 213*] 'development can be best described as an apparatus that links forms of knowledge about the Third World with the deployment of forms of power and intervention'; and he still calls this a discourse. Hajer's [*1993: 47*] better, clearer, umbrella term 'discourse coalition' covers 'the ensemble of a set of story lines, the actors that utter these story lines, and the practices that conform to these story lines, all organized around a discourse', in our sense (1) above.

4. Given Hajer's [*1993: 45*] concept of discourse, for him '[d]iscourses frame certain problems'; whereas with the linguistics concept of discourse, it is frames that set the scene for discourses.

REFERENCES

Abel, N. and P. Blaikie, 1986, 'Elephants, People, Parks and Development: The Case of the Luangwa Valley, Zambia', *Environmental Management*, Vol.10, No.6, pp.735–51.

Apthorpe, R., 1986a, 'Development Policy Discourse', *Public Administration and Development*, Vol.6, No.4, pp.377–89.

Apthorpe, R., 1986b, 'Social Labelling and Agricultural Development: Communal Lands or Council Lands in Zimbabwe?', *Land Use Policy* (Oct.), pp.348–53.

Apthorpe, R. and A. Krahl, 1987, 'Development Studies: A Contribution to Self Questioning', *Development and Peace*, Vol.8, No.2, pp.235–42.

Arnold, T., 1937, *The Folklore of Capitalism*, New Haven, CT: Yale University Press.

Backhouse, R. *et al.*, 1993, 'Exploring the Language and Rhetoric of Economics' in W. Henderson *et al.* (eds.), *Economics and Language*, London: Routledge, pp.1–20.

Barrett, M., 1995, 'Discoursing with Intent', *Times Higher Education Supplement*, 12 May.

Barry, B., 1990, *Political Argument*, London: Routledge (2nd edn.).

Bullock, A. and O. Stallybrass (eds.), 1977, *The Fontana Dictionary of Modern Thought*, London: Fontana/Collins.

Clay, E.J. and B. Schaffer (eds.), 1984, *Room For Manoeuvre: An Exploration of Public Policy Planning in Agriculture and Rural Development*, London: Heinemann Educational Books.

Connolly, W.E., 1993, *The Terms of Political Discourse*, Oxford: Blackwell (3rd edn.).

Corbridge, S., 1992, 'Third World Development', review article, *Progress in Human Geography*, Vol.16, No.4, pp.584–95.

Corbridge, S., 1993, *Debt and Development*, Oxford: Blackwell.

Crush, J., 1995a, 'Preface, Introduction', in Crush (ed.) [*1995: xi–xiv*].

Crush, J., 1995b, 'Introduction: Imagining Development', in Crush (ed.) [*1995: 1–23*].

Crush, J. (ed.), 1995, *Power of Development*, London: Routledge.

Dijk, T. van, 1990, '"Discourse and Society": A New Journal for a New Research Focus', *Discourse and Society*, Vol.1, No.1, pp.5–16.

Escobar, A., 1995a, *Encountering Development*, Princeton, NJ: Princeton University Press.

Escobar, A., 1995b, 'Imagining a Post–Development Era', in Crush [*1995: 211–27*].

Fairclough, N., 1992, 'Discourse and Text: Linguistic and Intertextual Analysis within Discourse Analysis', *Discourse and Society*, Vol.3, No.2, pp.193–217.

Fischer, F. and J. Forester (eds.), 1993, *The Argumentative Turn in Policy Analysis and Planning*, Durham, NC: Duke University Press.

Foucault, M., 1984, *Discipline and Punish*, Harmondsworth: Penguin.

Forester, J., 1993, 'Learning from Practice Stories – The Priority of Practical Judgement', in Fischer and Forester [*1993: 186–209*].

Fortmann, L., 1995, 'Talking Claims: Discursive Strategies in Contesting Property', *World Development*, Vol.23, No.6, pp.1053–63.

Gasper, D., 1991, 'Policy Argumentation', *Proceedings of the Second International Conference on Argumentation*, Amsterdam: SICSAT, pp.834–49.

Gastil, J., 1992, 'Undemocratic Discourse: A Review of Theory and Research on Political Discourse', *Discourse and Society*, Vol.3, No.4, pp.469–500.

Hajer, M., 1993, 'Discourse Coalitions and the Institutionalization of Practice', in Fischer and Forester [*1993: 43–76*].

Hoben, A., 1995, 'Paradigms and Politics: The Cultural Construction of Environmental Policy in Ethiopia', *World Development*, Vol.23, No.6, pp.1007–21.

Honderich, T. (ed.), 1995, *The Oxford Companion to Philosophy*, Oxford: Oxford University Press.

McCloskey, D.N., 1985, *The Rhetoric of Economics*, Brighton: Wheatsheaf.

McCloskey, D.N., 1988, 'Towards a Rhetoric of Economics', in G. Winston and R. Teichgraeber (eds.), *The Boundaries of Economics*, Cambridge: Cambridge University Press, pp.13–29.

McCloskey, D.N., 1994, *Knowledge and Persuasion in Economics*, Cambridge: Cambridge University Press.

Marglin, F.A. and S. Marglin (eds.), 1990, *Dominating Knowledge: Development, Culture, and Resistance*, Oxford: Clarendon.

Mitchell, T., 1995, 'The Object of Development – America's Egypt', in Crush (ed.) [*1995: 129–57*].

Moore, D., 1995, 'Development Discourse as Hegemony', in Moore and Schmitz [*1995: 1–53*].

Moore, D. and G. Schmitz (eds.), 1995, *Debating Development Discourse*, London: Macmillan.

Nelson, J.S. *et al.* (eds.), 1987, *The Rhetoric of the Human Sciences*, Madison, WI: University of Wisconsin Press.

Nott, K., 1977, *The Good Want Power: An Essay on the Psychological Possibilities of Liberalism*, London: Cape.

Peattie, L., 1987, 'An Idea in Good Currency and How it Grew: The Informal Sector', *World Development*, Vol.15, No.7, pp.851–6O.

Porter, D., 1995, 'Scenes from Childhood – The Homesickness of Development Discourses', in Crush (ed.) [*1995: 63–86*].

Rein, M. and D. Schön, 1993, 'Reframing Policy Discourse', in Fischer and Forester [*1993: 145–66*].

Ricoeur, P., 1979, 'The Model of the Text: Meaningful Action Considered as a Text', in P. Rabinow and W. Sullivan (eds.), *Interpretive Social Science: A Reader*, Berkeley, CA: University of California Press.

Rittel, H.W. and M.M. Webber, 1973, 'Dilemmas in a General Theory of Planning', *Policy Sciences*, Vol.4, No.2, pp.155–69.

Roe, E., 1989, 'Folktale Development', *The American Journal of Semiotics*, Vol.6, Nos.2/3, pp.277–89.

Roe, E., 1991, 'Development Narratives', *World Development*, Vol.19, No.4, pp.287–300.

Roe, E., 1994, *Narrative Policy Analysis*, Durham, NC: Duke University Press.

Roe, E., 1995, 'Except–Africa: Postscript to a Special Section on Development Narratives', *World Development*, Vol.23, No.6, pp.1065–69.

Sachs, W. (ed.), 1992, *The Development Dictionary*, London: Zed.

Tonkin, E., 1982, 'Language versus the World: Notes on Meaning for Anthropologists', in D. Parkin (ed.), *Semantic Anthropology*, London: Academic Press, pp.107–22.

Walton, D.N., 1989, *Informal Logic*, Cambridge: Cambridge University Press.

Watts, M., 1993, 'Development I: Power, Knowledge, Discursive Practice', *Progress in Human Geography*, Vol.17, No.2, pp.257–72.

Watts, M., 1995, '"A New Deal in Emotions" – Theory and Practice and the Crisis of Development', in Crush (ed.) [*1995: 63–86*].

White, L., 1994, 'Policy Analysis as Discourse', *Journal of Policy Analysis and Management*, Vol.13, No.3, pp.506–25.

Wilson, B.A., 1986, *The Anatomy of Argument*, Lanham, MD: University Press of America.

Wood, G., 1985, 'The Politics of Development Policy Labelling', *Development and Change*, Vol.16, No.3, pp.347–73.

Reading Development Policy and Policy Analysis: On Framing, Naming, Numbering and Coding[1]

RAYMOND APTHORPE

Reducing policy to writing, then expanding again through reading, are constitutive as well as interpretative acts. The focus of this study is on 'emancipatory reading' of development policy writing, which deserves its own place in the spectrum of methods of analysis in development policy studies. Particular attention is paid to discourse analysis of development policy's discursive activities. Singled out are the increasingly recognised stalwarts 'framing' and 'naming'; in addition 'numbering' and 'coding' merit being added to these.

INTRODUCTION

> ... any discourse is didactic in so far as it provides sets of directions as to how it can legitimately be read [*Burton and Carlen, 1979: 76–7*].

> the aspiration of emancipatory reading (is) to dispel the discursive hold of a text ... [its ability] to withhold attention from its own constitutive methods so that it appears to have been shaped by the reality it refers to [*Green, 1983: 47, 54–5*].

'I must admit', says a participant emerging from a policy-making meeting, 'there is still a lot of work to be done in terms of negotiation of language.' Policy-stating, whether in writing or speaking but *particularly* in writing, is one of the constitutive acts of policy. Another is what Bryan S. Green calls non-literal, 'emancipatory', reading, the primary purpose of which is 'to curb the constitutive power of a text to formulate the reader it requires' [*1983: 18*]. This study views policy as being analysis as well as policy, and analysis as being policy as well as analysis. Deeply to read policy and analysis of policy is to find devices of framing, naming and numbering, the sense-making codes of composition, and the ways in which analysis and policy are driven as well as served by them. These devices and codes operate within and beyond the

Raymond Apthorpe, Five Houses International, PO Box K410, Haymarket, Sydney, Australia, NSW 2000, Fax: 61-2-261-1222.

writing immediately in view. So a closer reading requires a total picture of reason, rules, responsibility, authority and community as well as just text, subtext and context.

Uncomfortable about his fellow economist McCloskey's 'slashing and witty attack' on economics' dominant methodology, Heilbroner says his colleague would be better advised to apply his valuable time, energy and reputation 'to economics and its substance not [wasting it on] its style' [*Heilbroner, 1986: 48*]. Heilbroner gets McCloskey's target right, namely 'the pretentious scientism in which economists couch their mutual persuasions, a scientism that lingers on as their near official language of economic discourse long after its inadequacies have been recognised by philosophers and scientists'. But his own attack is completely off-target. McCloskey's quarry is not scientism as embellishment or masking. For the manner maketh the scientistic matter; aesthetics is not an optional extra. Economics' 'deepest problem' says Heilbroner [*ibid.: 47–8*] is 'failure to recognise the inescapably ideological character of [economics'] thought'. Similar recognition is, however, part of McCloskey's [*1983*] justification of his analysis of the rhetoric of economics and of our justification of discourse analysis (hereafter DA) of development policy writing.

Framing and naming in all regards, plus numbering and coding, sum up much of what we must examine for emancipatory reading of policy and for analysis with emancipation. This paper aims to show that a three-dimensional reading is required, namely comprehension on the plane of structure, of wording and willing as vocabulary, tense and grammar; on the plane of function, of language as distributions of authority and power; and on the plane of performance, of speech as communication, code and plausibility. The study treats aspects of each of these three planes.

The aim of the whole is to identify some key DA concepts for development policy studies. First, we present the ideas of a 'language of discourse' and of examination via DA of its usage and effects. Then DA will be related to public policy discourse in general, and development policy discourse in particular; including with reference to expressed concerns with 'human aspects of development', as in 'structural adjustment with a human face' and 'human development reporting'. Next, framing and naming are introduced, as perhaps the dominant discursive activities faced in DA (see Gore in this collection), with examples drawn from poverty studies. Following this, and again with reference to poverty alleviation policy, numbering in development policy and analysis is considered, not as policy-driving but as policy-driven. This leads on to the further core concern of stylistic codes of composition and criticism. Neo-classicism and realism as leading and rival modes of statement and justification in social science and development policy are introduced. The study concludes with observations on DA and teaching development studies, and general suggestions on necessary methodological steps.

'LANGUAGE OF DISCOURSE' AND 'DISCOURSE ANALYSIS'

> The pretended privilege of the real world over the world of ideas is
> nothing more than the privilege of one discursive order over another
> in which unconditioned descriptive statements condition theoretical
> ones; since the confrontation takes place within discourse, it cannot be
> anything else [*Tribe, 1978: 7–8*].

Analysts and practitioners in any professional field engage with floating ideas
(which also sink at times), which serve as rallying points around which
positions and counter-positions can be presented and argued. Such
communication and contestation is made possible by what is commonly
known as a 'language of discourse'. This defines the 'universe(s) of discourse'
considered appropriate to be constituted and explored and the discursive
modes deemed appropriate to treat these.

    Within such languages and universes of discourse are the logic(s) of
framing, naming, numbering and coding as well as other elements in discourse,
demonstration and justification. They serve as sets of institutions and
mechanisms of meaning which permit plausible description and disputation to
be undertaken within certain bounds. For the most part these bounds are
accepted as given by those who, by habit or design, work within them. Within
them, items and argumentation can be ordered and seriously proposed,
contested, defended, rebutted. Such contest may be implicit or explicit, or
concealed or open, or difficult or easy to detect and determine. Nevertheless,
positions are taken or enhanced according to rhetoric 'not [as] mere ornament
or manipulation or trickery [but] in the ancient sense of persuasive discourse'
[*Nelson, Megill and McCloskey, 1987: 3*] in all areas of policy and social
science. Languages and universes of discourse allow, first, general
intelligibility to be established, so as to permit understanding and writing; and
second, plausibility and implausibility, so as to permit reading and
understanding to keep a running hold on general ideas as particular issues and
agendas come and go.

    The policy and academic field of development and development research
is no exception. For example, the economist and planner Sukhamoy
Chakravarty, reflecting on the way in which a model of growth is useful in
vastly different contexts, thanked Harrod and Domar for having provided the
profession (of development economists) 'with a language of discourse …
which was valid no matter whether one was talking about advanced or early
stages of development. [Also] the Harrod-Domar model … seemed [to some]
to give policy conclusions which fitted in with the commonsense of the

profession' [*Chakravarty, 1980: 102*]. Writing about why ('despite its undoubted social and political roots') economic theories of inflation dominate, Hirschman [1981: 177] took the view that this is 'not because the participants in the discussion are deeply convinced that they have got hold of crucial variables, but rather that they have developed intricate analytical structures which lend themselves to ever further elaboration, some empirical testing, and – most important – to the formulation of policy advice'.

These considered reflections of two eminent development economists on their trade touch on key points about matters of praxis and discourse, artefacts of professional culture and organisation, expectations and demands made of professionals. Sociologically speaking, languages – and universes – of discourse are relations between people over time and in particular situations and places in respect of ideas, words and other lexical elements and logic practices. The extra- and non-linguistic merge with the linguistic, the social with the scientific. It is the shared habits of discourse which make powerful, relevant and plausible argument possible. If there is no language of discourse there is no possibility of coming to significant agreement or rebuttal.

Thus to think about, in particular, the doing and contesting of framing, naming, numbering and coding becomes indispensable. We will require Foucaultian and Barthesian 'order of discourse' ideas in addition to anthropological concepts such as 'collective representations' and other versions of DA. Notably, since Voloshinov and then Pecheux [*1982*], a fertile strain of DA has focused on 'discursive formations'.[2] Policy can be emancipatorily read between its discursive formations. For example, DA asks what is 'basic' about 'basic facts', and takes the view that 'basic' is not unarguable observation but a consequence of discourse and argumentation. A different argumentation turns up different facts, some of which are 'really significant' facts as seen by this different argumentation. So the question is: basic *to which* position? *to which* argument? Always such 'basic' facts are deemed too important to be left uncontrolled. Therefore they are never allowed to speak for themselves (indeed how could they unless they had voices?). Always in policy and analysis of policy, 'basic facts' are spoken for or against. The controversy thus aroused is often the best indication of the significance attributed to them.

In addition, what Donati [*1992: 153–4*] describes as 'political discourse analysis' pays 'special attention not to the parts where plain, rational, argumentation is carried out but rather to the most imaginative parts, the metaphors, the "strange" constructions though which ... [frames and] contexts are elicited'. Political DA, just as he says,

> is not interested in abstract categories like who is 'for' and who 'against' (but rather) in the reasons why one one might be 'for' or 'against'; that

is, in what people understand of a text or an issue; in how the use of metaphors highlights some aspects of an issue and hides others, thus working as an argumentative and persuasive device; in how framing resonates with people's cultures, thus rendering the persuasion more or less likely, especially when discourse sounds [as often happens] 'non-rational'.

Discourse and DA in their various incarnations (see the Introduction to this collection) have not yet been given the prominence they deserve in development studies, and in development policy studies in particular. But while DA has not yet arrived here as distinctive sets of methodical procedures, it is unmistakably now in the course of arriving. This is despite few liking its appellation and many suspecting the upstart pretensions ('reveries of Proudhonists' [*Jameson, 1990: 98*]) of some versions.

The versions of DA appropriate for development policy studies are those appropriate to its objective: to make a constructive difference to policy. They do not deny that there is any such thing as 'reality itself'; but they accept that it must be read, re-read, and then read differently again. The language of discourse through which the universe at issue is reached and realised is *not necessarily* accepted. For what are contested are orderings and rival orderings of what is 'really significant', 'really true', *about* reality and policy. Policy argumentation, for instance, asks 'what is the main problem', 'what is the best solution', 'what are the links perceived or not perceived between problem and solution' and 'which are the best estimates as to likely outcomes of intervention and why?'.

Policy considered through its discourse is, so to put it, an open book. Readings of policy are likely to be as controversial as are its writing, no matter how finely crafted the ultimate product. So how to read closely development policy and related theory must arise as a methodological challenge in development studies.

DEVELOPMENT POLICY DISCOURSE

The chief function of any political term is to marshall political support or opposition. Some terms do so overtly, but the more potent ones, including those used by professions, do so covertly, portraying a power relationship as well as a helping one. When the power of professionals over other people is at stake, the language employed implies that the professional has ways of ascertaining who are sick, dangerous or inadequate [in development discourse 'underdeveloped'] ... and procedures for diagnosis and treatment [that] are too specialised for the lay public to understand or judge [in development, for example, 'structural adjustment']. It is of course the ambiguity in the relationship, and the ambivalence of the professional and in the client, that gives the linguistic usage its flexibility and potency. That is always true of symbolic evocations and it distinguishes radically such evocations from simple deception [*Edelman, 1984: 47–8*].

Bernard Schaffer's and my shared Orwellian, Barthesian, and Foucaultian interests in development studies crystallised at the turn of the 1980s. What I termed 'development policy discourse' served as both a point of departure for critical examination and as a quarry to be captured: otherwise it would capture you. The move to considering development policy through a focus on its discourse arose because of discontent with (a) the hegemony of development economics as a single-disciplinary approach in what pretended to be an inter-disciplinary field (even before the 'crisis in planning' perceived at the end of the 1960s and the subsequent resurgence of neo-classicism and 'the market' in development economics, which thus grew closer and closer to resemble ordinary orthodox economics); (b) the poverty of (economic) development policy to come up with poverty alleviating policies; and (c) the numerous weaknesses of policy analysis when this turned (or failed to turn) to administrative, social and spatial issues.

The first draft of my study 'Development Policy Discourse' [*Apthorpe, 1986*] was jointly written in 1983 with Bernard Schaffer. Sadly we were not able to continue the collaboration, for he died in 1984. We believed that some much needed room for manoeuvre in development research could be gained through discourse analysis. Our hope was that critical concerns expressed through policy discourse analysis might be more widely and carefully heard than just more rounds of head-on ideological and disciplinary critique. That was, however, not how the study was received at first.[3] In professional worlds, such as international development policy, which are highly doctrinaire (and ideological and paradigmatic), the scientific reputation of a research paper often relates to perceptions of where a researcher is labelled to stand politically (or religiously or ethnically, or whatever). Dividing lines between 'policy' and 'political' analysis may be faint or feigned. As Bryan Green [*1983: 169*] put it in another context, 'the political character of policy reports is so obvious and strong that the real analytic problem is not to demonstrate this extra-theoretic relation but to prevent policy reports from being understood as nothing but elements of political practice'.

Tentatively, too tentatively, the 1986 paper approached development policy discourse as a form of general policy discourse. There is indeed not just one language of discourse in development to pick out [*Apthorpe, 1984*], but also more than one way of describing such languages. Some descriptions focus on academic *discipline*. Thus usually economics language and arguments can readily be recognised as such in contradistinction, say, to sociological or geographical, mixed in actual practice though one may be with another. But there are cross-cutting *stylistic* patterns: for example, some economic and some sociological, some social anthropological and some political science argumentation may all be neo-classical (in the sense to be discussed later). Examples include current mainstream economic rationalism in economics, certain received systems- and structural-functional approaches in sociology and social anthropology, and fellow-travelling rational choice theory in political science and public administration. Other concerns give other types of description: focusing, for example, on whether a discourse is secularly or religiously 'official' or not.

That overgeneralisation can bring incoherence is urged by Gasper in his contributions to this collection. He shows where and how serious shortcomings of discourse analysis arise through inadequate setting of initial concepts and analytical terms and procedures of reference. The early discussions of development discourse were insufficiently differentiated. I may add, though, that a focus on plurality of languages was already central in my earlier [*1984*] study in Clay and Schaffer's collection, *Room for Manoeuvre*, which also introduced plausibility codes.

The 1986 study tried to introduce discourse analysis into development policy studies through a substantive analysis of development-speak. Development policy-talk was portrayed as being about 'helping' by 'giving' (and, as I now add, 'promising') through 'aid' made available under certain conditions. Development policy's 'donative' and 'promissory' features are, however, not exclusive to it. While this study takes the analysis further partly by more formal examination of some core concepts, our field is a continuing prime candidate for attention to the language of the helping professions. This language serves power in subtle ways, having political import even when it is presented as apolitical [*Edelman, 1984*].

Non-governmental agencies' style of discourse tends to be humanistic, but so is that of national and international governmental agencies when arguing for emergency relief aid. The higher the floor in *any* type of organisation's secretariat, the more will its discourse tend to emphasise 'bottom up' values and approaches and even 'human aspects'.[4] The typical intent in using the term 'human' – as in 'the human factor' [*Ortiz, 1970*], UNDP's 'human development', UNICEF's 'human face' and so forth – is unmistakably to convey compassionate concern. Less obvious is what is crowded out by such caring concern: social analysis that would be recognised as such by professionals in social anthropology, sociology, social psychology. Orthodox economic development policy discourse skips social analysis; rather it provides a-social analysis, pseudo-social analysis, sometimes anti-social analysis. Neo-classicism in the human sciences is averse, anyway, to inter-disciplinarity: 'rigour' and so on would be 'adulterated' – its rigour of form is at the expense of rigour of content.

Similar objections arise to much of what passes for 'social development' writing by economists in development research, such as work on 'human capital'. What it achieves is economistic and/or moral argument in favour of allocating resources to 'social sectors' (such as health, education and welfare). When in the 1960s development economists were entering such modes of policy argument with the aid of the economic theory of human capital, undoubtedly something positive was achieved for the credibility of the development discourse involved. In the 1980s, once again there were notable entries of 'human aspects' into the then current development files, for instance, with regard to structural adjustment policy. Likewise 'social indicators' searches have been far from insignificant; consider, say, their contribution to UNDP's 'human development index'. But these are sectoral, not social and, for the most part, exclude participants' concepts of standards and rankings. Little of such work is social in the sense of being about social states and conditions of social organisations, social institutions, social movements, and how they work and what they mean to their members and participants. For the most part social indicators are about social goods and services seen as inputs or outputs, and involve expert, not participatory, attributions of socio-economic status to statistical, not social, categories. Confusing social organisations with social institutions is another common feature [*van Arkadie, 1989; Apthorpe, 1990*], found even in the so-called 'new institutional economics'. Development policy analysis ought not to be commissioned out to economists only, however humanistic. University discipline is, however, by no means the only determining force. Methodological individualism [*Toye, 1993; van Donge, 1994*] can make itself felt in any discipline, and mechanistic 'systems approaches' [e.g. *Hoos, 1972*] are common in top-management consultancy from whichever disciplinary point of view; and such consultancy is known too for its lack of social class analysis. So, much social – not to speak of economic – analysis in development policy is crowded out by such discourse. However, as with 'lack of policy', 'lack of social analysis' must be interpreted with care. What is involved may range from complicity [*Fairhead and Leach, 1995*] and subservience on the one hand, to avoidance, whether studious, forgetful or deceitful on the other.[5]

FRAMING AND NAMING IN THE ANALYSIS OF POVERTY – ECONOMIC RATIONALISM AND HOLISTIC HUMANISM

... a complementary process of naming and framing. Things are selected for attention and named in such a way as to fit the frame constructed for the situation. Together the two processes construct a problem ... new descriptions of problems tend not to spring from the solutions of the problem earlier set, but to evolve independently as new features of situations come into prominence [*Schön, 1979: 261, 164*].

A language of discourse offers a mode of communication. Less obviously, but equally importantly, it contributes to constituting what can be thus communicated, and what such communication can be about. Framing is a core discursive activity in this regard: 'through frames ... facts, values, theories and interests are integrated' [*Rein and Schön, 1991: 262*]. 'Discourse is the place where efforts at defining public reality are made so that it can achieve a collective validity. Frames are the basic tools – or weapons – used in these efforts' [*Donati, 1992: 151*].

Rival ways of naming and framing set policy agendas differently. For example, economistic writing on development aid and poverty alleviation tends not to cover the situations of political and economic refugees and other disaster-displaced people (the 'conjunctural' poor) [*Iliffe, 1987: 146*]; they are treated under separate headings as 'emergencies' calling for 'relief'. Policies become divided accordingly, and linkage of 'development' with 'relief' is then often seen as heavily problematic and perhaps also counterproductive.

Poverty framed and named as economics and mechanisms, and poverty framed and named as politics and institutions, are very different theories of poverty, and likely to lead to different policies. Humanism in policy discourse may strongly differ from economism with regard to the 'deciles' and 'quintiles' and similar styles of statistical expression. Economistic argument uses these extensively in its disaggregating and distributional analyses of inequality. In rival frames these statistical styles are uncharacteristic, sometimes even unacceptable. Instead social, cultural, national and ethnic, not abstract statistical, groups and classes count. Humanism's focal concerns and policy issues are with social and political movements, and with tendencies seen to have mainly cultural and historical roots and reasons for being and for being important. Humanists believe these run deeper than the veneer of a regime's latest allocative failures 'to use resources efficiently' and 'deliver the goods'.

Another area of characteristic difference concerns, for want of a better term, multifocality. Economism's statistical calculations typically are of total quantities, levels or amounts of a single condition, a kind of amalgam. Sometimes it builds a kind of half-way house to plural conceptualisation as for example, when 'poverty' is seen to have different 'faces' or 'aspects' and thus to require a variety of indicators. This is normally as far as economistic framing prefers to go. 'The economy' in economic rationalism is singular, 'disaggregated' though some features may be on occasion. Framing and naming in this singular mode allows issue-concerns to be handled in mechanistic models and metaphors.

If economic rationalism were to confront itself with a range of qualitatively different pover*ties* [*Max-Neef et al., 1989*], problems would arise. Consider for example neo-classical economics' hallmark theory, automatic 'trickle down' (which it will not let go of despite repeated findings of its own research that this does not happen). It is not in the characteristic style of economistic approaches to ask *which kinds* of economic growth mechanistically trickle-down (apart from labour-intensive growth which is trickle-down virtually by definition), *which kinds of* poverty are diminished thereby, and which not. Neo-classicism abhors subplots, undercurrents, ironies, satires – along with subaltern dissent.

Economic rationalism's argumentative realms are deeply imbued with the scientist notion of 'automatic' or 'mechanical' linkage: no automatic linkage, then no scientism, therefore no economic rationalism. So if automaticity cannot empirically be established as between one set of variables, then it must be sought – and found – as between another. If poverty decline is not a function of economic growth, then it must be, say, of lower population growth or higher human capital investment or whatever. In such theory and argumentation, functional and mechanical relations are made to combine in a kind of floating 'economistic present' time or space, much as neo-classical anthropology writes in an imaginary 'ethnographic present'. What is involved, however, is found on closer inspection to be not a matter of temporal or spatial 'tense' at all, but an abstraction-at-large outside historical time and geographical space.

A further sharp contrast is with regard to quantification. Economistic arguments engage in heated and technical debate about 'scientific' and 'robust' measurement. Their struggle is to find ways of measuring even what is stoutly resistant to measurement. Humanistic argument does not depend so heavily on measurement for justifying its premises, findings and recommendations. For instance, when addressing the role and function of the public sector and development, it does not make economic rationalist measurements of 'cost efficiency' its central focus. Rather it spotlights national and cultural identity, and the country-wide potentiality and capacity of state and governmental structures for policy reform. In pursuing this focus of interest, recourse to figures is not missing, but it fears giving too much attention to numbers, especially early in a study, for risk of framing it unpermissively and thereby ruling out too much too soon.

NUMBERING IN POVERTY STUDIES

The false start which pseudo-investigation usually takes is the plausible one of asking a question. We are all apt to begin by referring to the arbitrament of 'the facts' some question in which we happen to be particularly interested, a question which has all the appearance of strict impartiality, but which is almost invariably what the lawyers call a 'leading question', if only because it is necessarily put in a phraseology involving a particular environment or set of conditions. Almost always we find, when we look back upon it after further experience, that the very terms in which the question was couched implied an answer of a particular kind or at least excluded answers of some other kinds about which we had not been thinking [*Sidney and Beatrice Webb, 1975 (1932): 34–5*].

We proceed to further aspects of numbering in development and other policy discourse by taking as an illustration the question: which measurements of poverty 'are best'? While one mode of data and measurement can be highly appropriate and persuasive for one purpose, it may not be suitable for another. 'Robustness' and similar scientistic desiderata may have little to do with it. This is because measuring and numbering in policy and policy studies is policy-driven and not, as it is normally presented, policy-driving. Indicators are sought as vindicators, not just descriptors.

My claim is not that scientism in policy and policy analysis is never aware of its limits; nor that data availability or requirements never 'come before' determination of policy; nor that policy determination is one thing, statistics quite another. Rather, through the framing and naming already introduced, and the codes of composition to be discussed in the next section, policy in its textwork interacts with numbering, not neutrally and transparently but complexly and opaquely.

Four common approaches to measurement jostle in the area of poverty: headcount, absolute, relative and participant (self-rating). Development policy writing abounds with statistical arguments for and against each of these, justified in terms just of technical qualities. But choices in policy and policy analysis are not on technical statistical merit alone, or even mainly. What matters more in all policy practice is suitability of fit of the genre of measurement with the premises and promises of the policy which is seen to require it. We can briefly take these types of measure one by one.

The headcount is often decried in poverty studies because it does not distinguish between 'poor' and 'very poor'. But for the same technical reasons, headcounts can be seen as ideal – for instance, for the administrative and allocative purposes of supply and delivery of emergency relief, say, for refugees, or a drought and famine-afflicted population. Graduated shades of poverty are not what emergency relief is about, just disastrous deprivation and need.[6] Headcounts will be much less suitable measures for the poverty of displaced people in, say, their second generation of displacement, in which the sheer fact of physical uprooting and destitution and disablement is not likely to be a principal feature for policy (where 'principal' means 'immediate' in the two senses of ease of observation and recency). Yet, for earlier than second-generation situations headcounts can be considered too informative, politically. To governments they may be too revealing of nationally and internationally sensitive situations, as refugee situations ordinarily are. To refugees' representatives in camps they may be too accurate for comfort of their arguments that they need more relief than agencies are providing.[7]

'Absolute' measurement of poverty refers to a poverty datum line. People above the line are deemed to be not in poverty; people below, to various degrees according to determined criteria. (The headcount version does not distinguish degree.) Now while this approach appears frequently in scientistic writing, there is abundant evidence that cut-off points or lines chosen are crucial. The amount of absolute poverty perceived is highly dependent on both the circumstances of its occurrence and the instruments and criteria used to measure it [*Scott, 1971; Booth, 1992; Glewwe and van de Gaag, 1990*]. Change the criteria against which the datum line has been determined even slightly, and the resultant picture can change dramatically. The proposition, as in poverty studies, that 'the methods paint the picture' is particularly true here. Given then that in case after case 'absolute' proves on re-reading to be close to 'negotiable' and 'negotiated', one might expect that this mode would have by now disappeared from development policy studies. But this has not happened. This mode persists unchanged because even in scientistic writing, other types of consideration may be uppermost – the non-numerical aspects of numbering. The reality is that policy drives the practice of numbering, rather than numbering practice driving the policy. Policy which promises to eradicate poverty must conceptualise and measure in terms of eradicability in order to be plausible. Poverty eradication policy and analysis 'demand' constructed minimum basic needs lines because without them such policy cannot be shown to be 'working' or not.

'Relative measurement' of poverty looks at inequality. Poverty is here not just a condition found below a datum line or cut-off point. Rather it is a matter of, say, bottom deciles compared with top deciles. Relative measures such as Gini and similar coefficients do not figure in basic needs poverty alleviation policy and policy analysis: they cannot show whether absolute poverty is being alleviated or not. Policy-driven recourse to relative measures tends to be led by the politics of a socialistic or social reformist agenda. Policy aiming to reduce relative poverty will have to address society at large, and not just that part of it deemed to be in absolute poverty. The politics of relative poverty alleviation policy are so different from those of absolute poverty reduction as to affront even the very (English, not French or German) word 'policy', for not being 'political'. Relative poverty reduction policy is (like self- or group-rated poverty to which I turn next) commonly, perhaps inescapably, branded as party-political.

Arguments for or against consensual, participant or self-rating measurement, are in the same way rarely settled just on technical merit. Arguments for
this mode, which is akin to public opinion polling, are that 'the people
themselves' know their own situations better than experts can. Arguments
against self-rating tend to be that such methods are 'subjective' – despite the
available statistical evidence that, technically speaking, they are as objective as
any other type of measurement.

For each of these measurement approaches, genre appetites appear more
determining than other considerations. The matter should be taken further
through examination of cases. There are, of course, considerations other than
those of genre. But once again data determination is not just the neutral and
transparent (and 'robust', etc.) statistical and scientific exercise that it is made
out to be. Thus the technical and statistical requirements of policy data are as
the glaze on a Ming bowl. A mis-glaze, an erroneous calculation, a badly
chosen indicator, a missed case for a vindicator, spoils the appearance and
value. For this reason, as standard texts say, indicators should be based on
available data, be specific and sensitive, reliable and valid, have good
coverage, be appropriate for action and so forth. But even with a defective
glaze a Ming bowl may fulfil at least a part of the purpose for which it was
intended – display; and in our case a flawed indicator can still further a
particular policy purpose.

Some economic (and economistic) theory in poverty research appeals
specifically to what it terms 'stylised facts' – factually incorrect simplifications accepted for purposes of theorisation; holding thus that what is true is
'existent' only 'stylistically'. Yet *all* data are constructions, as well as findings,
in social science and policy. How a picture is named and framed makes a
difference to the picture (see Gore in this collection). ' ... in a world in which
"naming" is becoming the equivalent of "bringing into existence", the
weakness of actors is too often a deprivation or deformation of the power of
naming. The flow of signs is meaningless, if there is no access to the dominant
codes' [*Melucci, 1992: 55*].

CODES OF COMPOSITION: NEO-CLASSICISM AND REALISM

An operative code may be as complex as primitive myth, as subtle as
an artistic genre, as overt as a written grammar or as mundane as the
competencies which sustain conversational glossing practices ... A
social report in order to produce reality and knowledge effects must
be articulated through an existing stock of knowledge containing
codes operative beyond the reading process which the person who
reads can use without question ... A text must play upon pre-existing

plausibility structures in order to achieve referential realism ... [*Green, 1983: 72,104*].

As performances of composition, philosophies, codes or styles do not reduce just to individual elements which may be listed item by item, precisely because what is involved is composition. Taking them apart, as in conventional approaches to exposition, is decomposition. The ways of describing dominant codes as pre-existing plausibility structures [*ibid.*] which are operative behind the literal reading process vary considerably. When syntaxes and grammars are approached as sense-making *codes* or *styles* of presentation and disputation, however, then obviously a focus on *stylistics* is appropriate. Currently 'neo-classicism' (in France known usually as just 'classicism') is enjoying an ascendancy, and is easily recognisable. To take this as an example, what is neo-classicism stylistically?

In brief, first and foremost neo-classicist style is strong on deductive and generalising statement. It contrasts sharply with realism's inductive and particularising style.[8] It depends largely on complex calculation to 'get right' the proportions and margins that it so highly values. In contrast, to achieve its priorities, realist discourse depends more on figurative and pictorial presentation of selected individual cases than on figures and balances. Both neo-classical and realist argumentation, whether institutional or geographical [Pain, this collection; *Ferguson, 1990; Mitchell 1995*], can be descriptive as well as prescriptive about development, but in such different styles as 'not really' to be about the same thing.

In art and architecture neo-classical composition has been described as arising when

> the diagonal gives way to the vigorously frontal view and sinuous complexities of Rococo [give way] to the elementary clarity of a simple perspective box ... Volumetric clarity ... perfect balance and uniformity ... universality is one of neo-classicism's prime aims ... pure spheres, cubes, cylinders and pyramids are representatives of this [*Honour, 1968: 25, 109*].

All this is true also of neo-classicism as style in social science, with its rigour and recourse to equilibrium theory, linearity and columns [*Francis, 1961*] and the like. Presentations that are realist in style seek to make their mark through a minimum of generalisation and deduction. But *both* – indeed *all* – codes have the aim of making a statement that in substance is true as well as real.

In other work this central conflict of composition, between realism and (neo-)classicism, may be approached and named slightly differently; as, for instance, with the pair of terms 'historicist' and 'technicist' representing 'two separate universes of discourse' in land reform policy analysis [*Lehmann,*

1978: 339–45]. But the core contrasts of framing that are drawn are substantively very similar. The best work in this area of criticism traces varieties and mixtures of, and tensions within, codes; for thumbnail and ideal-typical presentations fail to capture important shades. In land reform, one can contrast Walrasian and Marshallian strands within neo-classicism in economics [*Atkins, 1988: 935–56*]. Further, while categorical contrasting of codes is a necessary preparation for fundamental criticism, different policy conclusions may be reached by similar routes and vice versa [*Lehmann, 1978*].

Nor is there a simple disciplinary basis to these two rival codes, so criticising neo-classicism is not the same thing as criticising economists; special pleading for sociology is not necessarily special pleading for realism, and so forth. Orthodox, mainstream economics is strongly – and as 'the market paradigm' rules – increasingly neo-classical but *any* discipline may choose to go more one way than another as regards 'mechanistic' or 'humanist' and 'institutionalist' metaphors and models. *Any* disciplinary approach in policy or policy analysis may aim more for control than understanding. *Any* instrumentalist stance may bring preoccupation with 'mechanisms'; but to think mechanism is to think certainty, surety and predictability as well as just instrumentality. (Which particular types of mechanisms or knobs on development machines are preferred may show disciplinary aspects, with economics preferring economic instruments, and other disciplines, say, social, cultural or spatial.) Thus dominance, deserved or undeserved, of one persuasion (or occasionally discipline) over another is a problematic idea. One may not be 'wrong' because another is 'right'. Much depends on context and situation, what is uppermost in an intervention or analysis, and the extent to which policy is seen as proposition and style not decision-making and number-crunching.

DISCOURSE ANALYSIS AND TEACHING DEVELOPMENT STUDIES

> ... the conceptual framework of discourse analysis [allows] us conveniently in a postmodern age to practise ideological analysis without calling it that ... [and to reveal] the fundamental level on which political struggle is waged is that of the struggle of legitimacy of concepts: that political legitimation comes from that: and that for example Thatcherism and its counterrevolution was founded fully as much on the delegitimation of [the idea and word of] welfare-state or social-democratic [we used to call it liberal] ideology as on the inherent structural problems of the welfare state itself [*Jameson* (on Stuart Hall), *1990: 97*].

The emancipatory ways of some of the reading of framing, naming, numbering, and coding explored in this study and collection offer possibilities for more open communication across ideologies, cultures, continents and disciplines – and everything else: social classes, genders, sectors. Because it tackles issues not exactly head-on, DA is less likely to run into brick walls. This makes it invaluable, for example, as a class teaching aid in international development studies programmes.

Teaching in such programmes is like tightrope walking. The usual props to pedagogical authority do not apply. To be seen to be *relevant* is what matters more than anything else in such situations. The instructor must be seen to be learned, but if not relevant, then being learned and having the other usual grounds of authority is seen to count for very little. This means knowing case studies and, in particular, those of policies and projects in (all) the participants' own countries; and this is where lack of pedagogical authority starts. Even for very generalised purposes very much depends on case studies; but the instructor cannot be expected to know enough to satisfy everyone in the class about cases in every distant land. There will probably be no appropriate literature to hand on whichever particular case or cases it is. The different but, as you earnestly assure everyone, equally or even more interesting cases that you do know, satisfy no one.

In this situation, DA of current and recent policy discourses has telling advantages. It can involve and communicate widely as well as make something to communicate. In a multi-experience, multi-ideological, multi-national, multi-disciplinary, multi-everything situation, as international degree and master's programmes in development studies typically are, this is invaluable. And DA can often yield relatively quick results. By closely examining 'just' the writing on the paper, an immanent understanding becomes possible quite quickly. Bringing DA of the types outlined in this study and collection to bear gives you, and your students, much more to say, and to learn, other than metaphysics (such as: development is good, or, take your pick, bad for everyone or nearly everyone regardless of the case) or a drift into academic populism.

Many academics and trainers fall back on another resource: that the ruling policies, regardless of case or country typically, come from the same international agencies, aid bureaux, non-governmental organisations and similar sources. To fall back confidently on the ways and deeds of these is doubtless better than falling back on nothing at all – but to be without DA is to lack a high-yielding aid. As always, there are conditions: 'discourse' must not be autonomised and DA must be used in a combinatory, not an exclusionary, fashion, with its 'newness' not inordinately stressed and not presented as something altogether different from 'outdated' approaches that it allegedly 'supersedes'.[9]

CONCLUSION

Re-reading and reading emancipatorily, as this study has aimed to show, involves re-framing, re-naming, re-numbering, re-composing, re-describing, re-arguing. While of course these operations are not done all at once, or in this particular (or by any standard other) sequence of steps, they are by no means simply discrete and separate mental operations. Finding a single *mot juste* to convey the recursive moments of simultaneity (instantaneousness) and coincidence of 'rays' of insight is not easy. But clearly there is not just straightforward progression in any policy process from problem to solution, nothing so purely practical. Much policy in general, and most of development policy in particular, may be made up of answers in search of questions. Policy discourses fail overwhelmingly to reveal this; unless they can manage to escape from such capture they deprive themselves of room for manoeuvre to make a difference to policy.

Besides attention to styles of framing, naming, numbering and coding, DA on the lines I have advocated should include the following.

A clear decision right at the outset as to the purpose(s) for which recourse to DA is needed.

Acceptance that discourse '*per se*' cannot do anything 'by itself', so can be neither the sole villain of the piece nor its sole saviour.

Linkage of DA with argumentation analysis (see Gasper on argumentation in this collection).

Conceptualisation of 'basic', as in 'basic facts' or 'basic description', as a dependent not independent criterion (see Ferguson [*1990*], Mitchell [*1995*] and Pain, this collection).

Sensitivity to the extent to which development policies must be distinguished from even those development theories on which they may partly have been built (see Gore, this collection).

Ensuring that actual courses of events are not reduced to the policies, theories or models which they may closely or less closely have been shown to fit (see Gore, this collection).

Investigation of the extents to which under another name, in a different frame, continuities in development policies or development theories crowd-out change in policies or theories and come merely to re-affirm or re-establish what they purport to have changed (see Wickramasinghe [*1983*] and Moore, this collection).

Finally, we should remember that DA of development policy turns the searchlight on the social and cultural practices of practitioners, planistrators, researchers, that is, on ourselves and our (now seen as others') discourses. This is always less comfortable than just pottering about among the exotic social and cultural practices of peasants and other alterities.

NOTES

1. This study draws on (but also goes considerably beyond) my second and third lectures in the series 'Making Policy Analysis Matter: A Concern to Commit Social Anthropology to Current Public Issues', Ecole des Hautes Etudes en Sciences Sociales, Paris, July 1995, given at the kind invitation of Professor Jean-Claude Galey. A version of the first lecture of the Paris series, 'Policy Anthropology as Expert Witness', will appear in *Social Anthropology*, Journal of the European Association of Social Anthropologists [*1996, forthcoming*]; and a version of the third, 'Policy, Language, Power: Writing Development and Development Policy Studies' will appear in Shore and Wright (eds.) [*1996, forthcoming*]. I am greatly indebted to Des Gasper for emancipatory readings of drafts of the present contribution; and to Andras Krahl for discussions around his unpublished note, 'Discourse Analysis in Development Studies: The Underside'.

2. ' ... each discursive formation is embedded in turn in an ideological formation which contains non-discursive practices as well as discursive ones ... but the position of a discursive formation within a complex whole ... will typically be concealed from the individual speaker in an act of what Pecheux calls "forgetting"' [*Eagleton, 1991: 195–6*].

3. At the panel meeting of the Development Studies Association of the UK and Ireland in 1983, the majority reaction to our draft was this: looking semiologically and socio-linguistically, and as far as possible in its own terms and text, at what represented itself as an a-political discourse, evaded what essentially was needed – critique that was and could easily be seen to be political. Our perspective was deemed either to fail to address what was considered the essential problem, or to be too difficult to place ideologically and, for this reason, of little account.

4. The matter of language variations – which are not necessarily also discourse variations [*Contreras, 1989: 20*] – as between international development agencies and banks is another issue. Sometimes, however, their languages are more similar than different. I recently attended the launching of a poverty alleviation programme in a remote part of a country in Africa at which the World Bank representative delivered his address in the purest form of UNDP-speak. On other occasions the differences, especially on poverty alleviation policy, between positions and languages adopted by the World Bank and the UNDP are more striking.

5. The 'studious avoidance' of social class – and ethnic group – analysis in economic development theory and policy was much examined by Newton Gunasinghe [*1986*]. During a stay in Sri Lanka I traced a number of his works and contemplated a collection. The file disappeared from a suitcase that 'went missing' as I was departing (which when 'found' later had curiously not lost conventional 'valuables').

6. Headcounts are of considerable importance in relief policy practice [*Apthorpe, Ketel, Saleh and Wood, 1995*].

7. Of course, *any* type of data may be held back for reasons of institutional not technical sensitivity. In one country where I worked recently, research information revealing great income inequality between socio-economic categories was emerging (and in some statistical circles being 'leaked'), but publication was barred by the Minister concerned. Such income inequality and poverty was not officially admitted. I was hard put to advise the Minister responsible on how a true report on poverty in his country could be written. In the end I plumped for a report on 'vulnerability', but I believe that, after my departure, that was not deemed suitable either. In another country, absolute poverty figures disaggregated by region were officially regarded as too sensitive for release and access was made very difficult and expensive.

8. The stylistics of realism are explored further in my 'Policy, Language and Power: Writing Development Policy and Development Policy Studies' in Shore and Wright (eds.) [*1996, forthcoming*].

9. If 'discourse' is autonomised and as a result becomes 'potentially unrelated to reality and [something which] can be left to float off on its own, to found its own subdiscipline and develop its own specialists [*Jameson, 1990: 98*] the result is not a judicious use of DA in relation to other nostrums but an incestuous overdose.

REFERENCES

Apthorpe, R., 1984, 'Agricultures and Strategies: The Language of Development Policy', in E.J. Clay and B.B. Schaffer (eds.), *Room for Manoeuvre: An Exploration of Public Policy Planning in Agriculture and Rural Development*, London: Heinemann Educational Books.
Apthorpe, R., 1985, 'Development Indicators: Some Relativities of Subjectivity and Objectivity', in J.G.M. Hilhorst and M. Klatter (eds.), *Social Development in the Third World: Level of Living Indicators and Social Planning*, London: Croom Helm.
Apthorpe, R., 1986, 'Development Policy Discourse', *Public Administration and Development*, Vol.6, No.4, special issue on 'Institutions and Policies: Essays on Bernard Schaffer's Grammar of Official Provision'.
Apthorpe, R., Ketel, H., Salíh, M. and A. Wood, 1995, *What Relief for the Horn? SIDA-Supported Emergency Operations in Ethiopia, Eritrea, Southerm Sudan, Somalia and Djibouti*, Stockholm: SIDA.
Apthorpe, R., 1990, *see* Economic and Social Commission for Asia and the Pacific (ESCAP).
Apthorpe, R., 1996, forthcoming, 'Policy Anthropology as Expert Witness', *Social Anthropology*, Journal of The European Association of Social Anthropologists.
Apthorpe, R., 1996, forthcoming, 'Policy, Language, Power: Writing Development and Development Policy Studie', in Shore and Wright (eds.) [1996, *forthcoming*].
Arkadie, van B. (and discussion by J. Nellis, Pranab Bardhan *et al.*), 1989, 'The Role of Institutions in Development', Annual Conference of World Bank in Development Economics, Washington, DC: World Bank, pp.153–92.
Atkins, F., 1988, 'Land Reform: A Failure of Neo-Classical Theorization?', *World Development*, Vol.16, No.8, pp.935–46.
Booth, A., 1992, 'Counting the Poor in Indonesia', *Working Paper No.7*, School of Oriental and African Studies, Department of Economics, University of London.
Burton, F. and P. Carlen, 1979, *Official Discourse: On Discourse Analysis, Government Publications, Ideology and the State*, London: Routledge & Kegan Paul.
Chakravarty, S., 1980, 'Relevance of Growth Models to Development Planning', *The Pakistan Development Review*, Vol.XIX, No.2, pp.101–12.
Contreras, A.P., 1989, 'The Discourse of Development: Some Implications of Local Power/ Knowledge in the Philippine Uplands', *Philippines Sociological Review*, Vol.37, Nos.1–2. Jan.–June, pp.12–23.
Donati, P.R., 1992, 'Political Discourse Analysis', in M. Diani and R. Eyermann (eds.), *Studying Collective Action*, London: Sage.
Donge, van J. K., 1994, 'The Continuing Trial of Development Economics: Policies, Prices and Output in Tanzanian Agriculture', *Journal of International Development*, Vol.6, No.2, pp.157–84.
Eagleton, T., 1991, *Ideology: An Introduction*, London: Verso.
Economic and Social Commission for Asia and the Pacific (ESCAP), 1990, *Major Issues Relating to a Regional Social Development Strategy for Asia and the Pacific: A Conceptual Framework*, New York: United Nations.
Edelman, M., 1984, 'The Political Language of the Helping Professions', in M. Schapiro (ed.), *Language and Politics*, Oxford: Blackwell.
Fairhead, J. and M. Leach, 1995, 'False Forest History, Complicit Social Analysis: Rethinking Some West African Environmental Narratives', *World Development*, Vol.23, No.6, pp.1023–35.
Ferguson, J., 1990, *The Anti-Politics Machine: 'Development', Depoliticization and Bureaucratic Power in Lesotho*, Cambridge: Cambridge University Press.
Francis, R.G., 1961, *The Rhetoric of Science: A Methodological Discusssion of the Two-by-Two Table*, Minneapolis, MN: University of Minnesota Press.

Glewwe, P. and J. van der Gaag, 1990, 'Identifying the Poor in Developing Countries: Do Different Definitions Matter?', *World Development*, Vol.18, No. 6, pp.803–14.

Green, B.S., 1983, *Knowing the Poor: A Case Study in Textual Reality Construction*, London: Routledge & Kegan Paul.

Gunasinghe, N., 1986, 'Open Economic Policy and Peasant Production', *Upanathi*, Vol.1, No.1, Jan., pp.37–67.

Heilbroner, Robert L., 1986, 'The Murky Economists', *The New York Review of Books*, 24 April.

Hirschman, A.O., 1981, 'On the Social and Political Matrix of Inflation: Elaborations on the Latin American Experience', in A.O. Hirschman, *Essays in Trespassing: Economics to Politics and Beyond*, Cambridge: Cambridge University Press.

Honour, H., 1968, *Neo-classicism*, London: Penguin Books.

Hoos, I. R., 1972, *Systems Analysis in Public Policy: A Critique*, Berkeley, CA: University of California Press.

Iliffe, J., 1987, *The African Poor*, African Studies Series 58, Cambridge: Cambridge University Press.

Jameson, F., 1990, 'Postmodernism and the Market', in R. Miliband and L. Panich (eds.), *The Retreat of the Intellectuals*, Socialist Register, London: The Merlin Press.

Lehmann, D., 1978, 'The Death of Land Reform: A Polemic', *World Development*, Vol.16, No.8, pp.935–46.

McCloskey, D.N., 1983, 'The Rhetoric of Economics', *Journal of Economic Literature*, Vol.XXI, June, pp.481–518.

Max-Neef, A., Elizalde, M., Hopehayn, M. *et al.*, 1989, 'Human Scale Development: An Option for the Future', *Development Dialogue*, No.1, pp.5–81.

Melucci, A., 1992, 'Liberation or Meaning?: Social Movements, Culture and Democracy', *Development and Change*, Vol.23, No.3, pp.43–77.

Mitchell, T., 1995, 'The Object of Development: America's Egypt', in J. Crush (ed.), *Power of Development*, London: Routledge, pp.129–57.

Nelson, J.S., Megill, A. and D.N. McCloskey, 1987, *The Rhetoric of the Human Sciences: Language and Argument in Scholarship and Public Affairs*, Madison, WI: University of Wisconsin Press.

Ortiz, S., 1970, '"The Human Factor" in Social Planning in Latin America', in R. Apthorpe (ed.), *People, Planning and Development Studies: Some Reflections on Social Planning*, London: Frank Cass.

Pecheux, M., 1982, *Language, Semantics and Ideology*, London: Macmillan.

Rein, M. and D. Schön, 1991, 'Frame Reflective Policy Discourse', in P.E. Wagner, C.H. Weiss, B. Wittrock and H. Wollmann (eds.), *Social Sciences and Modern States: National Experiences and Theoretical Crossroads*, Cambridge: Cambridge University Press.

Schön, D.A., 1979, 'Generative Metaphor: A Perspective on Problem Setting in Social Policy', in A. Ortony (ed.), *Metaphor and Thought*, Cambridge: Cambridge University Press.

Scott, W., 1971, *Concepts and Measurement of Poverty*, Geneva: UNRISD.

Shore, C. and S. Wright (eds.), 1996, forthcoming, *The Anthropology of Policy*, London: Routledge.

Toye, J., 1993. 'The New Institutional Economics and Its Implications for Development Theory', in J. Martinussen (ed.), *New Institutional Economics and Development Theory*, International Development Studies, Occasional Paper No.6, Denmark: Roskilde University.

Tribe, K., 1978, *Land, Labour and Economic Discourse*, London: Routledge & Kegan Paul.

Webb, S. and B. Webb, 1975, *Methods For Social Study*, London School of Economics and Political Science: Cambridge University Press (original edition 1932).

Wickramasinghe, G., 1983, 'Reproducing Old Structures Through Reforms: The Experience of Land Reforms in Sri Lanka', *Sri Lanka Journal of Agrarian Studies*, Vol.4, No.1, pp.1–10.

Analysing Policy Arguments

DES GASPER

The complexity and distinctiveness of policy discourse bring a need for methods and advice in both specifying and assessing policy arguments. The study reviews, links and systematises work in three areas: (1) general advice from 'informal logic' on the exploration and analysis of sets of propositions that make up broad arguments; (2) commentaries on important elements and tactics in policy argument-ation in particular, with special attention to aspects of 'framing'; and (3) proposed methods to specify and appraise whole positions in policy argument, including the 'logical framework approach' and Fischer's 'Logic of Policy Questions'.

I. ARGUMENTATION AND POLICY ANALYSIS

While training in systematic practical argumentation is valuable for almost any subject, it may be especially important for policy-oriented work. Public policy discourse is notably complex and, further, has important distinctive features, including the need to incorporate value inputs, considerations of legitimacy, and assessments of the constraints on public action. I propose that we should stress not only any distinctive components and structures, but emphasise some themes that reflect the field's complexity. These themes include the underdefinition of problems and criteria, and the resulting importance of activities of problem formulation and closure.

There is a temptation in discourse analysis to plunge deep into philosophy and linguistic and literary theory. Yet the test lies not in the elegance of an abstracted case, but in our ability to provide new insights in particular instances, and to develop and convey to others some means by which they can generate insights themselves. Much current discourse theory seems of limited use to students of public policy. Its distinctions do not reflect the specifics of our field; they require specialist background and become inaccessible to nearly all policy analysis readers and practitioners. Further, while the complexity of policy argumentation calls for systematic methods of examination, it limits the value of any generic format for analysing all arguments or even all policy arguments. We have partly to develop our own variants of argument analysis.

Des Gasper, Institute of Social Studies, PO Box 29776, 2502 LT The Hague, The Netherlands; e-mail, gasper@iss.nl.

This study is a brief overview of some tools for analysing and assessing policy arguments. I will suggest that the following – overlapping, complementary, and non-exhaustive – contributions are useful in analysing and teaching policy argumentation: (i) some general tools of so-called *'informal logic'* that have been systematised in the past generation; (ii) work that identifies and discusses important *elements of specifically policy argumentation*, and associated tactics, dangers, and stylistic devices; and (iii) methods to try, first, to specify and, secondly, appraise *overall systems or structures of policy argument*.

We need to increase sensitivity in the definition and handling of concepts, and in patterns and types of inference, but also in less familiar areas: firstly, 'formulation', the overall shaping of extended arguments in complex fields, which involves issues such as the specification of boundaries and alternatives; and secondly, 'colligation' and synthesis, the pulling together of available elements towards a conclusion.

II. ELEMENTS OF ARGUMENT ANALYSIS

Toulmin [*1958*] and Scriven [*1976*] suggested that when we try to upgrade practical argumentation we must look largely outside formal logic, for that subject has been concerned with laws, not maxims or tentative assessments. It rarely analyses multi-part real arguments, but instead generally restricts itself to assessing given, isolated parts or artificial arguments; in other words, to quite limited or already clearly ordered sets of propositions, a far cry from real wide-ranging policy arguments. In contrast, Scriven noted that practical argument analysis (also known as 'informal logic') has two phases: first, specifying the content and structure of a real, untidy position, and only secondly, assessing them. The first phase is neither trivial nor already given to us. In analysing policy arguments we normally have to spend considerable time identifying their components and linkages before deciding which parts should be appraised in detail.

Scriven's own format for analysis reflects direct experience in the tangled argumentative world of programme evaluation, and deserves attention. He indicated the following steps (which can be iterative) in the process of *specification* of arguments and positions. A careful, even plodding, approach proves justified here. The steps help us look for components and structures, but do not pre-empt our findings:

(1)   clarification of meanings (not total definitions but distinctions sufficient to the use-in-context);

(2)   identification of conclusions (including unstated implications);

(3)   portrayal of structure (the precise connection of premises, inferences and conclusions);

(4)   Identification of unstated assumptions (the most defensible premises needed to make the argument complete and consistent).

Typically it will be worth first enumerating significant propositions and terms (for example, concepts such as 'efficient' or 'fair' may need examination). One can then construct a diagram or set of diagrams to show interconnections in the overall argument [*Dubnick, 1978*].

Argument *assessment* involves criticism of the premises and inferences that have been identified. Criteria here include (a) (sufficient) clarity; (b) consistency – both logically and with accepted facts; (c) scope – that is, the range of the consistency; (d) simplicity – including absence of special pleading; (e) applicability and refutability; (f) comparison with other relevant arguments. This final criterion might appear unduly to extend the scope of assessment; in fact it keeps matters more manageable and relevant by setting practical parameters, and making assessment relative not absolute. It is easier to defend or attack things if they are considered in isolation; but to reject one argument may mean having none, or implicitly accepting another, and should be assessed in the light of that.

FIGURE 1
SCRIVEN'S SCHEMA FOR ARGUMENT ANALYSIS

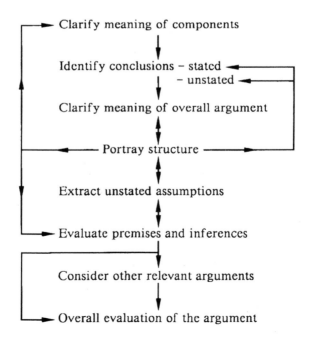

In Figure 1 I summarise Scriven's *procedure* for specifying arguments, as a flow-diagram. We should distinguish his procedure from the use of flow-diagrams for summarising already specified arguments, as Dubnick suggested and as is increasingly practised [*Cole, 1995; Cole, Cameron and Edwards, 1983; Edwards, 1985*]. This sort of summary helps in the clear presentation of a case, but may not coerce one to study the logic of the connections or whether the summary is a good one. Scriven's procedure emphasises painstaking specification, with stages of feedback and iteration, and formalised assessment as well as description.

So, to assess arguments we must first work out what they say and how. Even prior to that we need to find and identify them. Stakeholder analysis helps in spotting different parties and viewpoints involved in an issue. Similarly, unless one identifies the positions that are being responded to, one may miss the meaning of an argument. One's initial listing of viewpoints may, of course, be refined during later analysis.

III. SPECIFICATION OF POLICY ARGUMENTS

Many authors list types of element or component in policy arguments. Pen [*1985*] noted these: (1) proposed observations – although these may be defective, and are bound to be selective; (2) logical statements; (3) empirical statements on relations between observables; (4) methodological statements; (5) images and metaphors used for the integration or 'colligation' of the above elements into 'stories'; (6) value judgements that could be expressions of taste or, truly, judgements; (7) policy recommendations that are produced by a further stage of what Pen calls super-colligation, pulling together values and facts towards normative conclusions.

What we need besides such lists is a way to look at how elements function and connect within an argument as a whole. Toulmin's 'The Uses of Argument' [*1958*] offered something more helpful here than the classical syllogism, and has been applied in later policy analysis theory and cases [e.g. *Mason and Mitroff, 1981*]. Classical logic's focus on determinate inference mean that it is less relevant for us than jurisprudence, which has non-definitive conclusions, exceptions to rules, and so on. Toulmin thus spoke of 'warrants', that support a belief but do not deductively oblige it. He also added to the standard syllogism the categories of 'qualifier' and 'rebuttal', and distinguished between 'grounds' and 'warrants' as types of premise. Grounds are factual statements (purportedly), whereas warrants are the considerations used to move from these empirical particulars towards a conclusion. Warrants in turn require backing of some sort. Figure 2 shows a modified variant of the format adapted by Dunn [*1981*] for policy analysis.

The format illustrates that arguments have structures, and gives one

FIGURE 2

TOULMIN-DUNN SCHEMA FOR SPECIFYING POLICY ARGUMENTS

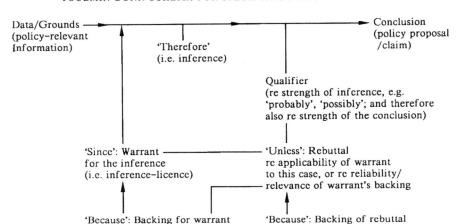

generalised picture of structure. It is a tool for looking at any case at issue presently, but not a universally sufficient pattern.

Toulmin *et al.* [*1979*] use it to show how the character of 'grounds', 'warrants' and so on vary between fields.[1] Even within one field there are various types of warrant. For policy analysis, Dunn [*1981*] illustrates the use of each of: (i) authority; (ii) insight, judgement and intuition; (iii) established analytical methods; iv) standard general propositions; (v) pragmatic comparisons with other cases; and (vi) ethics. An exercise for students is to look for the types of warrant, as well as of backings, grounds and so on, in a selected study or report.

Goldstein [*1984*] confirms how eclectic are the warrants and backings used in arguments in planning. This reflects its interdisciplinary history and tasks, and the need to combine empirical and normative considerations. In drawing inferences from grounds (data about current or projected situations, such as needs and preferences), the warrants used can include positive theories, normative theories about appropriate allocations or procedures, and existing laws. Their proposed backing may include views on method, broad positive and normative conceptions of man and society, the legal constitution, established professional approaches, and so on.[2]

Toulmin and Dunn's format remains too simple to be a complete layout for arguments. 'Grounds' may themselves need backing; there can be several types and layers of warrants and backing; and discourses contain whole sets of propositions. Neither is the format a full procedure for analysing arguments to identify their detailed structures. There is a danger that, after students have learnt it, they may try to force everything into a single strait-jacket and be diverted from analysing the particular features of an argument. One must stress that the format is just a starting point.[3]

Toulmin–Dunn provide a way of looking at a particular proposition or well-knit set of propositions that is more relevant than the standard syllogisms in logic texts, although these may still offer us something important. However, one cannot analyse complex policy positions or debates in the way one would dissect a single page or poem; one must be selective. From Scriven and others we have some advice for analysing the more extended sets of propositions that make up broad arguments. What we require are approaches that combine the insights of Toulmin–Dunn and Scriven and then connect them more thoroughly to key particulars of the policy analysis field.

A helpful proposal is Hambrick's 'Guide for the Analysis of Policy Arguments' [1974], which probes further the nature of warrants, backings, rebuttals and qualifiers in policy arguments. It tries to identify the types of premise involved in any claim that a policy measure will lead to desired impacts and be worthy of support. Such a proposition involves a combination, explicit or implicit, of cause–effect claims and normative claims. This is obvious (although not highlighted in Dunn's format, which simply re-labelled Toulmin's format devised for any type of argument). Hambrick adds other categories: (a) 'grounding propositions', that is, intellectual background (not the same as Toulmin–Dunn's 'grounds'); (b) 'time–place propositions', that is, the context of application for the proposed claims; (c) 'constraints propositions', that is, claims about feasibility; and (d) comparison with alternatives. We will look further at alternatives, constraints and 'grounding' in a subsequent section.

In Figure 3 I take Hambrick's guide beyond a list of elements by putting it in a diagrammatic sequence. In Stage 1 an initial if–then proposition draws on positive data and warrants, and on grounding warrants and backings from theory and methodology (as do other propositions). In Stage 2 normative warrants and backing turn the if–then proposition into a means–ends proposition, which in Stage 3 is tested by a number of possible rebuttals (for example, whether there are better alternatives available), to see how far it is sustainable as an action proposal.

Hambrick's main distinctive stress is thus on what I have called Stage 3, the testing of a means–ends proposition in various ways. Two other increasingly well-known approaches focus somewhat differently: the 'logical framework' approach elaborates the cause–effect chain in Stage 1; and Taylor's model of normative argument, as applied by Fischer [1980] to policy arguments, goes deeper into the normative backing in Stage 2, and can be used similarly to examine grounding propositions. Both models, however, represent to some extent similar elements as in Hambrick's guide. We can consider them in turn.

FIGURE 3

HAMBRICK'S FORMAT FOR THE STRUCTURE OF POLICY ARGUMENTS

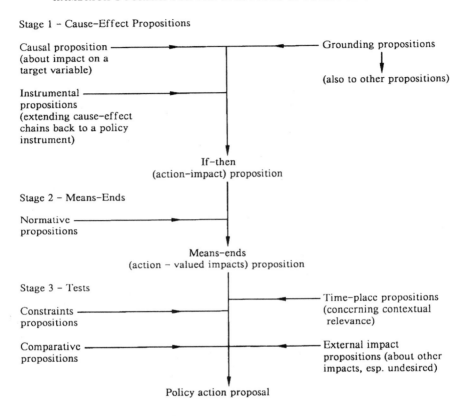

Stage 1 – Cause-Effect Propositions

Causal proposition ——————————————————— Grounding propositions
(about impact on a
target variable)
                                                   (also to other propositions)

Instrumental ——————————————
propositions
(extending cause-effect
chains back to a policy
instrument)

If–then
(action-impact) proposition

Stage 2 – Means-Ends

Normative ——————————————
propositions

Means–ends
(action – valued impacts) proposition

Stage 3 – Tests

Constraints ——————————————— Time-place propositions
propositions   (concerning contextual
                                       relevance)

Comparative ——————————————— External impact
propositions   propositions (about other
                                       impacts, esp. undesired)

Policy action proposal

The '*logical framework approach*' (LFA or 'logframe') in project analysis was developed around 1970 for USAID, and has since been adopted by most of the major official international aid agencies. It attempts (i) to distinguish various levels of project objectives, starting with inputs, through to those about eventual or broader development impacts; (ii) to specify and check the causal linkages between the different levels; (iii) to identify the assumptions about the other factors that are needed for the connections between the different levels to be valid; and (iv) to specify means of measuring the degrees of fulfilment of the various levels of objectives. Elements (i), (ii) and (iii) concern us here. They try to indicate the sequence and structure of argument implied in a project or project proposal.

The original USAID version has four levels of objectives (Inputs-Outputs-

Purpose-Goal). The project's argument has to be put in the following form [*Coleman, 1987*]:

(1)   If the specified Inputs are provided and the specified Assumptions (notably about important conditions external to the project which could interfere with achievement of the Outputs) are fulfilled, then the specified Outputs will be achieved;

(2)   if the specified Outputs are present and a second set of specified Assumptions are fulfilled, then the specified Purpose will be achieved; and

(3)   if the specified Purpose is achieved and a third set of specified Assumptions are fulfilled, then the specified Goal will be achieved.

Assumptions analysis in LFA clearly corresponds to the 'Unless' clauses in Toulmin–Dunn, and to Stage 3 in Hambrick's format, the testing of a means–ends proposition; but the logframe format does not include a built-in set of questions to support this analysis. Many authors observe how, for this and other reasons, the assumptions column is typically completed perfunctorily and unhelpfully.[4] Similarly, the objectives column is frequently confused and arbitrary. Many completed logframes thus have an appearance of logic but lack the substance. The increasingly popular GTZ (German) version, which rejoices in the acronym ZOPP, is more useful. It distinguishes five levels, while reducing the degree of stress on means of measurement, but the relevant difference here is that it specifies the project's chain of means–ends links by first undertaking a problem analysis to establish a chain (or branching 'tree'-diagram) of hypothesised cause–effect links. The problem analysis gives a reasoned, non-arbitrary basis for the logframe's means–ends hierarchy.

Compared to Hambrick's guide, the LFA gives a more concrete means–ends format, but often less advice on how then to proceed with the analysis. Hambrick offers more in the way of procedure, questions and categories. The two approaches are thus fairly complementary.

Fischer's model involves 12 groups of questions implied in policy arguments (Box 1). The 12 are themselves grouped into four levels derived from Taylor [*1961*], moving up from (1) technical analysis in terms of given objectives, to (2) assessing the objectives in terms of available policy goals, to (3) assessing the goals in terms of accepted social ideals, and finally to (4) assessing the ideals. Some details of the model and the ways it is used are open to criticism [*Gasper, 1989*]; but these require a separate discussion. For our present purposes the model valuably suggests the scope for ordering and systematising normative policy arguments, and is becoming quite widely used.

BOX 1

FISCHER'S MODEL OF THE LEVELS OF POLICY EVALUATION

I have paraphrased Fischer [*1980: 206–12*]. The comments in parentheses are Fischer's on how to tackle the questions.

Level 1 (Technical verification of programme objectives):

1) Programme Objectives – Is the program objective logically derived from the relevant policy goals? (Refer to logical rules.)

2) Empirical Consequences – Does the program empirically fulfil its stated objectives? (Refer to empirical knowledge of consequences.)

3) Unanticipated Effects – Does the empirical analysis uncover secondary effects that offset the programme objectives? (Refer to knowledge of consequences.)

4) Alternative Means – Does the program fulfill the objectives more efficiently than alternative means available? (Refer to knowledge of alternative means.)

Level 2 (Situational validation of policy goals):

5) Relevance – Are the policy goals relevant? Can they be justified by appeal to higher principles or established causal knowledge? (Refer to knowledge of established norms and to causal conditions and laws.)

6) Situational Context – Are there any circumstances in the situation which require that an exception be made to the policy goal or criterion? (Refer to particular facts of the situation.)

7) Multiple goals – Are two or more goals equally relevant to the situation? (Refer to normative logic.)

8) Precedence – Does the decision-maker's value system place higher precedence on one of the conflicting criteria? Or does it lead to some contradictory prescriptions? (Refer to normative logic.)

Level 3 (Vindication of political choice):

9) System Consequences – comparison of goal-system's consequences with accepted social ideals in the situation. (Refer to causal conditions and laws.)

10) Equity. (Refer to normative logic and accepted social ideals.)

11) Ideological conflict. (Ditto.)

For questions 10 & 11, there should be discussion of how far the policy's goals and the supporting social ideals are compatible with equitable resolution of conflicts.

Level 4 (Choice of Social Order):

12) Alternative Social Orders – comparison with alternative social orders, if 10 & 11 so imply. (Refer to knowledge of fundamental needs and to normative logic.)

Fischer's model was devised more for assessment than for description, and so we look at it further later. However, checklists of elements or issues that policy arguments *should* cover may also help us also in description, for they provide questions with which to probe what is covered in an argument and what is not. (Hoppe has used Fischer's model in this way.) They similarly help us in generating propositions. The Fischer–Taylor approach of distinguishing broad *levels* helps in describing the levels of normative backing to an argument, *systems* of grounding propositions, and the world-views and 'paradigms' used in different policy stances.

The Fischer model provides more questions than does the LFA. It bears a superficial similarity to LFA, for the prevalent USAID version of LFA also contains four levels. However the top two USAID levels seem roughly to correspond to the bottom two Fischer levels:

FISCHER

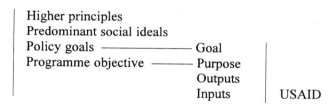

So Fischer's model is stronger for probing the Goal level and beyond, and LFA for levels of Purpose and below. This is consistent with the acknowledged weakness around Goal level in the use of LFA [*Cracknell and Rednall, 1986*]. The use of four levels in both cases probably reflects the attraction of four as a reasonable balance between on the one hand complexity and highlighting of layers and interconnections, and on the other hand simplicity and manage-ability, especially for large-scale use. Dividing a programme into four (or five) levels is usually a simplification; correspondingly in practice the dividing lines between levels are often left unclear.[5]

How may one counter the real danger that once people have learnt an approach they will insist on 'finding' examples of its categories in every argument, and only of those categories? And further, for example, in the use of the LFA, insist on identifying a project's means–ends chain(s) as five-level (or four-level if they have been taught the German version), regardless of the specifics of the case; or, because only one slot is provided in a diagram, identifying only one Purpose or Output when there are several.

I suggest that a picture of imputable sequences of argument in actual project and policy analyses makes a useful complement. The idea is to minimise leading people to preset answers, and to emphasise the creative and variable stages of formulation and final synthesis that can produce a range of structures and tactics. Hopefully this picture balances specificity (and hence practical usefulness) with generality (and so a wide range of application).

Here is a set of activities into which one may analyse the contents, explicit and implicit, of appraisal and evaluation arguments:

(1)   Formulation and framing
      1a – definition of the exact type of assessment question asked
      1b – interpretation of key terms and categories
      1c – defining the scope of materials to which the question is put (this
      involves further questions about alternatives, constraints, boundaries)

(2)   Objectives and criteria
      2a – specification of objectives and criteria
      2b – justification of them (but the presence and form of this stage depend
      on 1a above)

(3)   Data collection: on outcomes, etc.

(4)   Data analysis and interpretation.

(5)   Synthesis
      5a – partial synthesis; as in making predictions, or interpreting what are
      costs and benefits; etc.
      5b – full synthesis: evaluation, prescription, conclusion.

The stress on formulation and synthesis is seen by the first and last stages, which we will examine in sections IV and V below. Much in Hambrick's propositions on grounding, constraints and alternatives corresponds to 'formulation'; there is little in his schema to match 'synthesis'. Yet policy conclusions generally do not follow simply or unequivocally from the materials mustered in their support; further stages of interpretation and judgement are required.

The set of stages above can be useful in both analysing and improving arguments. It is not a necessary sequence for actually constructing, specifying or assessing positions; these sequences could well be more complicated.[6] It is more a format for grouping the multiple strands and clusters that argument analysis will reveal, or that brainstorming produces. (See Apthorpe and Gasper [*1982*], with reference to evaluations of service co-operatives in developing countries.) The stages cited are interactive; for instance, definition of scope and specification of objectives affect each other. Which stages are worth distinguishing depends on the case; for example, interpretation of what are costs and benefits can be sufficiently creative to deserve separate attention. (See Gasper [*1987*] on project analyses.)

One should look broadly at a position in and across its stages, not only at isolated statements. Specifications of positions may reflect an approach to their assessment, for example, a predisposition to defending or condemning (see my paper on essentialism in this collection). Scriven argues that one should lean towards charitable interpretations and, hence, more defensible specifications. This gives priority to developing knowledge rather than criticising as an end in itself. Attacks on weaker specifications of arguments are also more easily dismissed.

In this section I have argued that Toulmin's popular format is not enough to show the mechanics of policy argumentation. We need, too, the more open-ended exploratory methods of Scriven and others, to look at individual cases and patterns, and more reference to the specifics of policy, where Pen and others offer lists of typical components. I have extended Hambrick's work into a sketch of how components fit into an overall policy argument and compared this with the 'logical framework' approach and Fischer's model. The three have different emphases and can be seen as complementary.

In all of these cases there remains the danger that approaches devised to help us think more carefully will lull us into not thinking. I have therefore added a complementary sketch of an imputable set of activities in evaluation arguments, with emphasis on how positions are framed and synthesised from available materials. It directs attention to key issues rather than relying on a fixed format that may be thoughtlessly imitated. The following two sections look further at this framing and synthesis.

IV. FORMULATION AND FRAMING

Policy argument includes as overlapping activities the framing of techniques and the application of social philosophies [*Braybrooke and Lindblom, 1963; MacIntyre, 1977*]. We see this clearly in Fischer's schema. Techniques may only operate within a frame of assumptions and, on the other hand, general principles only become operational through many technical steps. This inter-section needs to be handled in an orderly consistent way, and policy argument analysis tries to unravel the linkages involved. Important issues may otherwise fall neglected between the disciplinary stools of the social scientist and the social philosopher, and sophisticated lower-level materials and higher-level philosophies may be sloppily combined.

Rein's influential discussions of 'framing' in policy analysis take 'frame' as a comprehensive category, such as 'paradigm' in its 'disciplinary-matrix' sense, that is the core set of shared ideas on which the work of a group is based.[7] While examining such paradigms has become common in universities, 'the university environment and culture ... has the tendency of driving [such] inquiry into a metalevel where the philosophical assumptions ... [are] examined ... and runs the risk of deepening the separation between thought and action' [*Rein, 1983: 106*].

I will therefore highlight aspects of argument framing which have an active and practical nature: matters of inclusion, exclusion and attention, including how the burden of proof is distributed, and the perception of alternatives and constraints. There is a case for limiting the word '*framing*' to these areas to help differentiate terms. We used '*formulation*' earlier as a label for a broader concept; the more limited meaning seems better suited, too, to the root metaphor for framing that Rein [*1983: 96-7*] employs – that of visual perspective – than is a sense that covers every aspect of one's approach.

Since choice of broad theoretical/policy paradigm does not settle all other choices, one may highlight these overlapping component areas in formulation: (a) the choice of purpose and standpoint of an argument; (b) the above sense of 'framing'; (c) the choice of terms and categories, and (d) the key images and metaphors used. The first concerns, for example, at what level of a 'logical framework' one is presently arguing and why; who is the client/audience, and what is the context. It is now relatively familiar, as are issues of paradigm choice. Choice of key images (such as 'growth pole') has also been well treated [*Rein and Schön, 1977; McCloskey, 1985*]. Here I will look instead at framing and the boundaries adopted in analysis.

Policy analysts would do well to consider the following *seven connected aspects of framing* when they examine a policy position, rather than consider how to fit it into the categories of, say, the speech-act theory or classical or modern rhetoric. The seven concern the sort of, often, unstated assumptions that were referred to in Scriven's checklist. Limits of space preclude extended examples:

(1) In tracing and weighing of effects, issues of *time horizons* and *discount rates* have become prominent, thanks to environmentalists' attack on the valuations in mainstream economics [*Goodin, 1982*]. The issues are vital because, to exaggerate only slightly, 'any argument can be turned to any effect by juggling with the time scale' [*Elster, 1984: 34*]. All institutions and movements argue, for example, that bad short-term effects will be outweighed by long-term improvements. In the extreme, a supposedly 'infinitely' better future justifies anything that furthers its eventual attainment. At the other extreme, use of a high discount rate may, in effect, render the long-term future of no importance.

(2) The overall issue of the proper *scope* of analyses has been considered in planning theory's debates about comprehensive versus bounded rationality, the range of factors to include in project analyses and so on. Where in open systems should one draw the boundaries of analysis? Matters of scope in identifying *causes* link closely to choices of level of analysis and of broad policy paradigm. Some types of possible *effect* are often ignored if it is believed that all options may equally plausibly claim them, or that action on such matters is better assigned to other policies. On the other hand, Hirschman [*1967*] noted that while analysis cannot go on forever, it must consider those 'side-effects' of projects, such as impacts on self-reliance, management

capacity, commitment and adaptability, that are in fact vital in their future operation.

Also enlightening here is work by historians conscious of the necessity of selection in their accounts and analyses and of corresponding criteria. Some connections are traced but not others; some contributory factors are highlighted as causes but not others. The issue is not that this is done – for neither causes nor effects may be traced in totality or without end – but how consistently and defensibly [*Stretton, 1969*]. The convenience of an author, rather than his or her special insight, may underlie claims of necessary bounds to the argument, as signalled by 'in the final analysis' and similar phrases. These require probing to see if they have more content than just 'where I want to stop (or happen to have stopped) the analysis'.

Critics of foreign aid from both Right and Left have insisted that aid be seen as contributing to a wider system, which they respectively identify as public sector socialism or dependent capitalism; and they then simply assess aid by assessing that system. Whereas liberals who have sought to identify precise project impacts are faced with problems such as that aid flows can release domestic resources for other uses that are very hard to identify. They have sometimes concluded [e.g. *Wood and Morton, 1977*] that evaluation is an unending task, with rapidly diminishing returns. The greater the scope in any policy analysis, the greater, often, is the indeterminateness. The need then is for defensible principles of delimitation. These can be legal, political, ethical, administrative, economic and procedural-methodological. And this is the heart of policy analysis [*Self, 1975*].

(3) Focusing includes distribution of the *burden of proof*. Has a policy or a danger to be sufficiently proved or sufficiently disproved? What is the balance adopted between the risks of Type I and Type II errors? (that is, the risks of rejecting a true claim/good proposal, and of accepting a false claim/bad proposal [*Gasper, 1987*]). Similarly, why are certain things taken as not needing explanation, as being 'normal' or 'natural' and so on?

(4) These designations of a 'base case' are of special interest in valuative argument: what is the *baseline* against which something is judged positive or negative, an improvement or a retrogression? It is a commonplace that revolutions are more likely after an earlier period of improvement, just as loneliness can become intolerable after a taste of contact. Conflicts often involve different views over how things would be in the absence of the feature that is in dispute, and these typically depend much on conceptions of how things *could* and *should* be.[8] In investment analysis, for example, the specification of the 'without-project' case is generally more important for the results than are the refinements of cost-benefit analysis that have received so

much attention from theorists [*Stewart, 1978*].

(5) We need to ask more generally what comparisons are made. The conceived *alternatives* often determine the evaluation of a situation. Thus Bienefeld [*1982*], when arguing how relatively casual some academic assessments of Tanzanian performance have been, drew out a variety of tacit or under-argued optimistic assumptions used by critics from the Left and Right on the feasible alternatives that were available, supposedly.

Struggles to legitimate one base case and set of categories rather than another sometimes involve controlled comparisons of the performance of different systems, but with the control used to ensure certain conclusions. The alternative to the inherently efficient and enlightened system that the advocate favours is often depicted as a a collage of its bad features, so that it can be ruled out from further consideration. The actual performance of one's preferred system may then be more easily defended. Rulers have a special fondness for TINA, the claim that 'There Is No Alternative' to their current policy. TINA is also an assertion about constraints, and leads to the Panglossian claim that one is in the best of all *possible* worlds.

(6) A linked aspect of alternatives concerns the ideas used about the range of *means* that are available and legitimate, and how they work. In practice 'policies in taxation, welfare, subsidization and so forth ... [operate in ways that are] complex, unintended, hard to alter' [*Schaffer and Lamb, 1981: 75–6*]. Past disputes in cost-benefit theory thus often centred – implicitly – on what are the constraints in using *other* policy tools: which variables are manipulable and which must be accepted as given [*FitzGerald, 1978*].

(7) Layard [*1972*] has suggested more generally that underlying most normative disputes is the question of which factors are to be taken as given, as constraints. Definition of *constraints* is thus the other crucial face of framing. The answers necessarily reflect both theories and values, for to call something a constraint means claiming that there is an unsatisfactory rate-of-return from trying to change it; and so they are often controversial. Compared to the project level, some argue that at broad policy levels the criteria of (economic) efficiency and optimisation become more obscure and potentially misleading, and constraints more numerous instead, so that analysis can usefully centre on them [*Majone, 1975; Seers, 1983*]. Neo-liberals have instead believed they can define, and enforce, efficiency economy-wide, nation-wide, and world-wide (see Gore in this collection).[9]

One needs to be suspicious of alleged constraints but assertions, or presumptions, of absence of constraint must be treated sceptically, too [*Goodin, 1977; Gasper, 1987*]. The allegations are likely to be emphatic in an attempt to avoid debate. 'The government of India, for example, *simply cannot* command the resources that would guarantee each one of [the] inhabitants of India a standard of living adequate for the health and well-being of himself and his family [sic]' [*Cranston, 1973: 67;* my emphasis]. Yet the governments of Sri Lanka and China can substantially do it. As Bentham noted, 'the plea of impossibility offers itself at every step, in justification of injustice'.

Having noted in sections III and IV some key structural elements, we can turn more to how they link up in arguments. Just as the scope of policy argumentation means we must study its framing, so when we look at extended discourses we must consider overall texturing and pattern, not just the strength of individual links.[10]

V. STYLE, STORY-TELLING, AND COLLIGATION

One can investigate 'style' in various ways. Sillince [*1986*] tries to identify language forms corresponding to different policy contexts. He discusses four language styles he sees in urban and regional planning: hortatory, administrative, legal and bargaining. It is useful, too, to simply list various stylistic devices, for sensitisation rather than memorisation. McCloskey [*1985*] and others give illustrations, and government plans are a rich source (see Box 2). George [*1990*] shows some distorting devices used to present 'Government as Intrusive Alien' and 'Taxes as Burdensome Impositions' in many of the most used introductory American economics textbooks; the cases hinge on the 'details' of choice of terms and choice of comparisons.

Of special interest are the devices by which authors rule out certain things

---

BOX 2

PURPOSEFUL TALK – THE BOTSWANA TRIBAL GRAZING LAND POLICY

'Efforts will be made to develop means for the progressive restriction of TGLP herds to their ranches' – i.e. for enforcement of a longstanding legal condition in the ranch-leases – says the sixth National Plan for Botswana (1985: para.4.65). We can break this sentence into three parts:-

    1. Efforts will be made

    2. to develop means

    3. for the progressive restriction of ...

Each part contains words of action, and the overall effect is thus one of purposefulness. (Mention of the past non-implementation of legal requirements is left until later.)

    But suppose we remove the first part of the sentence, to leave something like 'Means will be developed for the progressive restriction of TGLP herds ... '. Interestingly, the result now seems more purposeful, not less. Alternatively we could remove the second part, which gives us 'Efforts will be made to progressively restrict ... ' Finally, suppose we remove both the first and second parts, and just say 'TGLP herds will be progressively restricted to their ranches [as required by law] ... ' There are now fewer purposeful words and yet a more powerful meaning.

as needing to be discussed or taken further. Exclusion can be tacit, or by invoking precedents, authority, 'likeliness', 'obviousness' and so on. Exclusion is part of framing, but is especially marked in the concluding stages of extended arguments when authors may be in a hurry to arrive at claims.

The project of McCloskey and others to identify the forms of 'the rhetoric of the human sciences' [*Nelson et al., 1987*] has encountered some resistance, not least the belief that it is 'merely looking at style'. However, the way the components of an argument are selected and handled is *both* style and substance of the argument. If one does distinguish, then McCloskey suggests that we see style as 'the details of substance' rather than as surface ornament [*1988: 286*]. Until recently their research project has not given much attention to the organisation of positions in policy-oriented argumentation (although see Throgmorton [*1991*]).[11] So in the previous sections, especially that on formulation, I have highlighted some major 'details' of the substance of policy argumentation.

Two further important lines are the work on 'colligation' and 'storytelling'. Practical argument often involves synthesis of judgements from a variety of experiences and of types of argument. The latter type of synthesis is especially common in policy, since one must relate disparate sets of ideas (economic, sociological, political, administrative). Colligation refers to the construction of overall arguments, where one has 'to connect or link together, tie, join, to relate (isolated facts, observations etc.) by a general hypothesis' (*Collins Dictionary*). It 'is ubiquitous ... because only [so] can one tie ... research to the uses to which [social science] is put' [*Ward, 1972: 181*]. In policy argument it involves further layers, with the use of ideas about purposes and values, as implied in Pen's ugly label, 'normative super-colligation'.

The term 'storytelling' likewise conveys the need for selection and construction from what materials are actually available (rather than just hoped for). Unfortunately its connotations of narrative sequence, and of casualness or even deception, make it controversial as a general label. We refer here though to the sort of disciplined interpretive description practised by the good historian. (In contrast, mathematical economists' 'stories' are often fables.) Explaining actions requires relating them to contexts that may never be fully or non-interpretively described. These inevitably partial explanations are colligated into an overall account of behaviour. Story-telling is then not just one more phase or technique but the purposeful knitting together and application of all the relevant phases and techniques, including resolving disputes between them. Besides being used to understand past events, and in scenarios of possible future implementation problems, narratives may help in coming to agreed policy proposals [*Kaplan, 1986*].[12]

Analysis of the available 'stories' in a particular case involves analysing arguments by means such as we mentioned earlier, and something more.

Criticism and improvement of 'story-telling' require awareness that selections, and hence criteria of selection, are inevitable and may need to be clarified; and likewise for the stitching together of incomplete materials into conclusions.

'Storytelling' is empirical, for without information there is little to select or stitch. Unfortunately the term has obscured this to some. Several commentators have been enraged into inattention, as are others by McCloskey's use of the word 'rhetoric'.[13] Many authors have presented ways of countering the dangers and for assessing 'stories' [*Ward, 1972; Rein and Schon, 1977; Wilber, 1978; Kaplan, 1986*]. The criteria in their lists are largely familiar. For example, Kaplan speaks of truth, richness, consistency, congruency and unity;[14] although not all the criteria (for example, fertility, elegance, consistency with felt convictions and expert belief) are part of the older philosophy of science, and they are often overlooked in the enraged attacks that allege rejection of all criteria. Kaplan and others propose instead to make our actual practice of argumentation more explicit and systematic.

VI. ARGUMENT ASSESSMENT

Aspects of assessment have emerged in earlier sections. Much follows directly from careful argument specification: for example seeing how far terms are used consistently, or what alternatives have been considered. Often one may take it as a compliment to be told one has 'only' identified 'simple' errors, for in reality, inconsistencies and failings may involve elements that are spread wide and deep within positions, amongst thousands of words not already collated and displayed. All errors appear simple when broken into steps, but the identification may be far from simple; having some methods is important. Flawed policy arguments are not in general knowingly constructed and then defended; instead, appealing or convenient arguments are defended, and these then need to be deconstructed.

Corresponding to *universal criteria* of assessment are standard lists of *fallacies*. Toulmin *et al.* [*1979: 158–85*], following Aristotle, distinguish 'fallacies of ambiguity', which trade on obscurity in key terms; and 'fallacies of unwarranted assumptions' or unwarranted inferences, which involve inconsistency with rules of logic or accepted facts or other premises. Thouless [*1974*] and others provide similar compilations. It is neither sufficient, nor indispensable to study such lists. Much of the important pitfall orientation is subject-specific, but they help as much to increase alertness as to provide specific tools. Toulmin, for example, lists 18 fallacies with some sub-variants, and Thouless provides 38; these are practical lists, neither uselessly vague nor immensely academic. They should be combined with the study of subject-specific pitfalls as in Majone's [*1989*] proposal for 'craft training' in policy analysis.[15]

We noted earlier that the content and character of 'grounds' and 'warrants' vary between fields. Toulmin concluded that 'all the canons for the criticism and assessment of arguments are in practice field-dependent' [*1958: 38*], and illustrated this at length in a later textbook. It can be misplaced, for example, to criticise ethical or policy arguments for not being mathematical or natural science arguments. 'Context determines criteria' [*Toulmin et al., 1979: 120*].

Some authors argue that certain criteria are implicit in the (or a) particular context of policy argument. 'Political evaluation, as a [specific] subuniverse of evaluative discourse, specifies a "point of view"' [*Fischer, 1980: 113*]. There are various interpretations of what this entails: for example, reference to 'the public interest'; or, according to Anderson [*1979*], to efficiency, justice, and appropriate authority (although the meaning of each is, of course, open to debate).[16]

MacRae [*1993*] offers five worthy though pedestrian criteria for assessing policy proposals relative to given goals and values, in other words, within a group of like-minded people. Proposals should (1) not omit reference to relevant valuative criteria; (2) not elevate means into ends; (3) compare alternative policies, including the *status quo* and doing nothing; (4) not omit relevant information; and (5) consider relative quantities. A multi-criteria matrix can ensure that the pros and cons of each relevant alternative are considered for each relevant criterion. He also offers a few points, equivalent to pieces of a professional ethics, concerning what tactics are unacceptable in debate between groups with different goals, and how to constrain them.

The Fischer model (see Box 1 above) shows this layering of types of policy discourse in a deeper and clearer way, and much more. His 'A Logic of Policy Questions' [*1980: 206–12*] provides a general heuristic for considering how particular families of questions correspond to certain levels of the evaluation of policy arguments (see Box 1 above). We noted that some of its questions match Hambrick's, but with more probing of normative and grounding propositions, and more on warrant-backing hierarchies than in the Toulmin–Dunn model. It gives one serviceable frame for looking at whole positions, not just the mechanics of single propositions or proposals. The 'Logic of Policy Questions' is now quite extensively used in teaching and research in the Netherlands [*de Graaf and Hoppe, 1989; Hoppe et al., 1990; Hoppe, 1993*].

Its emphasis on desirable elements of a policy argument still needs to be complemented by methods to identify actual tactics, links and structures, like the formats we saw earlier. In addition, full operational classifications of questions have to be specific to particular policy contexts. Finally, Fischer's framework reflects a certain philosophy of valuation, derived from Taylor [*1961*] and others. Thus he speaks of 'A' rather than 'The' logic of policy questions. By going in-depth into one widely used philosophy he is able to give more precise, even if not universally binding, illustrations of how policy argumentation synthesises positive and normative aspects.[17]

After noting criteria of assessment, we must consider practical matters of strategy. Outside the closed worlds of mathematics and formal logic, and given the presence of multiple criteria which can pull in different directions, assessment is a matter of reasoned judgement and not always of decisive demonstration; and what is reasonable generally depends on the context.

First, since it usually does not suffice to point out an individual fallacy here or there in a component argument of a position, Scriven's canons of assessment in section II above went beyond clarity and consistency, to matters such as scope and comparison with other relevant arguments. The criteria for assessing wider story-telling come in here, too. Some quantification and weighting of criteria may sometimes be useful as a check, since our unaided powers of aggregation tend to be unreliable. Assessment is not absolute, but may clarify differences and their sources, shift balances, and help sift out arguments.

Second, for real-world debates, where the strands of argument may spread virtually without limit, Scriven advised focusing one's energies. Concentrate on the parts of an argument that support the main conclusions, not necessarily on the weakest parts; and concentrate on strong variants of positions. Since positions are frequently underspecified, priority should usually go to encouraging their improvement rather than trying totally to tie them down for absolute judgement at one moment. In practice most positions will accept implicitly some criticism and an assessment of 'could do better', as is seen by their evolving after the criticism.

Next, immanent criticism is often helpful, using the position's own terms, as opposed to transcendent criticism, which draws on clearly external criteria and intellectual resources. Immanent criticism works within a position, but does not imply acceptance of the whole position. Positions are layered; parts of them, such as methodological criteria, may have priority and be used to rule against some other parts. Also, the immanent/transcendent distinction is not absolute, since positions are usually not sharply defined and bounded. The layered systems have fuzzy bounds. Positions exist as both (A), the stated representations, and (B), the representations' sources, that are somewhat vague, and neither totally stated nor perfectly represented by (A). Appeal to the quasi-internal resources in (B) is an important aspect of criticism which aims to persuade [*Nussbaum and Sen, 1987; Walzer, 1987*]. Whether it is then called immanent or transcendent could vary with context. Scriven's advice was thus to give less priority to judging the current representations than to improving their portrayal of their sources. Rigorous criticism is still vital in this, but some of the emotions it arouses might thereby be reduced.

Fourthly, the debating aspect to assessments is fundamental, as it is for policy argumentation itself. Indeed we saw that debate, in the form of possible rebuttals and comparison with alternative views, is integral to all practical argumentation as elucidated by Toulmin and Scriven. Arguments attempt to persuade an audience; they respond, even if implicitly, to previously stated views; and their meanings always go beyond the conscious control of the author [*Throgmorton, 1993*]. Assessments of the quality of arguments involve interchanges between parties, where 'face' can be as important as 'faiths'.

The selective interchange in debates is potentially a way of concentrating on matters that are more important in the given context, but it can also facilitate conflict. People usually cannot resist concentrating on others' peripheral apparent inconsistencies, to imply their own superiority, since that is often easier than demonstrating it.

Also common are crossed transactions where responses are directed at implications it is feared others *might* draw from a statement, rather than directed (as in complementary transactions) to its actual content.

Examples of complementary transactions:
   Stimulus – co-operatives aren't suitable in cases A to H.
   Responses – (i) I agree; (ii) I don't agree; (iii) I agree for cases A to D, but not for cases E to H; (iv) for reasons x,y, and z, I think you should review your arguments and criteria.

Examples of crossed transactions:
   Stimulus – co-operatives aren't suitable in cases A to H.
   Responses – (i) co-operatives aren't to blame for lack of suitability; (ii) I deny that co-operatives are a flawed and inferior form of organisation; (iii) so you reject co-operatives (see Apthorpe and Gasper [*1982*]).

Many a time, transactions reinforce differences rather than reduce them; so some policy analysis techniques keep parties out of direct contact, to reduce the peripheral conflicts. The above set of crossed responses is prone to be followed by 'you renegade', and more. Provoked by the tactics and tone of debates around evaluations of formal rural service co-operatives in India, Baviskar and George [*1988*] provided a thoughtful set of suggestions on controversy management. Debates around other policies and organisations are equally heated and in need of help.

Finally, assessors must not be surprised by the apparent persistence of identified fallacies, nor by the denial of change even if and when fallacies are abandoned. On one occasion one thing is said, on another something evidently inconsistent, but the two may have a common inspiration: a belief in the essential desirability of the policy being discussed, and a common effect, namely, its vindication. Even a feeling of consistency may then be retained. In the short run, the 'open texture' of concepts[18] may help cover inconsistencies and defence of idealised essences; but in the longer run it may provide a yet more valuable service. For when adaptation is felt advisable, open texture eases an evolution under cover of claiming – indeed perhaps still comfortingly feeling – that one's essential position has not changed, even though by operational tests one's effective position clearly has. 'But of course we have always believed in [our new position].'

VII. CONCLUSION: TACTICS BUILD STRUCTURES

I have presented argumentation in policy analysis and planning as selective and creative, so I have tried to outline an active flexible approach in argument analysis. This is not a grand theory but some usable themes and methods that should help to draw forth skills, not depress them under a supposedly total map of policy argumentation. The approach aims to be flexible where there can be differences in structure and elements between cases, but to stress issues in 'opening' and 'closing' that arise in every case. I have tried, too, to present argument specification and assessment in a broader context, to help in identification, generation and improvement of arguments, not just the examination of given and fixed positions.

In a complex field, none of the methods mentioned, or others, or all put together, will guarantee correct or insightful analyses, and they may be misused. However, in general they should help. Many may be viewed as similar to the aids one uses when learning a language or some other skill. Once one has mastered such aids, one may go on to more novel tasks and refer back only occasionally.

My concern has been to introduce modest but helpful tools. There is little point in asking policy analysts to master the latest models from speech-act theory or whatever, elaborated without reference to the specifics of their field. We need instead to mobilise and complement their 'trade'-skills. With students, too, we should foster skills that will help them to grapple with cases by themselves, during their courses and later. While the literature on policy argumentation has more to offer (see Fischer and Forester [1993]), I have considered that one priority is to present a practical approach to analysing arguments. The second priority has been to highlight a few important issue clusters that may be vividly conveyed in teaching. A kit of 'watch-out-fors' and 'think-carefully-abouts' should supplement the standard tools. Argument analysis must include sensitivity both to use of language and to wider structures. The issue cluster of framing was emphasised accordingly. There and elsewhere, policy argument analysis can and should give attention both to broad conceptions and precise details and, vitally, show how those conceptions are realised through the mere 'details' of argument. Tactics build structures.

NOTES

1. If rewriting *The Uses of Argument*, Toulmin has said he would stress further how the very substance of the things at stake varies between fields, and hence how each field is distinctive [*Toulmin, 1990*].

2. Goldstein suggests that in utilitarian arguments the grounds include individual preferences, market prices and so on; the warrants are from orthodox welfare economics; and the backing is utilitarian social philosophy (with more or less liberal amendment). In systems arguments, grounds include estimated and/or projected system conditions; the warrants are the models used in the system, and the posited goals, usually for system maintenance, backed by the associated methodology. In procedural arguments, the grounds are facts about the procedure by which a conclusion is reached (for example, majority voting held under certain conditions); the warrant is a purported principle of good procedure; and the backing is a supportive social philosophy. He noted, too, the prominence of qualifiers and rebuttals in policy and planning arguments, given our limited theories, orientation to an uncertain future, and typical need to act before research may fully mature.

3. Figure 2 refines the schema by noting that there may be a rebuttal not only to a warrant, but also to a backing.

4. See Cracknell and Rednall [*1986*]; Wiggins and Shields [*1995*]. Location of the assumptions column at the far right of the logical framework diagram contributes to its neglect, at least in the USAID and related versions that place two other columns between the means-ends hierarchy and the associated assumptions. People obliged to fill in a logframe are, in addition, often exhausted by the time they reach this fourth column. A more sensible location would be directly adjacent to the means–ends hierarchy, on its left.

5. The orthodox case for standardisation and associated simplification holds that, unless principles of analysis are incorporated into compulsory administrative routines, they are unlikely to have widespread and sustained impact [*Cracknell and Rednall, 1986*]. Bureaucracy favours standardisation for large-scale use by ordinary staff, and for ease of comparison and central supervision; one's judgement on standardisation may depend on how much faith one has in people's independent thinking. The LFA also seems more used in aid programmes than in domestically funded programmes in either rich or poor countries; the resolution (on paper) of objectives is easier to enforce when the players have such unequal power.

6. Thomas [*1972*] presents a similar picture, and notes that it is a 'reconstructed logic'. He then contrasts it with a pragmatic 'logic-in-use' for actually making and testing value judgements.

7. In fact Kuhn's other, neglected sense of 'paradigm' is equally important here: 'exemplar' paradigms are concrete instances of exemplary practice, that embody ideas that can be recognised but are not easily or satisfactorily formalisable, including ways of 'seeing' situations or of deciding which formalisations should be applied and how. The meaning of exemplars is notably open-textured and open to evolution [*Kuhn, 1977*]. Exemplar is not only the older meaning, but also not prone to the potential danger with the other sense (that is, a way-of-thinking or disciplinary matrix) of inducing lack of care when we examine others' ideas.

8. The choice of base case can be vital in bids to define the term 'justice'. In the classic liberal view of Locke, a man has exclusive right to the products of his own labour, including land that he opens up, provided that there be 'enough and as good left in common for others'. Many enclosure movements in fact reduced the standard of life of those who had benefited from communal rights of access. Hence, property holders and their advocates often seek a modified reading of Locke's proviso. The relevant baseline for those who are excluded by the privatisation of common property is taken as their well-being in an original 'state-of-nature', in which resources were not scarce but where living standards were conveniently low. It is easier to defend privatisation when 'the baseline for comparison is so low' [*Nozick, 1974: 181*]. Yet if one argues – as do many defenders of privatisation – that the long-run position of the excluded be considered, and that short-term losses may be outweighed by longer-term gains, then the baseline for the comparison should not be static. It should be what others' standard of life would be over time without the privatisation, for example, with socialisation when that has been an historically relevant alternative. The baseline then could well rise over time and not flatter private holding in the way that Nozick's argument does [*Paul, 1982*].

9. While economists are trained to think of constraints, they can forget even economic constraints, for example, the need for states to raise revenue on a scale beyond the scope of allocatively 'neutral' methods. There are also numerous constraints of law and administrative procedure, and political, behavioural and administrative capacity limits. Some development economists find absurd the idea that a government could wish to pursue an objective (for example, redistribution) but be effectively barred from using an available means (say taxation) [Stewart, 1975]; they read this as just a disguised statement of lack of concern, for they presume that a government is like an individual. However, existing tools may be so burdened with other tasks, or so inert and difficult to change, that introduction of a new tool (such as social cost-benefit analysis in investment choice) might enable those using it to advance the objective to some degree.

10. I have not discussed the social framing of argumentation, including selection and grouping of participants, a key aspect of argument generation. Mason and Mitroff [1981] and Fischer and Forester [1993] put argument analysis in this perspective.

11. For an example of 'the new rhetoric' – that is, an integration of classical rhetoric's study of style with analysis of other aspects of argumentation – applied to programme evaluations, see Appendix A of House [1980]. Much of the early work on 'rhetoric of economics' was on the Keynesian versus monetarist versus new classical controversies in macroeconomics [e.g. Klamer, 1984], but emphasised rather universally posed policy issues of intervention versus non-intervention and discretion versus fixed rules. Attention to more intricate and substantive policy argumentation becomes unavoidable in work on sectors such as health or roads; see Colvin [1985].

12. Although often consensus on objectives and criteria is unattainable, agreement on actions is sometimes still attainable through composing and scrutinising a narrative that reviews past experience, explains current dilemmas, and presents corresponding proposals. Value criteria may be left partly implicit, only suggested by the account; for the proposals may be compatible with a range of values and objectives and hence acceptable to a range of people.

13. See reviews of Pen [1985] by Cohen [1986]; and of Klamer et al. [1988] by Blaug [1989]. McCloskey [1994] gives a magisterial rejoinder to his critics.

14. Incongruency is when adjacent elements seem to conflict, without adequate explanation being given. Unity means that the sections of a story clearly show their relationship to each other.

15. Sillince [1986] gives examples from planning, for 18 types of fallacy, mostly based on Thouless. In some instances one might query whether the fallacy is well presented, distinct from others, and well exemplified, or even whether what is described is always a fallacy. This is partly inevitable when one comes to complex real cases; and it offers an opportunity to engage students, not spoonfeed them. They can also consider what type of fallacy each is: (1) conceptual; (2) inferential; or (3) failure to look at relevant factors; (4) introduction of irrelevant factors or (5) a 'Type III error' of addressing the wrong question. Dunn [1993: 261] contrasts 'first-order errors.. the choice of the less valid of two or more causal inferences [for example, Type I and Type II errors], and 'second-order errors.. the selection of the less appropriate of two or more world-views, frames of reference, or problem definitions'.

16. Dunn [1981: 232–9] has a similar list of criteria, but is non-committal on whether they are obligatory. He also presents extensive sets of more general criteria relevant to knowledge claims, covering (a) types of possible warrant or backing, and (b) types of possible rebuttal [1993b: 270–82]. Similarly, Dunn [1990] collates a large number of possible weaknesses: the classical fallacies in deduction, plus the fallacies possible in asserting causality (standard in discussions of experimental design), plus the sorts of 'practical' criteria (clarity, scope and so on) we saw earlier from Scriven; he does not advance as clearly as Fischer does to substantive considerations of what a *policy* argument should have covered but did not.

17. Taylor's proposal was that testing a normative judgement requires four stages: 'verification', 'validation', 'vindication', 'rational choice'. Fischer valuably suggests which types of social science and philosophy correspond to the four levels. It is debatable, however, to take Taylor's model as a universal prescription (let alone description). It reflects the work in moral philosophy of Kurt Baier, Herbert Feigl and R.M. Hare, and is consistent with a type of rule-consequentialism. This is why it provides four, rather than more or fewer levels. It fits some socio-cultural-political set-ups and issue areas better than others, and 'it is possible to have as many forms of policy analysis as there are systems of political thought' [Anderson, 1987: 26].

Even given its philosophy, the four levels in fact overlap and flow into each other, rather than being sharply distinct (see the Appendix to Gasper [*1989*]). Some applications mainly use just two aggregated levels [*Hoppe et al., 1990*]: policy discourse that employs given normative beliefs concerning a policy, and discourse concerning those beliefs.

18. This means our inability to specify a full and exact set of necessary conditions that together are the sufficient condition for use of a term; instead, meanings develop in the process of use. See Gasper on 'Essentialism' in this collection.

REFERENCES

Anderson, C.W., 1979, 'The Place of Principles in Policy Analysis', *American Political Science Review*, Vol.73, No.3, pp.711–23.

Anderson, C.W., 1987, 'Political Philosophy, Practical Reason and Policy Analysis', in F. Fischer and J. Forester (eds.), *Confronting Values in Policy Analysis*, Beverly Hills, CA: Sage, pp.22–44.

Apthorpe, R.J. and D.R. Gasper, 1982, 'Policy Evaluation and Meta-Evaluation: the Case of Rural Cooperatives', *World Development*, Vol.10, No.8, pp.651–69.

Baviskar, B. and S. George, 1988, 'Development and Controversy', *Economic and Political Weekly*, Vol.XXIII, No.13, A.35–43.

Bienefeld, M., 1982, 'Tanzania: Model or Anti-Model?', in M. Bienefeld and M. Godfrey (eds.), *The Struggle for Development*, Chichester: Wiley, pp.293–322.

Blaug, M., 1989, Book review, *Economic Journal*, Vol.99 (Sept.), pp.856–7.

Braybrooke, D. and C. Lindblom, 1963, *A Strategy of Decision*, New York: Free Press of Glencoe.

Cohen, A.J., 1986, Book review, *Journal of Economic Literature*, Vol.XXI (Sept.), pp.1218–19.

Cole, K., 1995, *Understanding Economics*, London: Pluto Press.

Cole, K., J. Cameron and C. Edwards, 1983, *Why Economists Disagree*, Harlow: Longman.

Coleman, G., 1987, 'Logical Framework Approach', *Project Appraisal*, Vol.2, No.4, pp.251–9.

Colvin, P., 1985, *The Economic Ideal in British Government*, Cambridge: Cambridge University Press.

Cracknell, B. and Rednall, J., 1986, *Defining Objectives and Measuring Performance in Aid Projects and Programmes*, Report No.EV384, Evaluation Department, Overseas Development Administration, UK.

Cranston, M., 1973, *What are Human Rights?*, London: Bodley Head.

Dubnick, M., 1978, 'Comparing Policy Alternatives', *Policy Studies Journal*, Vol.6, No.3, pp.368–75.

Dunn, W.N., 1981, *Public Policy Analysis: An Introduction*, Englewood Cliffs, NJ: Prentice Hall (Second Edition 1993).

Dunn, W.N., 1990, 'Justifying Policy Arguments', *Evaluation and Program Planning*, Vol.13, pp.321–9.

Dunn, W.N., 1993, 'Policy Reforms as Arguments', in Fischer and Forester [*1993: 254–90*].

Edwards, C., 1985, *The Fragmented World*, London: Methuen.

Elster, J., 1984, *Ulysses and the Sirens*, Cambridge: Cambridge University Press.

Fischer, F., 1980, *Politics, Values and Public Policy*, Boulder, CO: Westview Press.

Fischer, F. and J. Forester (eds.), 1993, *The Argumentative Turn in Policy Analysis and Planning*, Durham, NC: Duke University Press.

FitzGerald, E.V.K., 1978, *Public Sector Investment Planning for Developing Countries*, London: Macmillan.

Gasper, D.R., 1987, 'Motivations and Manipulations: Practices of Project Appraisal and Evaluation', *Manchester Papers on Development*, Vol.3, No.1, pp.24-70.

Gasper, D.R., 1989, 'Policy Argument', *Working Paper No.47*, Institute of Social Studies, The Hague.

George, D., 1990, 'The Rhetoric of Economics Texts', *Journal of Economic Issues*, Vol.XXIV, No.3, pp.861–78.

Goldstein, H.A., 1984, 'Planning as Argumentation', *Environment and Planning B: Planning and Design*, No.11, pp.297–312.

Goodin, R., 1977, 'Ethical Perspectives on Political Excuses', *Policy and Politics*, Vol.5, pp.71–8.

Goodin, R., 1982, 'Discounting discounting', *Journal of Public Policy*, Vol.2, pp.53–72.
de Graaf, H. and R. Hoppe, 1989, *Beleid en Politiek*, Muiderberg: Coutinho.
Hambrick, R.S., 1974, 'A Guide for the Analysis of Policy Arguments', *Policy Sciences*, Vol.5, No.4, pp.469–78.
Hirschman, A., 1967, *Development Projects Observed*, Washington, DC: Brookings.
Hoppe, R., 1993, 'Political Judgement and the Policy Cycle: the Case of Ethnicity Policy Arguments in the Netherlands', in Fischer and Forester [*1993: 77–100*].
Hoppe, R. *et al.*, 1990, 'Belief Systems and Risky Technologies', *Industrial Crisis Quarterly*, Vol.4, pp.121–40.
House, E., 1980, *Evaluating with Validity*, Beverly Hills, CA: Sage.
Kaplan, T.J., 1986, 'The Narrative Structure of Policy Analysis', *Journal of Policy Analysis and Management*, Vol.5, No.4, pp.761–78.
Klamer, A., 1984, 'Levels of Discourse in New Classical Economics', *History of Political Economy*, Vol.16, No.2, pp.263–90.
Klamer, A. *et al.* (eds.), 1988, *The Consequences of Economic Rhetoric*, Cambridge: Cambridge University Press.
Kuhn, T. S., 1977, *The Essential Tension*, Chicago, IL: University of Chicago Press.
Layard, R., 1972, 'Introduction', in R. Layard (ed.), *Cost-Benefit Analysis*, Harmondsworth: Penguin, pp.9–69.
MacIntyre, A., 1977, 'Utilitarianism and Cost Benefit Analysis', in K. Sayre (ed.), *Values in the Electric Power Industry*, Notre Dame, Indiana: Notre Dame University Press, pp.217–37.
MacRae, D., 1993, 'Guidelines for Policy Discourse', in Fischer and Forester [*1993: 291–318*].
McCloskey, D., 1985, *The Rhetoric of Economics*, Madison, WI: University of Wisconsin Press.
McCloskey, D., 1988, 'The Consequences of Rhetoric', in Klamer *et al.* [*1988: 280–93*].
McCloskey, D., 1994, *Knowledge and Persuasion in Economics*, Cambridge: Cambridge University Press.
Majone, G., 1975, 'The Feasibility of Social Policies', *Policy Sciences*, Vol.6, No.1, pp.49–70.
Majone, G., 1989, *Evidence, Argument and Persuasion in the Policy Process*, New Haven, CT: Yale University Press.
Mason, R.O. and I.I. Mitroff, 1981, *Challenging Strategic Planning Assumptions*, New York: Wiley.
Nelson, J.S. *et al.* (eds.), 1987, *The Rhetoric of the Human Sciences*, Madison, WI: University of Wisconsin Press.
Nozick, R., 1974, *Anarchy, State and Utopia*, New York: Basic Books.
Nussbaum, M. and A. Sen, 1987, 'Internal Criticism and Indian Rationalist Traditions', *Working Paper 30*, World Institute for Development Economics Research, Helsinki.
Paul, J. (ed.), 1982, *Reading Nozick*, Oxford: Blackwell.
Pen, J., 1985, *Among Economists*, Amsterdam: North Holland.
Rein, M., 1983, 'Value-Critical Policy Analysis', in D. Callahan and B. Jennings (eds.), *Ethics, the Social Sciences and Policy Analysis*, New York: Plenum, pp.83–112.
Rein, M. and D. Schön, 1977, 'Problem Setting in Policy Research', in C. Weiss (ed.), *Using Social Research in Public Policy Making*, Lexington, MA: Heath, pp.235–51.
Schaffer, B. and G. Lamb, 1981, *Can Equity Be Organized?*, Farnborough: Gower.
Scriven, M., 1976, *Reasoning*, New York: McGraw-Hill.
Seers, D., 1983, *The Political Economy of Nationalism*, Oxford: Oxford University Press.
Self, P., 1975, *Econocrats and the Policy Process*, London: Macmillan.
Sillince, J., 1986, *A Theory of Planning*, Aldershot, Hants.: Gower.
Stewart, F., 1975, 'A Note on Social Cost-Benefit Analysis and Class Conflict in LDCs', *World Development*, Vol.3, No.1, pp.31–9.
Stewart, F., 1978, 'Social Cost-Benefit Analysis in Practice', *World Development*, Vol.6, No.2, pp.153–65.
Stretton, H., 1969, *The Political Sciences*, London: Routledge & Kegan Paul.
Taylor, P., 1961, *Normative Discourse*, Englewood Cliffs, NJ: Prentice Hall.
Thomas, L.G., 1972, 'A Model for Making and Testing Value Judgements', in L.G. Thomas (ed.), *Philosophical Redirection of Educational Research*, Chicago, IL: University of Chicago Press, pp.239–57.
Thouless, R., 1974, *Straight and Crooked Thinking*, London: Pan.

Throgmorton, J., 1991, 'The Rhetorics of Policy Analysis', *Policy Sciences*, Vol.24, No.2, pp.153–79.

Throgmorton, J., 1993, 'Survey Research as Rhetorical Trope: Electric Power Planning Arguments in Chicago', in Fischer and Forester [*1993: 117–44*].

Toulmin, S., 1958, *The Uses of Argument*, Cambridge: Cambridge University Press.

Toulmin, S., 1990, 'Logic, Rhetoric and Reason', Keynote address, 2nd ISSA International Conference on Argumentation, University of Amsterdam, 19–22 June.

Toulmin, S. et al., 1979, *An Introduction to Reasoning*, New York: Macmillan.

Walzer, M., 1987, *Interpretation and Social Criticism*, Cambridge, MA: Harvard University Press.

Ward, B., 1972, *What Is Wrong With Economics?*, London: Macmillan.

Wiggins, S. and D. Shields, 1995, 'Clarifying the Logical Framework', *Project Appraisal*, Vol.10, No.1, pp.2–12.

Wilber, C.K., 1978, 'The Methodological Basis of Institutional Economics: Pattern Model, Storytelling, Holism', *Journal of Economic Issues*, Vol.12, No.1, pp.61–89.

Wood, R. and K. Morton, 1977, 'Has British Aid Helped Poor Countries?', *ODI Review*, No.1, pp.40–67.

Re-reading 'Mountainous', 'Isolated', 'Inaccessible' and 'Small': The Case of Bhutan

ADAM PAIN

This study examines the theme of being 'mountainous' that runs through Bhutan's development policy. It investigates the way in which predominantly negative connotations of the descriptive language have been used almost to the exclusion of possible positive ones. It notes the surprising absence of concerns over 'smallness' in the policy debate and argues that an emphasis on the positive attributes of being 'mountainous' and 'small' would lead to alternative policy options.

I. INTRODUCTION

This study has several intertwined themes but the central strand that runs through it is that much of the terminology that has been used to describe and frame policy discourse in Bhutan – and the particular theme of being 'mountainous' – has tended to be interpreted only from a negative stance. The conceptual framework of policy has emphasised only the negative connotations of the descriptive language – for mountainous read 'isolation' and 'inaccessibility' – to the exclusion of possible positive ones. Because of this, policy has tended either to labour under these as intractable constraints or sought to mitigate them through various policy interventions: the development of road systems to reduce inaccessibility, for example. Language and its interpretation has influenced policy formulation and prescription. Yet, as this study argues, there are many positive elements of being mountainous that could be harnessed and used towards broader government objectives. Being mountainous could be seen as an advantage, particularly if you are small.

Related to the emphasis on the negative dimensions of being 'mountainous' is the way in which this appears to have excluded consideration of other possible 'constraints', notably of being 'small'. By all criteria Bhutan is a very small country with a land area of 46,500 square kilometres: being 150 kilometres north to south and 300 kilometres east to west and comprising a population of some 600,000. Being small, as will be discussed in section III, is widely considered to pose particular problems of development [*Streeten, 1993: 197–8*] but this has not been an issue of debate in Bhutan. However, lurking

Adam Pain, Ministry of Agriculture, Thimphu, Bhutan.

behind the policy frames [*Rein and Schön, 1991*] of both 'mountainous discourse' and 'smallness discourse' are some less tangible issues, in particular frames of scientific knowledge which are touched on in relation to the knowledge and understanding of 'mountainous attributes' in section II.

A major purpose of this study, however, is to develop what Roe [*1995: 1067*] has called 'counter scenarios', and to challenge the negative views of being mountainous. As Roe has argued, this pattern of thinking needs to be reversed and attributes of being mountainous need to be re-interpreted as the very factors that will provide the opportunities for successful mountainous development.

First, I shall present the evidence for the view that mountains are largely seen as constraints. In Chapter 1 of the *Seventh Five Year Plan, 1992–1997*, of the Royal Government of Bhutan there is a section on constraints on development which reads as follows:

> The development of the Bhutanese economy is however constrained by several factors:
>
> (a) Bhutan is geographically isolated from other countries in the region being a landlocked country, and is distant from the nearest sea port in Calcutta, India. This isolation makes the transport of goods into and from Bhutan costly.
>
> (b) Because of the extremely mountainous terrain, the area of land which is suitable for agricultural production is relatively small. This limits the potential for increasing output from the agricultural sector and increases the risk of environmental degradation.
>
> (c) The population is distributed in remote scattered settlements, to take advantage of the limited land suitable for agricultural production.
>
> (d) The above factors have made the provision of roads and communication networks difficult, and the delivery of health and education services costly.
>
> (e) Unlike most other developing countries, Bhutan has a relatively small population and the supply of manpower is a major constraint.
>
> (f) As most of the population have been subsistence farmers until recently, the level of monetisation has remained low [*Royal Government of Bhutan, 1991: 9*].

The purpose of this study is not to question how closely the above statements or apparent 'facts' approximate to the truth. It is more an examination of the language characteristics used in describing Bhutan and how the status of being mountainous (which by all objective criteria Bhutan is) is interpreted in terms of isolation and inaccessibility. It has become accepted as a dominant piece of development language with a set of normative meanings with implications for policy and practice.

A discussion of the implications of 'development' as an organising concept and as a value-laden dominant problematic [*Ferguson, 1990: xiv*] is not the major issue for the purposes of this paper. Suffice it to say that the Royal Government of Bhutan's policy is framed within the normative models of development and modernisation. The avenues through which it is seeking to raise the living standards of its population are those of promoting self-reliance, fostering sustainability, promoting efficiency and development of the private sector, popular participation and decentralisation, human resource development and regionally based development [*Royal Government of Bhutan, 1991: 23*]. For the Royal Government, being mountainous is a disadvantage for pursuing these routes to development. But what is being 'mountainous'?

II. BEING MOUNTAINOUS: CONCEPTS AND EVIDENCE

A mountain is a natural elevation on the earth's surface which, by convention, must be more than 1,000 feet (although 'The Mountain' in Denmark does not achieve this dizzy height). By definition therefore the adverb 'mountainous' implies many mountains.

By tradition the territory of tourists, climbers and ecologists, mountains and their agriculture have become a development theme and a problematic in their own right. This is most clearly reflected in the establishment of an international institution (the International Centre for Integrated Mountain Development, ICIMOD, in Nepal) with a mandate to focus specifically on mountain development. The arguments put forward to justify the incorporation of mountains as a special development problem are not hard to find. (See, for example, Conway's preface in Jodha, Bankskota and Partap [*1992: ix*].) They can be summarised as follows.

The benefits of earlier development activities are considered to have reached mountain inhabitants least and indeed to have often made them more economically marginal. New plant varieties that established themselves in fertile, flat well-watered areas resulting in major increases in grain production, failed to insert themselves in agricultural systems in mountains. Most seriously, market forces still manage to penetrate mountain areas through improved access and this, combined with population growth, has led to the removal of forests and vegetation cover, to severe erosion on steep slopes and ultimately to the severe degradation of the mountain environment.

With mountains thus becoming legitimised as a focus for development (and not just a development hinterland), a whole new terminology and language has been created to define mountain characteristics in relation to development and it is these that must be examined. One of the key exponents of a mountain perspective and the architect of a framework for describing mountain specificities is N.S. Jodha, based at ICIMOD. His 1992 paper is an effective summary of a framework and theoretical stance developed over the preceding years. He describes the mountain perspective as follows:

> The mountain perspective ... means simply explicit or implicit consideration of specific mountain conditions or characteristics and their implications while designing and implementing activities in mountain habitats. In fact, the preliminary enquiries into factors and processes contributing to the ... negative changes [see Conway above] indicated that the latter are largely a consequence of disregard of specific mountain characteristics and their operational implications by public and private interventions in these areas [*Jodha, 1992: 43*].

A mountain perspective, incorporating mountain specificities, is therefore seen by ICIMOD as central to the language of policy, the process of policy formulation and ultimately to the design of development interventions.

Jodha has characterised and labelled six important mountain specificities which can be used to separate mountain habitats from other areas, although it is recognised that some of these can also be found in deserts and other habitats. He differentiates four 'first order' specificities of inaccessibility, fragility, marginality and diversity or heterogeneity and two 'second order' specificities of niche or comparative advantage and human adaptation mechanisms; the latter being responses or adaptations to first order specificities [*ibid.: 44*]. It is these specificities that need to be examined.

Inaccessibility

Inaccessibility is described by Jodha as the diagnostic physical feature of mountain environments, reflected in isolation, poor communication and restricted mobility. These can all be traced to specific physical features such as altitude, terrain conditions and seasonal hazards (snow, storms, landslides and so on) [*Jodha, 1992: 44*]. Although the socio-economic dimensions to inaccessibility are acknowledged, it is primarily conceived as a physical and therefore an unarguable reality and constraint.

The application of inaccessibility in an absolute sense must be seen in relation to concepts of 'development' and of a so-called 'modern' capitalist economy. Lack of direct access to education, health, general government services, electricity, roads and markets are seen as a disadvantage. From the point of view of a government trying to deliver services, inaccessibility combined with a scattered population represent a real economic cost and raise real problems of inter-spatial equity.

But inaccessibility is also a relative concept and it is not difficult to identify the advantages that can be associated with it. Historically, as is clear for Bhutan, it provided protection and promoted self-reliance. Mountains by definition have limited and clearly defined routes of access and thoroughfare and so provide control over trade routes and, thus, trading opportunities. Inaccessibility can also be regarded as an opportunity consistent with objectives of long-term maintenance of environmental conditions, preservation of genetic diversity and maintenance of comparative advantages (for example, with respect to the cultivation and production of medicinal plants). Inaccessibility is therefore in some respects an effective 'trade barrier' with all the advantages to a domestic economy that this implies, and is particularly advantageous to a small country.

Inaccessibility and its concomitant 'remoteness' is also a 'positional' good, to use Hirsch's [1977] term: its scarcity in the western world and the degree to which it is sought after by those who value it and are willing to pay for access to it, turns it into a high value product for those who can market it. The profitability of the tourist market in Bhutan, with charge rates of around US$200 per day, is testament to that. Bhutan has also deliberately pursued a policy of not only charging highly but also restricting access to a limited number of tourists each year, thereby maintaining the value of access to Bhutan as a 'positional good'.

What inaccessibility means in practice in Bhutan is highly variable both between and within *dzongkhags* (districts). There is also a seasonal dimension as access can be cut off in winter (through snow) or summer (through landslides). Certain districts, such as Gasa in the north, have no vehicular access, no direct telephone links and limited education facilities (but are important for tourist trekking). Others, such as Chukha (a western *dzongkhag*) are on the main road between Thimphu (the capital) and Phuntsoling (a border town with India in the south of Chukha) but have *gewogs* (blocks or sub-district administrative divisions) that are several days' walk away from the *dzongkhag* headquarters.

Inaccessibility is therefore a relative concept, the application of which has both advantages and disadvantages. It is also one which is highly variable in its expression. The challenge that it provides for government policy and institutions is that of supporting *dzongkhag* and *gewog* economies in a way which balances the advantages of inaccessibility with its limitations.

Fragility

Fragility, the idea that something can easily shatter, perish or is constitutionally weak, is a widely-used term with respect to mountain environments. It has been argued that on account of altitude, steep slopes, underlying geology and biotic factors, mountains have very limited capacity to tolerate even a small degree of disturbance and that they are highly vulnerable to irreversible damage. Moreover, when deterioration does occur, it will take place at a rapid rate.

Accepting for the moment the truth of the above proposition, the major inferences that have been drawn from the concept of 'fragility' are that mountain environments are highly vulnerable to deleterious change and that every effort must be made to preserve their environmental integrity. Yet the existence of production 'pockets', be they of paddy tracts or dryland within mountain environments, could be seen as a direct consequence of fragility; the accumulation and concentration of erosion outputs or fertility, primarily in valley bottoms, which can be harnessed for production activities. It is precisely the so-called 'fragility' of mountains that has led to a mosaic of environments and a corresponding availability of a range of production opportunities. Without 'fragility' and the movement of nutrients, opportunities for production would be much less.

However, the very proposition of 'fragility' needs to be questioned. What exactly does it mean? How can it be applied and is it measurable? Are there degrees of fragility that would enable comparisons to be made between different mountain systems so that one particular mountain can be considered more fragile than another? It is difficult to see how this could be done with any degree of precision. As there is no real measurement of fragility, the term loses meaning in its application. The fact that the term 'fragility' has come to be used so widely in mountain development discourse is indicative more of a particular 'structure of knowledge' [*Ferguson, 1990*] of environmentalism and mountains rather than a coherent scientific case.

It is possible to tease out the concept of fragility into two separate components which do have a specific meaning, are measurable to some extent and which have been used elsewhere within ecology. The two components, which have been used to describe the behaviour of animal and plant populations, are 'stability' and 'resilience'. Stability refers to the extent to which a population size (of animals or plants) oscillates around a mean value. Highly stable populations show little departure from the mean value; highly unstable ones show a wide departure. The idea of stability also recognises the fact that variability over time is a widely occurring natural phenomenon, and consequently one needs to examine natural environments as dynamic entities. The resilience component refers to the ability of populations to cope with fluctuations and their capacity to deviate from a mean (of population size, species diversity and so on) only to return later to that mean value. In other words, how far can you stretch a piece of elastic before it breaks.

With respect to mountains (and other environments), therefore, one could conceptualise a range of possibilities, the boundaries of which would be differentiated by systems with (a) high stability and high resilience, (b) high resilience and low stability, (c) high stability and low resilience and, (d) low stability and low resilience. Only in the last of these is the concept of 'fragility' likely to be applicable. What is the evidence that mountains have low stability and low resilience?

This question raises a wider set of issues in relation to the very nature of evidence and the methods that are used to collect it. This issue has been well discussed by Thompson et al. [1986]. In developing an institutional theory to explain environmental perceptions in the Himalayas, they sought data and expert opinion on deforestation, the rate at which forests reproduced themselves and their rate of utilisation. Not only did they find it impossible to draw up a coherent picture and obtain consistent data on these two variables but they also uncovered major uncertainties about such questions as 'what is a forest?' and 'what is deforestation?'. They summarised their position as follows:

> Our conclusion is that the uncertainties surrounding the key variables in the man-land interactions in the Himalayas (and, worse still, the uncertainties as to what the key variables *are*) render 'the problem' unamenable to the traditional problem-solving methods of applied science. The problem, we conclude, is that there is not *a* problem, but a multiplicity of contending and contradictory problem definitions each of which takes its shape from the particular social and cultural context that it helps to sustain [*Thompson et al., 1986: 6*].

This may sound remote but it is of major practical importance. The history and general failure of soil erosion management in Africa demonstrates all too well how institutional attitudes and prejudices (initially colonial, but subsequently adopted by independent states) translated into so-called objective research and development interventions on soil erosion, ultimately creating more problems, both social and technical, than existed in the first place. This is not to deny the existence of erosion or that (some) mountain environments can suffer irreversible change. What is being argued is that issues of stability and resilience must be handled with great caution. To start off with generalities and pre-conceptions of 'fragility', embedded in a view of mountains as constraints, is not helpful.

What does this mean for Bhutan? Although it is widely stated that soil erosion exists, there is little evidence to support this, even when adopting the normative frame of scientific method in relation to soil erosion measurement (soil erosion plots, catchment sediment loads and so on). Evidence of enhanced soil erosion, divorced from inherent geological instability and natural processes, is non-existent. The major source of evidence for erosion is visual (and highly subjective, informed by a mountainous perspective of 'fragility') and relates mainly to the construction of roads and other physical infrastructure such as irrigation canals. This does not mean that there is room for complacency.

Major changes in the agrarian economy are taking place. The development of export industries of potato, horticultural forestry products and potential medicinal plants does have implications, as yet not fully realised, on fertility management systems (rates of extraction of natural fertility) and land use changes. Aerial photographic evidence of these changes is scarce at present but these changes are occurring. Accordingly resource management at the farm level and the relation between this and resource utilisation outside the farm boundaries will need to become an increasing focus of development policy and action.

Marginality

Being remote and physically isolated are seen as contributing to the third key mountain specificity, 'marginality'. To be marginal is to be on the edge, not just in a passive sense but also in a more active exploitative way so that social and economic relations between the edge and the centre are seen to be unequal [*Jodha, 1992: 45*]. As is widely recognised, marginality has both physical and economic dimensions. Poorer people are usually spatially marginalised to the least productive environments (on dryland, higher slopes, less fertile soils) and often forced by economic circumstances to undermine the very basis of their sustenance.

Within the context of Bhutan, marginality is likely to be closely associated with the negative aspects of inaccessibility. Yet economic differentiation within Bhutan's agrarian economy is probably not very high at this juncture. Market pressures have not led to major divisions between those who have and those who do not have land; there is not much evidence for landlessness. Pressures for survival have not pushed people to the point that their economic survival depends on an excessive degree of resource exploitation. What little data there is on household level economies and consumption patterns does not indicate major problems of food availability or household level nutrition. The evidence from nutrition surveys shows specific problems of iodine deficiency, Vitamin A and Iron, which are more a reflection of consumption preferences than absolute food shortages.

There clearly are both poorer regions with less economic potential and poorer people within these and other districts but, given that Bhutan as a whole is a mountain economy with no major geographical and economic divisions between plain and mountain as in other countries, marginality has less force in Bhutan than elsewhere. Furthermore, many goods and services (such as yak products, medicinal plants, forest products) traded by those who might be considered marginal by virtue of their location, remain highly valued and highly priced commodities within Bhutan's economy.

Notwithstanding Bhutan's historically marginal role in the region's economy (itself evidence of the strength of its basic economic self-sufficiency), there are many senses in which the Bhutanese economy and its mountain environment are potentially far from marginal, as illustrated below.

Diversity and Heterogeneity

Jodha [*1992: 45*] rightly acknowledges that the extreme degree of variability found in mountain environments leads to highly diverse biological and human adaptations and these should be seen as positive attributes of mountain economies. The evidence from Bhutan supports such a view. The physical variability in altitude, aspect and slope and the way in which these interact with soil and moisture regimes are fully reflected in the mosaic of vegetation within and between valleys. Micro-habitats created by such interactions are scattered throughout the landscape. This diversity is reflected in the distribution of crop varieties. The local distribution of indigenous rice varieties (or more strictly landraces that are heterogeneous in genetic composition) can be understood only in terms of specific adaptation to particular environments [*Chettri, 1992*]. The same is probably true of the indigenous varieties of the major legume species grown in the eastern part of Bhutan.

This diversity is further exemplified by the diversity (and integration) of farm level activities. Multiplicity of activities at the farm level, reflecting the utilisation of the different land facets that the landscape offers, is a common feature: it is as misleading to talk of a paddy farmer as it is to talk of a livestock producer. Most farmers do most things. The diversity of farm operations is in itself a risk-avoidance strategy, although there is no major evidence of substantial fluctuations of production at the farm level between one year and another.

The diversity of environments is a major advantage in relation to pest and disease control at the farm level. The lack of contiguous uniform environments growing genetically similar varieties combined with accessibility/mountain barriers means that major problems of pest and disease control have not occurred.

Yet despite the advantages arising from diversity, it is often only the problems that are noted: the variability that results from diversity, the complexity, the lack of uniformity and the difficulty of generalisation. Normative models of agricultural research and extension organisation, management and implementation, which have a tendency to seek to blueprint successful institutional designs and technology development processes [*Farrington and Mathema, 1991; RGOB, 1992*], have grappled unsuccessfully with the problems of scale, locality and decentralisation required by diversity.

Niche and Adaptation

Following Jodha's characterisation, two 'second order' specificities – the existence of niches and human adaptation mechanisms – arise from, or are responses to, the four 'first order' specificities of inaccessibility, fragility, marginality and diversity.

The fullest expression of niche specificity is to be found in the location of plant species. For Bhutan this means a unique flora, in type, number and diversity of species. Some of these have provided the basis of a major ornamental horticultural industry in the west and elsewhere. Others, such as medicinal plants, mushrooms, ferns, Daphne species (for paper), have provided the basis of localised economic opportunities. Niche also has major relevance to agricultural practice. The range of growing environments offers year round growing opportunities across districts and temporally-based comparative advantages for Bhutan and the regional economy.

Adaptation is both a plant species response to niche specificity as well as a human response in terms of management strategies to the opportunities which the environment offers. An important corollary to the existence of diversity and niches is the reality of localised, and therefore limited, abundance. The existence of scarcity within this diversity has led to important management strategies by communities. One of these is transhumance: the movement of livestock and households between one environment and another. The cultivation of rice in one location in one season (winter) and dryland crops in another (summer), as commonly happens with the movement of households – such as that between Haa and Chukka, is both a utilisation of the opportunities available as well as a response to the livelihood constraints of each environment. Similarly communal institutions, rules and management strategies for scarce resources, such as high quality leaf litter, are a key adaptive response to the opportunities and constraints presented by the environment.

Yet government policy, working within normative models of development and modernisation and with a perspective of 'mountains' as constraints, has had difficulty in handling human adaptation responses as positive attributes and advantages to be built upon. Extension policies have tended to emphasise prescriptive uniformity in programme design and content and to prioritise macro-policy considerations in terms of national grain production rather than localised opportunities. Transhumance practices, and traditional objectives and values in animal husbandry, have been viewed as obstacles which run counter to the development of a 'modern' livestock industry. Livestock by-products have been emphasised to the near exclusion of the central role of livestock in producing dung and fertility and thereby sustaining production under 'fragile' conditions. Village forests, which had been traditionally owned and managed by local communities and whose rules on rights and usage were firmly based on local knowledge, have been nationalised and negotiations on the return of such forests to village management hinge on the introduction of scientific management plans, developed on normative models of forest science, which cannot incorporate local knowledge of diversity and niche.

The challenge for government is to recognise that the opportunities presented by 'niche' and the associated human adaptation responses require a high degree of specificity of local knowledge which cannot be provided by central government services and that the development of such adaptive responses offers a way forward and not an impediment to the future.

III. BEING SMALL

As noted in the introduction, one constraint that we could expect to figure prominently with respect to the development of Bhutan's economy is that of being small. Bhutan, whose capital comprises 30,000 inhabitants, is clearly a small country. However, despite the fact that there is a particular strand in the development literature which emphasises the disadvantages of being small, 'smallness' in the case of Bhutan is nowhere mentioned as a constraint. Being mountainous has overridden all other considerations.

The disadvantages of being small have been summarised by Streeten [*1993: 197-8*]. These include the fact that small countries tend to have less diversified economies than larger countries in a comparable state of development. This is because smaller areas generally have less diversity of raw materials and their domestic markets fall below the economically optimum size for production. Consequently, small countries have tended to concentrate on products in which they have a comparative advantage and to export them. In relative terms, international trade can be much more important to smaller than larger countries because exports offer a chance of achieving economies of scale of production and thereby of increasing returns.

Other disadvantages of smallness claimed by Streeten include the lack of import protection as small internal travel distances lead to low transport costs. Moreover small countries are often more heavily dependent on foreign sources of supply. Consequently, small countries often have less freedom to set their macroeconomic policies because of their dependence on regional and neighbouring economies.

There are a number of countries, as Streeten points out, where being small has not hindered economic growth rates. The explanation for the high growth rates of Singapore and Hong Kong appears to lie in the fact that these are urban economies with no agriculture to slow development. However, the specific circumstances of these two city states cannot explain the success of other small country economies, such as Malta, Trinidad, Botswana, Mauritius and Jordan, and less tangible explanations have been offered in terms of the greater solidarity of smaller societies, diseconomies of scale in small country administration, the relative importance of remittance income from migrant labour and higher levels of foreign aid.

Many of the disadvantages of being small clearly apply to Bhutan. Nevertheless, the economy has achieved strong economic growth rates of some seven per cent during the 1980s. There is no remittance income from overseas workers and the value of its one major exportable natural resource, hydro-power, cannot be compared to the value of diamond exports in the case of Botswana. Bhutan is primarily an agrarian economy with a narrow range of export produce, the fortunes of which are heavily dependent on market conditions in neighbouring countries. Bangladesh's recent imposition of a tariff on the import of Bhutanese apples led to a rapid and substantial fall in their price and, thereby, a major drop in income for producers. Domestic markets in Bhutan are extremely small and the costs of production are such that Indian agricultural and industrial goods compete strongly and often dominate the market. For example, the cost of imported Indian rice may be half that of the domestic product. There is no possibility for Bhutan to set its agricultural prices independently from those of India. The room for independent pricing of hydro-electric power has been relatively circumscribed by virtue of the fact that India is also Bhutan's major aid donor and customer for electricity.

Yet the disadvantages of being small are scarcely raised as important development constraints for Bhutan. Rather, isolation, remoteness and being mountainous (or 'this unusual environment' [*RGOB, 1992: 3*]) are depicted as 'the obstacles' to development. Thus, Bhutan is seen to be geographically isolated – not small – and it is isolation that leads to higher transport costs and not smallness to lower ones. Its mountainous environment is seen to lead to a limited agricultural area, rather than to the promotion of diversity which runs counter to the disadvantages of being small. Bhutan's small population is viewed not in terms of a limited domestic market but as a constraint to the supply of manpower. However, a major policy objective of the Seventh Five Year Plan, that of promoting self-reliance, is precisely that which Streeten argues is a necessary strategic objective for small countries.

As noted above, smallness can also have advantages although the policy debate on 'smallness' as with 'mountainous' has tended to emphasise the negative dimensions. There are interesting comparisons to be drawn from small country agricultural research organisations and current thinking in international business where 'excellence' is increasingly viewed as being closely linked with 'smallness' in both scale and attitudes. Peters [*1992*] has argued that smallness is related to flexibility and innovativeness and that this should be built on. It is precisely these arguments that Eyzaguirre and Okello [*1993*] draw on when asserting that small country research systems should think and act differently from large country research systems, by emphasising opportunism, flexibility, information management and borrowing rather than just the traditional experimental role of research.

IV. CONCLUSION

It is ironical that historically Bhutan pursued an explicit policy of political self-isolation in which being mountainous was seen as a distinct advantage [*Rose, 1977*]. From the late eighteenth century, a combination of expansionist pressures from Tibetans in the north and the British in India from the south, led Bhutan to withdraw from all external relations in the interests of its survival as an independent nation. This self-imposed isolation was greatly helped by a series of mountain ranges which clearly delineated the territory of Bhutan and made access difficult from all directions. Being mountainous therefore greatly facilitated its isolation.

After the accession to the throne in 1952 of the third King of Bhutan, King Jigme Dorje Wangchuck, there was a slow but gradual policy of opening up the economy of Bhutan, by developing its infrastructure and particularly roads, and reducing its political isolation. From 1961 onwards a series of five year development plans have been implemented. Since that time, the mountainous environment has increasingly come to be seen as a constraint on Bhutan's 'development'.

The conclusion to be drawn from this study is not that mountain environments present boundless opportunities. One cannot deny that mountain environments are, relatively speaking, difficult places to live in and make livelihoods from. They do pose major problems for government policy and practice. Nor should it be thought that it is only from the vantage point of Bhutan that such an upbeat view of the potentialities of mountains can be upheld and that if one were sitting in Nepal, for example, one might have a more jaundiced view of mountain futures. Rather the focus of this article is on the positive attributes of mountain environments which can lead to different policy debate and objectives.

There remains the interesting question as to why this particular language about mountains has been developed and where it has come from. There are no simple answers to this. Part of the explanation lies in the shift in policy in Bhutan itself, from a self-isolationist stance to one where normative 'development' objectives were set, with the result that what had previously been seen as advantageous now became an impediment. The view of mountains as constraints has partly been a home-grown contribution.

There is no doubt, however, that this view has been reinforced by external 'expert' advice which inevitably incorporated comparisons of 'development' elsewhere. Although policy discourse in Bhutan with respect to mountains – inaccessibility, fragility – is shared by ICIMOD, the direct influence of ICIMOD is probably fairly small since the contact between ICIMOD and the Royal Government of Bhutan has been limited. Indeed ICIMOD has probably developed a more thorough 'mountainous discourse' than that adopted in

Bhutan and a careful reading of Jodha's work shows his sensitivity to the potentialities that mountains can offer. Nevertheless the very language that is used by ICIMOD, particularly with respect to issues of 'fragility', is framed largely in a negative manner and is interpreted accordingly in policy debate. To accept this without question can lead to the lack of recognition of alternative policy options.

It is surprising that 'smallness' has not emerged in general policy discourse in Bhutan as an issue and one can only assume that it has been submerged by the seemingly greater emphasis on 'mountainous'. Putting 'mountainous' and 'smallness' together and emphasising their positive attributes as a basis for policy, it is clear that being 'mountainous' could be seen as an advantage if you are 'small'.

REFERENCES

Chettri, G.H., 1992, 'Rice Varieties in Bhutan', M.Sc. thesis, University of Los Banos, The Philippines.

Conway, G.R, 1992, 'Preface', in Jodha, Bankskota and Partap [1992].

Eyzaguirre, P. and A.E. Okella, 1993, 'Agricultural Research Systems in Small Countries: Implications for Public Policy and Administration', *Public Administration and Development*, Vol.13, No.3, pp.233–47.

Farrington, J. and S.B. Mathema, 1991, *Managing Agricultural Research for Fragile Environments*, London: Overseas Development Institute.

Ferguson, J., 1990, *The Anti-Politics Machine*, Cambridge: Cambridge University Press.

Hirsch, F., 1977, *Social Limits to Growth*, London: Routledge & Kegan Paul.

Jodha, N.S., 1992, 'Mountain Perspective and Sustainability: A Framework for Development Strategies', in Jodha, Bankskota and Partap[*1992: 41–82*].

Jodha, N.S., Baukshota, M. and T. Partap (eds.), 1992, *Sustainable Mountain Agriculture, Volume 1: Perspectives and Issues,* New Delhi: Oxford and IBH Publishing Co. Ltd.

Peters, T., 1992, *Liberation Management: Necessary Disorganisation for the Nanosecond Nineties*, London: Macmillan.

Rein, M. and D. Schön, 1991, 'Frame-reflective Policy Discourse', in P. Wagner, C.H. Weiss, B. Wittrock and H. Wollmann (eds.), *Social Sciences and Modern States: National Experiences and Theoretical Crossroads*, Cambridge: Cambridge University Press, pp.262–89.

Roe, E.M., 1995, 'Except-Africa: Postscript to a Special Section on Development Narratives', *World Development*, Vol.23, No.6, pp.1065–9.

Rose, L.E., 1977, *The Politics of Bhutan*, Ithaca, NY: Cornell University Press.

Royal Government of Bhutan (RGOB), 1991, *Seventh Five Year Plan, 1992–1997*, Thimphu: Planning Commission.

Royal Government of Bhutan (RGOB), 1992, *Research Strategy and Plan*, Thimphu: Ministry of Agriculture and the International Service to National Research Systems (ISNAR).

Streeten, P., 1993, 'The Special Problems of Small Countries', *World Development*, Vol.21, No.2, pp.197–202.

Thompson, M. Warburton, M. and T. Hatley, 1986, *Uncertainty on a Himalayan Scale*, London: Milton Ash Editions, Ethnographica.

Methodological Nationalism and the Misunderstanding of East Asian Industrialisation

CHARLES GORE

This study argues that the controversy over the role of public policy in East Asian industrialisation should not be seen as a question of whether economic success can be attributed to states or markets, but rather as a conflict over policy frames. East Asian policies analyse national trends in a global context and have sought to achieve nationalist economic goals; the currently dominant development policy paradigm attributes national economic success mainly to internal factors yet seeks to promote a liberal international economic order. The study examines misunderstanding which arises when East Asian success is explained in the terms of the dominant paradigm, focusing on 'outward-oriented' as a key word, the World Bank study The East Asian Miracle, and the flying geese model of development.

INTRODUCTION

A central controversy in development policy discourse concerns the role of public policy in the rapid economic growth and industrialisation in East Asia. It is generally agreed that some East Asian countries have been the most successful developing countries in economic terms but a number of authoritative accounts [*Johnson, 1982; Amsden, 1989; Wade, 1990; Castells, Goh and Kwok, 1990*] show that their policies diverge from those advocated in the dominant development paradigm which has been elaborated over the 1980s and 1990s, particularly by the World Bank in its annual *World Development Report*. This study first examines the nature of the divergence between the East

Charles Gore, International Institute for Labour Studies, ILO. The author is grateful to Raymond Apthorpe, Ha-Joon Chang and Des Gasper for helpful comments on earlier versions of this article and editorial suggestions. Section II elaborates a seminar paper presented at IEDES, University of Paris, in 1987, entitled 'Adjustment – National or International?', which was informed by many discussions on development policy discourse with Raymond Apthorpe; he also at the time introduced me to the notion of a policy frame. Some elements of Section V were written in 1994 as background research for a chapter of UNCTAD's *Trade and Development Report 1994* on East Asian industrialisation, and have benefitted from discussions with Yilmaz Akyüz. The usual disclaimers apply, and the text does not necessarily reflect the views of the International Institute for Labour Studies, the ILO, or UNCTAD.

Asian approaches and the dominant development paradigm, and then analyses the anatomy of misunderstanding which arises in texts which interpret that experience within the framework of the dominant paradigm.

The standard way to analyse the controversy is to see it as a disagreement about the appropriate balance between states and markets in enabling and promoting national development. Here the controversy will be analysed at a deeper level, as a conflict over policy frames. By close attention to the meanings of key words and to structures of argumentation, this article seeks to show the precise nature of the conflict and the ways in which it is expressed.

A policy frame can be defined as 'a perspective from which an amorphous, ill-defined, problematic situation can be made sense of and acted on' [*Rein and Schön, 1993: 146*]. Differences in policy frames lead people 'to see different things, make different interpretations of the way things are, and support different courses of action concerning what is to be done, by whom and how' [*ibid: 147*].[1] Framing of national development policy issues involves both explanatory analysis ('what is') and normative evaluation ('what ought to be'), each of which can be done at either a national or global level. These alternatives are the source of the frame conflict between East Asian development policies and the dominant development paradigm.

I will argue that the dominant paradigm is founded on a global normative framework, in the sense that it is concerned with the promotion of a liberal international order, whilst its explanatory framework seeks to explain national patterns and trends by reference primarily to national factors, an approach to explanation which I shall label 'methodological nationalism'. In contrast, the policies of the successful East Asian economies are based on an explanatory framework which analyses national patterns and processes within a global context, and a nationalist normative framework which seeks national economic development through rapid industrialisation.

This argument is part of a broader thesis of historical and future trends in development policy discourse, which is summarised in Table 1.

TABLE 1

FOUR MAIN COMBINATIONS OF EXPLANATORY AND NORMATIVE FRAMEWORK
IN DEVELOPMENT POLICY DISCOURSE

| | | Normative Framework | |
		NATIONAL	GLOBAL
Explanatory	NATIONAL	Dominant development paradigm pre-1980	Dominant development paradigm post-1980
Framework	GLOBAL	East Asia-type development policies Latin American dependency 'theory' (some versions)	'Coming' paradigm shift

In stark terms, this thesis is that before the introduction of the adjustment policies of the 1980s, the dominant paradigm in development policy discourse was founded on a combination of analysis and evaluation which were both undertaken within a national frame of reference. But since 1980 a process has begun which may be described as the globalisation of development policy discourse, that is, a shift from a national to a global frame of reference. This switch has occurred in an incomplete manner: a peculiar combination of methodological nationalism in explanation and 'global liberalism'[2] in evaluation has become dominant. This combination is impossible to sustain, and a paradigm shift will thus occur. Initially wider copying of East Asian type policies is likely, but the coming paradigm shift, already in fact under way, will complete the globalisation of development policy discourse: both the normative and explanatory policy frames will become global in scope. In this shift, alternative global normative frameworks to the variants of global liberalism which underlie the present dominant paradigm will be elaborated, and more sophisticated global explanatory frameworks than the current alternatives to 'methodological nationalism' will develop.

In this study sections I–III will define the nature of the frame conflict between the dominant development paradigm and the East Asian development experience. Section I describes methodological nationalism as a form of explanation, identifying as its central feature the isolation and separation of internal and external factors as determinants of national economic performance, with primacy being given to the former. Section II examines the framework of the currently dominant development paradigm. It focuses on the changing meaning of the term 'structural adjustment', as an indicator of a shift in policy practice from a national to a global frame of evaluation in the dominant paradigm; and shows how the basic rhetorical forms associated with this shift are arguments that national policies which conflict with the norms of a liberal international economic order (LIEO) are harmful to national economic interests. This rhetoric is articulated through methodological nationalism. Section III examines the global/national frame of East Asian policies. It identifies five main axes of difference between these policies and those advocated in the dominant paradigm; and it attributes them to the different policy frame used, and the precise nature of the national goals of East Asian policy makers and of the international goals in the currently dominant paradigm.

Sections IV–VI will examine the anatomy of misunderstanding in texts which represent the East Asian development experience in the terms of the dominant paradigm. Omissions and occlusions are particularly apparent on the five axes of policy difference identified in section III. This will be illustrated by: the semantic confusion surrounding the description of East Asian economies as 'outward-oriented', the key word which was initially deployed to explain their success (section IV); the discursive practices used in the World Bank's policy research report, *The East Asian Miracle: Public Policy and Economic Growth*, a key text which presents a more subtle and informed view of East Asian policies but which still seeks to make them conform to the dominant paradigm (section V); and the shifts in the meaning of the 'flying geese' model of industrialisation, which is becoming particularly important now in explaining sustained growth in south-east Asia.

The article shows that a recurrent feature of development policy discourse is the redefinition of the meaning and the domain of reference of certain key terms. This has occurred for 'adjustment'; 'outward-oriented/looking'; 'export push' strategy; 'market-conforming'; and the 'flying-geese model'. These terms are not deployed in isolation but are part of systems of argument through which problems are defined as such, understood and tackled. The meaning of key terms and the structures of argument within which they are articulated reflect the ways in which development issues are framed; changes in meaning and structures of argumentation are indicators of frame shifts and frame conflicts. Close attention to discourse in these situations of frame shift and frame conflict enables identification of the nature of the policy frames.

The study's conclusion reviews the sorts of insight – both for discourse analysis and better policy design – which become possible through a focus on policy framing.

PART 1: THE NATURE OF THE FRAME CONFLICT

I. METHODOLOGICAL NATIONALISM AND THE INTERNAL/ EXTERNAL DICHOTOMY

Roche [*1992: 184–5*] states that much modern social science theorising, social policy, and political analysis tends to be 'methodologically nationalist', in the sense that 'they are designed on a basis which appears to take the nation state, its sovereignty and the powers of its government utterly for granted'. In the present context, this definition is not sufficient. Methodological nationalism will be defined here in a similar way to 'methodological individualism', as an approach to explanation.[3]

Defining Features of Methodological Nationalism

Explanations which are methodologically nationalist try to explain economic and social trends in countries, basically by reference to facts about the countries themselves. The focal object of enquiry is often described as the economic or social 'performance' of a country, usually in comparison with other countries. Specific performances are typically 'explained' by dividing causal factors into 'internal' and 'external' factors, and then attributing what is happening in a single country or set of countries within a region of the world (say, 'East Asia' or 'Latin America') mainly to internal factors.

The key defining feature of methodological nationalism is that it isolates and separates the influence of internal factors from external factors. Explanations within a global frame of reference in contrast emphasise the interaction between internal and external factors. Some of these alternatives certainly give primacy to international relations and minimise local processes. But the more sophisticated alternative explanations interrelate the 'internal' and the 'external' to such an extent that these terms become virtually meaningless.

Methodological nationalism as a form of reasoning can only be totally logical if national economies and societies are completely isolated and closed from outside influences. In practice, however, they are not; indeed, from the normative point of view of the dominant paradigm, being 'open' is, as we shall see, regarded as 'good'. The attempted resolution of this conundrum involves acknowledging that national economies are, to varying degrees, open economies, and recognising that external factors play a role. But this role is minimised through two discursive moves. First, it is assumed that national economies are abstract entities which are 'open' but not situated in relation to other economies. The existence of any structure in the world economy is downplayed and it is assumed that all countries face the same external environment. Secondly, the focus is on *differences* in performance between economies. With these two moves it can then be asserted that, although external factors certainly influence what happens within countries, all countries faced the same external environment and the differences in their performance must be attributed to internal factors.

A further twist is introduced by stating that differences in performance are due to the (internal) national capability to manage adverse external changes or to harness the benefits of positive external changes. Such external changes may be periodic 'shocks', or a more long-lasting process of 'globalisation', which in the frame of reference of the methodological nationalist, is understood as something which is happening *to* countries, a change in their 'external' strategic environment, rather than something in which they are implicated. Countries which have high internal capability to respond to shocks or to capitalise on the increasing cross-border flows of capital, goods, services and labour are said to have 'flexible' economies. 'Flexibility' is thought to increase with 'openness', and thus in effect the best way to cope with shocks is to increase exposure to them.

Whilst the basic feature of methodological nationalism is to explain national performance by reference to national factors, a particularly important theme in this approach is to focus on the purposive actions of national governments. Nation-states are taken to be like rational individuals with preferences, capabilities and responses to the stimuli and opportunities of their strategic environment. This is like methodological individualism projected to an international scale. It not only denies the effects on country performance of the structure of the world economy (comparable to assuming 'abstract' rather than 'situated' individuals), but also downplays the effects of all 'internal factors' other than domestic policy. Thus for example, all price distortions are assumed to be policy distortions; and the influence of such factors as country size or natural resource endowment are ignored. The approach magnifies the influence of national policy on country performance, as in the following typical non-sequitur: 'In the long term, the divergent performance of developing countries faced with similar external trends points to the overriding importance of domestic policy' [*World Development Report 1986: 26*].

A common method used in explanations which are methodologically nationalist is regression analysis which establishes the statistical relationships between indicators of national economic performance and a series of national variables, including indicators of the nature of national policy. The essence of this method is areal correlation between dependent and independent variables, to identify the extent to which variation of the former between a given set of national territories matches variation in the latter between the same territories, at certain points in time or over specific periods of time. Regression equations are used to identify the significance of different national factors, and graphs and charts, which can be made powerfully suggestive of strong relationships, are also presented.

An interesting feature of much of this empirical work is that at one and the same time it strengthens an idea of 'the Third World' and divides it into separate countries. Earlier cross-national studies of development patterns [e.g. *Chenery and Syrquin, 1975*] try to show national patterns of resource mobilisation and resource allocation for countries at different levels of development throughout the world, *both* industrialised *and* developing. Many of the more recent cross-national exercises which emphasise the effects of national policy on country performance typically, though not always, treat 'developing countries' as a group. But at the same time as 'the Third World' is recreated in this way, successful country cases are isolated; and more recently divergent regional performance is being highlighted. The global conceptual map in currently dominant development discourse emphasises contrasts between East Asia, Latin America, and Sub-Saharan Africa.

Some Clarifications

Methodological nationalism is not a substitute for methodological individualism. It coexists with it. Recent explanations using methodological nationalism extend analysis 'downwards' to explain the purposive actions of nation-states in terms of the interests of members of the bureaucracy or the rent-seeking activities of various sectional interests. Typically 'rational' policies are seen as associated with efficient and incorrupt bureaucrats who enjoy 'technocratic insulation', whilst 'irrational' policies reflect the power plays of entrenched interest groups which can be understood within the rational choice perspective of the new political economy.

There have been heated debates in the philosophy of social science about methodological individualism. Proponents of methodological individualism contrasted it with 'sociological holism' and 'organicism' which seek to explain social phenomena in terms of systemic social forces, not the activities of individuals. In a similar way, one alternative to methodological nationalism is a holism which argues that the behaviour of nation-states can only be understood as constituent elements of the world system. An extreme exemplar of holism is the work of Samir Amin in the 1970s who argued that analysis of underdevelopment could only be undertaken at a world scale, in terms of relationships between centre and periphery, and that national economies were misleading units of analysis for the periphery of the world economy as they have no internal dynamic [*Smith, 1982*].

Such a denial of the validity of national units as both an object of study and a framework for explanation is not, however, a necessary feature of all alternatives to methodological nationalism. There are also explanations of development patterns, processes and trends *within* nation-states which avoid an exclusive focus on 'national factors', and examine national dynamics in interaction with international centre-periphery relations, and/or with trends towards differentiation and uniformisation in the international economic structure. Such approaches have been elaborated in particular by theorists in the 'less developed' countries themselves concerned with problems of 'late industrialisation', including in *some* versions of the dependency perspective in Latin America and in East Asia.[4] Moreover another alternative form of explanation to methodological nationalism is actor-centred, focusing on the purposive behaviour of different kinds of transnational actors, in particular transnational corporations, usually depicted as either a cause of development or of distortion, and international financial institutions.

Overall, neither the holism of world systems theory, nor the transnational actor-centred explanations are convincing. The debate on methodological individualism has shown that it is possible to construct explanations which are neither 'methodologically individualist' nor 'sociologically holist', but inter-relate the individual and society [*Giddens, 1984*]. Similarly, the displacement of methodological nationalism requires a form of explanation which examines the interplay between agency and structure.[5]

II. 'ADJUSTMENT' IN THE TERMS OF DEVELOPMENT

Methodological nationalism has been characteristic of the dominant paradigms in international development policy research ever since the 1950s. Much theorising on development strategy in the 1950s and 1960s was based on abstracted sequences of economic change which had occurred in the past in already-industrialised countries and which were expected to recur, particularly if the right policy interventions were made, in 'less developed' countries. Such theorising most typically understood 'development' as a transition from a 'traditional' (rural, backward, agricultural) society to a 'modern' (urban, industrial) society, a process which was narrated in summary form as either 'stages of growth' or recurrent patterns of structural transformation. These patterns of development could be deduced by examining earlier transitions. But such abstracted histories filtered out the effects of the experience of the industrialised countries as colonial powers, and generally focused on the internal dynamics of change, perhaps adding that particular external relations were necessary to start the process or to close 'gaps' which threatened its breakdown.

There were, of course, counter-currents to this type of analysis. These were elaborated in particular by theorists in the 'less developed' countries of the world concerned with problems of 'late industrialisation', notably in Latin America and East Asia. But these ideas remained outside the dominant paradigm: the Latin American dependency perspective was strongly criticised as impractical (by the Right) and atheoretical (by the Left), and East Asian ideas were ignored or misrepresented.

Before the 1980s, the normative objectives at the centre of development discourse were, like the explanatory arguments, also articulated within a national frame of reference. The basic objective was promotion of 'national development'. What this actually meant was controversial. The orthodox economist's view that national development consisted of economic growth was challenged; others suggested that it meant increasing employment, reducing poverty, and enhancing basic needs satisfaction and participation. But these disputes actually served to construct the normative frame of development policy discourse as being nationalist. Whatever objectives were taken to be central, national objectives were the focal concern.

In the 1980s, while methodological nationalism in explanation persisted, a critical shift occurred in the normative frame of reference of the dominant development paradigm – from the national level to the global level – with the introduction of structural adjustment programmes and the related discourse. Now, although in rhetoric 'national development' (understood principally as economic growth plus poverty reduction) is still espoused as the main objective, in practice the central norm which is used to evaluate policies is their compatibility with the principles of a LIEO. The dominant paradigm at present thus combines nationalism in explanation with the pursuit of global normative objectives.

A Case for (Enforcing) a Liberal International Economic Order (LIEO)

Lal [*1980*], in an argument for a LIEO which also makes an interesting proposal on how such an international order can be achieved, illustrates how national development policies and adjustment programmes can be conceptualised within this new normative framework.

The argument assumes that a LIEO – defined as free trade in goods and services, free capital movements, and freely floating exchange rates – is optimal for the world as a whole, but Lal wants to show that it is also in the interest of 'rational' nation-states to adhere voluntarily to such an order. He defines 'rational' nation-states as those in which public policy is designed to raise economic welfare (consumption by current and future citizens), and he labels the pursuit of extra-economic goals as 'irrational'. On this basis he assesses the 'optimal tariff' argument as a justification for deviating from liberal principles and, finding it unrealistic, concludes that a LIEO is optimal for 'rational' nation-states.

But this leaves a conundrum. For actual nation-states resist such an order by imposing tariffs and quotas, restricting foreign ownership of domestic assets, and limiting domestic ownership of foreign assets. Within the structure of his argument, there is one obvious answer – nation-states behave 'irrationally'. Voluntary adherence to a LIEO does not occur, he suggests, because it is possible to use restrictions on foreign trade to achieve certain goals in domestic income distribution, and because powerful domestic sectional interests can gain from trade restrictions. Similarly free trade in assets is restricted because of concerns that 'foreign investors may attempt to subvert the host country's polity or culture, particularly if their investments are large relative to the size of the economy' [*ibid.: 12*].

The policies which Lal identifies as expressions of 'irrational behaviour' were often key elements of national development strategy from the 1950s to the late 1970s. But, such 'irrationalities', in Lal's terms, mean that a LIEO will not 'emerge spontaneously'. Thus 'some form of external enforcement of the liberal international economic order may be required in the real world' [*ibid.: 11*].

With this jump from the rationality of voluntary adherence to the necessity for 'some form' of external enforcement, Lal moves on to consider what this should be and makes a memorable proposal:

> Lacking a world government, and hence an apparatus for enforcing rules that nations fail to internalize for various irrational reasons, some have suggested that a rational hegemonic power should force other nations to be free ... A securer foundation, in my view, would lie in propagating rationality and thereby internalizing adherence to the liberal international order among nations of the world [*ibid.: 12–13*].

One caveat is added. In the face of strong domestic sectional interests who stand to gain from trade restrictions, he suggests that 'external constraints on resorting to protection might be desirable', besides the propagation of rationality. These external constraints could help 'to offset "extra-economic" considerations by stiffening the resolve of the government to resist sectional pressures that go against the national cosmopolitan interest'. 'Enforcement', he argues, 'may be particularly important for developing countries' [*ibid.: 11*].

The Meaning of 'Structural Adjustment'

While Lal's paper was not the historical origin of adjustment programmes,[6] his argument helps us to see those programmes as a way of promoting and reinforcing a LIEO on a country-by-country basis. But for the programmes to work like this, the term 'structural adjustment' had itself to be adjusted.

Between the mid-1970s and the early 1980s there was a double shift in usage and deployment of the term. The first transformation was to flip the *domain* to which the word applied, from industrial countries (where it was associated with state assistance to declining industries which could not compete with developing country producers), to developing countries. The second transformation was to alter the *meaning* of the term, to make it refer to one particular means (liberalisation) of achieving a general goal (altering the structure of production within countries so that external payments imbalances were corrected) rather than to that general goal, and to make the means itself the general goal. With this double shift, a term which in the mid-1970s referred to some measures in a new international economic order for fairer relationships between rich and poor countries, with a focus on *policy action in rich countries* to enable greater market access for developing country products [e.g. *ILO, 1976*], became deployed in the 1980s for enforcing a LIEO through country-by-country unilateral liberalisation, with the focus now on *policy action in developing countries*.

The shift in meaning was associated with an analysis based on the external/internal dichotomy and a change in the relative importance given to external and internal factors in explaining economic conditions in developing countries. When the term 'adjustment' was first applied to developing countries in the late 1970s, it was suggested that they were being adversely affected by changes in their *external environment*, such as increased oil prices, high interest rates, and stagflation in OECD countries. Developing countries, it was argued, had to 'adjust to new circumstances'. The external shocks had created increasing balance of payments deficits and these shocks were regarded as permanent. In these circumstances, the stabilisation programmes recommended by the IMF, to correct 'temporary maladjustments' in developing countries' balance of payments, were not considered sufficient. The short-term, demand-side, macro-, and financial measures of the IMF had to be supplemented by medium-term, supply-side, sectoral and micro-economic 'structural adjustment programmes' [*Yagci et al., 1985*].

Structural adjustment programmes thus sought to correct external payments imbalances through adjustments to the structure of production, and structural adjustment loans were first introduced and rationalised as financial support for such adjustments. As Anne Krueger put it, in an article which *criticised* the World Bank's first conception of adjustment lending to developing countries:

> The list of items envisaged for support includes (i) facilitating the adjustment of production to higher energy prices, (ii) emphasis on labour-intensive investments with 'a substantial impact on employment' and a 'short gestation period', (iii) export diversification (through encouraging investment, not through provision of incentives), (iv) either 'enhancement of export competitiveness' *or* 'redirection of investment to domestic markets in the face of changed costs structures or limited export prospects' and (v) altering fiscal and savings incentives [*Krueger, 1981: 279*]; (within-quote quotations from the World Bank Annual Report 1980; emphasis in original).

Krueger was critical because, according to her, 'the adoption of an outward-looking, or export-oriented strategy for development' [*ibid.: 272*] has played a large role in the success stories of newly industrialising countries (listed as the four East Asian Tigers, Hong Kong, Singapore, South Korea and Taiwan, *plus* Brazil), and a desirable function of foreign aid should be to make 'sizeable credits' available to support 'an attempted transition to a more liberal and outward-looking economy' [*ibid.: 279*]. However, the rationale of the new lending facility for structural adjustment was unfortunately 'a far cry from the vision of a major shift' [*ibid.: 279*]. Owing to 'political constraints' and the 'bureaucratic tendency towards fairness', the programme 'seems designed to support individual programmes and policies that, while improving resource allocation at the margin, are consistent with failure to alter overall policy design and implementation' [*ibid.: 280–81*].

By 1983, and partly in association with the design of a strategy to manage the debt crisis, the shift advocated by Krueger had occurred. Structural adjustment came to refer to policy reform aimed at trade liberalisation, price control liberalisation, privatisation, reduction in public spending and so on. These reforms were said to improve the efficiency of resource allocation within developing countries, by removing price distortions which were said to arise from policy distortions. The justification given for adjustment was no longer an adverse external environment. It was rather *domestic mismanagement* and, echoing Lal, the need to remove 'irrationalities'. And the term adjustment no longer referred to changing the structure of production, but rather a particular means of achieving that objective – economic liberalisation – which in fact became both the objective of adjustment programmes and what the term meant.

In rhetoric these measures have been justified as being in the national economic interest. But in practice they have promoted and enforced a LIEO. This is reflected in the design of the programmes. Broadly they have involved two types of measures: first, to change the pattern of price incentives ('getting the prices right'); and secondly, to remove the structural constraints on supply response which prevent economic agents taking decisions on the basis of those prices. But in both these policy areas, there have been specific limits to the type of price distortions and the type of structural constraints which have been tackled. In each case the limits conform with the orientation of 'structural adjustment' to global norms of a LIEO.

The main price distortions considered have been those attributable to government policy. Distortions arising from the imperfect way in which markets operate have been downplayed or ignored. Moreover, the standard used to identify distortions are international prices. The 'right' prices are regarded as those which bring incentives for domestic resource allocation in line with international opportunity costs. The structural constraints which have been addressed are similarly restricted to the overextension of the scope of government activity and the weakness of the public sector's administrative and managerial capacity. Tackling 'over-extension' has entailed the replacement of the commitment of the State to achieve substantive goals of national development by a commitment to provide an 'enabling environment' in which 'free' markets and the price mechanism are given a greater role in guiding economic activity. Structural constraints on supply identified by the 'old structuralists' of the 1950s, such as concentration of land ownership or regional dualism, are ignored in this 'new structuralism' [*Foxley, 1983*].

Internalising Adherence to a LIEO

After the double shift in the meaning of 'structural adjustment', 'rationality', in Lal's terms, has been propagated and adherence to a LIEO 'internalised' through both financial and discursive means. Associated with the new discourse was an aid regime in which the World Bank and IMF took leadership, setting a framework within which the activities of many bilateral donors could be integrated [*Gibbon, 1993*]. Access to aid funds became conditional on wide-ranging policy reforms, which unlike the IMF conditionalities of the 1950s to 1970s, went into details of policy.

For the weaker countries, the new conditionality represented a powerful 'external constraint', as Lal put it, which was a strong incentive to 'reform' along these lines. The power relations involved in the negotiation of adjustment programmes were not totally one-sided, and developing countries have had some room to manoeuvre to escape conditions [*Mosley, Harrigan and Toye, 1991*]. However, a particular structure of argumentation was developed in order to persuade governments that policy reforms which supported a LIEO were plain common-sense. This may well have been more powerful than financial carrots and sticks in propagating 'rationality'.

One element in the rhetoric was the assertion that 'there is no alternative to adjustment'. Given the double shift in the meaning of adjustment this implied that 'adjusting countries' would have to adopt policies which fitted the country-by-country enforcement of a LIEO. But the principal rhetorical form used were arguments that national policies, such as protectionist tariffs or selective industrial policy, which are in conflict with the norms of a LIEO are *harmful* to *national* economic interests, whilst national policies which correspond to those norms are *beneficial*. These arguments imply that it makes sense for all countries to adopt national policies which conform to certain desired international norms. And they thus encourage the *autonomous* adoption of domestic policies which conform to the norms and principles of a LIEO, and the 'internalisation' of these principles.

In making this rhetoric coherent, the choice of the terrain for defining national economic interest is critical. For much of the 1980s, this involved reduction of the definition of the economic interest of developing countries, from 'national development' to 'national economic growth' and particularly short-term economic efficiency. On this terrain, arguments have been elaborated that policy distortions, particularly associated with import substitution industrialisation, are detrimental for growth.[7] And – a more complex task – attempts have been made to show that national policies which 'free' markets and 'open' economies result in fast and sustained growth.

The explanatory form used has been methodological nationalism. The main thrust has been to relate policy distortions, or their absence, to the system of incentives for efficient resource allocation. (Important exemplars are World Bank [*1981*]; World Bank [*1983*]; and World Bank [*1987*].) A key discursive strategy has been the classification of national economies and national policies as 'inward-oriented' or 'outward-oriented', and the use of regression analyses to prove that outward-oriented policies (or export growth) are associated with higher economic growth.

These statistical demonstrations have contributed to what Krugman [*1995*] suggests is a main mechanism through which policy reforms have worked – a speculative bubble in which reforms increase investor confidence, and private financial inflows respond to reforms and their promised effects. High and sustained levels of aid funds, and rescue-packages at moments of crisis, have supported a few model cases ('success stories' in every sense). But even with some capacity to 'make truth', particularly through the effects on private investment of denial of the stamp of approval of international financial institutions, many evaluations of adjustment programmes indicate very mixed and limited success – even the evaluations by the World Bank itself [*World Bank, 1990; 1992*].

Against this background, new rhetoric, which focuses particularly on implementation failures, has emerged to sustain commitment to national policies which conform to a LIEO. One argument, which makes explicit the need for the 'internalisation' of rationality, is to suggest that adjustment programmes have not been implemented properly because of a lack of 'ownership' of the programmes at the national level. A related argument has been to suggest that where they have failed they have done so because they have not been carried out intensively enough, or for long enough time. Within the framework of methodological nationalism, this is difficult to refute, for there remains no alternative explanation.

The Changing Content of the LIEO

The programmes and discourse of adjustment reinforce at the national level the principles of a LIEO. But what this precisely means in terms of national policy depends on the specific content of the LIEO, and this too has been modified since the early 1980s.

Ruggie [*1982: 381*] describes the general form of an 'open' or liberal international economic order as follows:

> In the organization of a liberal order, pride of place is given to market rationality. This is not to say that authority is absent from such an order. It is to say that authority relations are constructed in such a way as to give maximum scope to market forces rather than to constrain them. Specific regimes that serve such an order, in the areas of money and trade, for example, limit the discretion of states to intervene in the functioning of self-regulating currency and commodity markets. These may be termed 'strong' regimes, because they restrain self-seeking states in a competitive international political system from meddling directly in domestic and international economic affairs in the name of their national interests.

Within this general form, a number of variants are possible. Thus the laissez-faire liberalism of the nineteenth century is different from the post-war liberal order. In the latter until the end of the 1970s, multilateral promotion of freer and non-discriminatory trade, the liberalisation of payments facilities and the loosening of capital controls, were limited by the requirements of domestic stability, a compromise which Ruggie calls 'embedded liberalism'.[8]

A key insight from Ruggie's analysis is that a central question about a LIEO is whether it simply entails liberalisation of a country's external economic relations or whether a liberal domestic economic policy is also required. At the start of the 1980s, the type of LIEO which defined the scope of adjustment programmes involved a laissez-faire liberalism in which the objective was to liberalise *both* external relations *and* domestic economic policy. But over time, this position was modified in the face of criticism and the search for more 'growth-oriented' adjustment. The emerging conventional wisdom about sensible economic reforms was synthesised as the 'Washington consensus' [*Williamson, 1993*]. And the new dominant consensus view about development was crystallised in the early 1990s as the 'market-friendly approach' [*World Bank, 1991*].

The 1990s 'market-friendly approach' advocates liberalisation of the external trade and financial policies of developing countries, but allows some degree of intervention in domestic markets to rectify 'market failures'. Such interventions must take place in a 'sound policy environment' (low fiscal deficits and inflation kept in check) and they must be 'market-friendly'. This means that governments should:

> *Intervene reluctantly.* Let markets work unless it is demonstrably better to step in ... .

> *Apply checks and balances.* Put interventions continually to the discipline of the international and domestic markets ... .

> *Intervene openly.* Make interventions simple, transparent, and subject to rules rather than official discretion ... [*ibid.: 5*].

Another important shift since the late 1980s has been the introduction of social dimensions of adjustment. This was partly a response to UNICEF's analysis *Adjustment with a Human Face* [*Cornia et al., 1987*]. But modifications to the dominant approach were only made to the extent that they were compatible with the underlying form of a LIEO. Thus they focused on guaranteeing minimum levels of consumer welfare rather than on meso policies which could modify the growth-poverty relationship. Moreover, though *Adjustment with a Human Face* promoted a more 'people-friendly' adjustment, it served at the same time to strengthen the policy frame of the dominant paradigm, by arguing that 'Adjustment is clearly necessary' [*ibid.: 289*] and focusing on what could be done at the national level to alleviate poverty and help groups whose basic living standards were vulnerable to adjustment measures.

III. THE POLICY FRAME FOR EAST ASIAN DEVELOPMENT

In contrast to the policy frame of the dominant paradigm, East Asian type development policies pursue nationalist objectives and seek to achieve their goals through an analysis of trends and policy options in a global frame of reference. The governments of the most rapidly growing East Asian economies, with the possible exception of the colony of Hong Kong, have not only given priority to the national interest but equated that with the promotion of national development. This has involved a goal-oriented approach to economic policy, with strong emphasis on rapid and sustained industrialisation.[9] For Japan during the post-war period until the 1970s, the strategic orientation was to catch up with more industrialised countries. Policy was 'production-oriented' rather than 'consumption-oriented' – geared to catching up in the sphere of production rather than of consumption – and consciously guided by international comparisons of production patterns, techniques and organisational structures between Japan and more advanced countries. In Taiwan, Korea and Singapore, national survival and security also influenced the industrialisation drive.

This goal-oriented approach to economic policy has led various observers to characterise the most successful East Asian economies as 'developmental states'.[10] But this description does not mean that states have somehow supplanted markets in the development process. On the contrary, a key feature of East Asian type policies is that they have sought to promote national development through the activity of private enterprise. This has entailed the search for, and implementation of, what Johnson [1982] calls 'market-conforming' policies; not telling business managers what to do, but seeking to increase the capabilities of firms by providing them with better means of production, to expand the set of market opportunities open to firms, to diminish risks associated with seizing opportunities, and to alter the relative risks and rewards of particular courses of action. Such policies are not market-replacing, but rather market-augmenting and market-accelerating.

These policies have, like some Latin American dependency theory, been formulated in a global frame of reference concerned with the process of late industrialisation. But whereas Latin American theory directed attention to how international centre-periphery relations blocked or distorted development in peripheral countries, East Asian theory, developed in particular in Japan, analyses how late industrialisers can catch up with more industrialised countries through national policies which use those international relationships. There is no assumption that the pursuit of the national interest necessarily involves protectionism, trade controls, and controls on capital movement. But there is equally no blind adherence to free trade and free capital movements. Norms of global liberalism are not totally ignored, for multilateral obligations have required phased adherence to certain principles of international economic relations. But these are delayed as far as possible if they conflict with the achievement of national development goals.

The resulting type of understanding of the development process is well illustrated in the ideas of the Japanese economist, Kaname Akamatsu, who identified and named the 'wild-geese-flying' pattern of development. This pattern explained the sequence of transformations, including in the structure of production and trade, direction of trade, and policy measures, which occurred in 'newly rising countries' (*shinkookoku*) as they, like Japan, began industrialising behind already industrialised countries but before other under-developed countries [*Akamatsu, 1961; 1962*]. It was the first theorisation of how growth occurred in newly industrialising countries, and related this to an analysis of trends towards differentiation and uniformisation in the international economic structure as such countries developed. Significantly, one of the papers outlining this theory in English was entitled 'A Theory of Unbalanced Growth in the World Economy'.

Akatmatsu uses the term 'wild-geese-flying' because he found that the graphs of imports, exports and production for the new industries successively introduced into Japan (cotton yarn, cotton cloth, spinning and weaving machinery, machinery and tools), when plotted on the same axis, appeared to resemble a line of flying geese. For each industry in turn, rising imports of particular industrial products are followed by import substitution as that industry becomes established in the country, after which export expansion begins.

Domestic production of imported consumer goods is identified as 'the take-off stage in the wild-geese-flying pattern' [*Akamatsu, 1962: 209*]. This occurs through 'a struggle of economic nationalism' [*Akamatsu, 1961: 13*] in which 'there should be fostered a domestic consumer goods industry powerful enough to win in the competition with imported consumer goods and to recover the home market from the hands of foreign industries' [*ibid.: 13*]. National economic policy is important to promote this through protectionist measures, and to promote the accumulation of capital and the technological adaptability of the people in the country seeking to industrialise. As these consumer industries grow, they develop into export industries, and at that point a further process of import substitution begins with regard to capital goods industries. These industries, in turn, become export industries.

For both consumer goods and capital goods, less industrialised countries initially provide important markets, but as production progresses from crude and simple goods to complex and refined goods, more advanced countries become significant markets. And over time, exports of simple consumer goods begin to decline as other less advanced countries themselves start production of these goods, initiating their own wild geese flying pattern and competing with the early 'newly rising countries'. Different countries, at different stages of this process, can be seen, in Akamatsu's words, as 'a wild-geese-flying order' [*Akamatsu, 1962: 17*].

Akamatsu's theorisation illustrates a mode of analysis which places the process of national development in a global framework. It is not presented here as being *the* East Asian model of industrialisation.[11] Various other elements are involved, not least to translate Akamatsu's understanding of the development pattern in newly industrialising countries (with some policy ingredients) into full development strategies for such countries. As Akamatsu stresses, there is nothing inevitable in the progression which he identified. The elaboration of a strategy which promotes it requires understanding of the underlying mechanisms driving the evolving pattern, and various further policy ingredients. These include: macroeconomic policies to support rapid growth and industrialisation; industrial policy to boost profits, investment and innovation in particular firms and industries at particular moments in time, including competition policy, national innovation systems, and the creation of rents; the management of urban growth in the city-states; and the facilitation of structural adjustment (in the sense it was understood in the 1970s) and outward direct investment in particular industrial sectors at the end of their sequence of development from imports to import substitution to export expansion.

The mode of analysis which Akamatsu's work illustrates, when coupled with the pursuit of national development through rapid industrialisation, leads to policy emphases different from those founded on a combination of methodological nationalism and global liberalism.

First, a focal concern of national policy in the dominant paradigm is promotion of economic growth and consumer welfare through a system of incentives for efficient resource allocation. This orientation is seen in the argument which relates a LIEO to national economic growth. East Asian type policies, in contrast, do not take capital accumulation for granted, but are concerned with accelerating and sustaining it, including through productivity growth and the sequencing of resource allocation in a way which is dynamically efficient [*Akyüz and Gore, 1996*].

Secondly, East Asian type policies are not simply export-oriented. In a national policy formulated in a global context, national demand is taken to be a part of global demand (global is not external), and consideration is given to both demand *and* supply. Policy thus does not simply promote exports but manages the relative mix of domestic and foreign demand *and* the relative mix of domestic and foreign supply through consideration of the size of the domestic and foreign markets, the changing structure of demand in these markets, *and* the availability on the supply side from domestic production, the import capacity of the economy, and the organisation of importation [*ESCAP, 1990*]. Close attention is paid to the changing competitive situation of particular industries in an international context and opportunities for catching up through the adoption and adaption of technological best practices.

Thirdly, whereas a key tenet of national policy founded on the norms of global liberalism is that the national economy should be open, the East Asian type analysis leads to the conclusion that a country's external relations should be characterised by selective openness, with the degree of openness varying between types of external relationship (trade relations, industry by industry; technology relations; capital movements; movement of people and so on) and varying over time, determined according to whether it supports the achievement of national goals or not. Singh [*1994*] describes this form of integration into the world economy as being 'strategic' rather than 'close'.

Fourthly, another key tenet of national policy founded on global liberalism is that domestic policy should be neutral between sectors. But the analysis underlying East Asian development policies leads to the conclusion that industrial policies can articulate the interrelationship between internal and external factors in the growth process so as to produce positive effects. For example, the industrial rationalisation policies designed to increase the international competitiveness of Japanese firms in the 1950s and 1960s were concentrated in sectors in which the potential for growth and dynamic development was greatest, namely those with a high income elasticity of demand and those where the potential for productivity improvement through technological progress was high [*Shinohara, 1982*]. A deliberate effort was also made to increase the proportion of industrial output in sectors in which world demand was growing fastest and being exported to markets where demand was growing fastest [*Yoshihara, 1962*]. In sum, rapid export growth was not simply achieved through being open, nor through export incentives on their own.

Fifthly, the global framing of East Asian type policies has involved analysis of changing economic relationships with *both* more advanced countries *and* less advanced countries. Regional economic relationships are taken account of, and also developed, as part of East Asian national development policies. These relationships include direct investment and trade linkages, and also indirect linkages, through competitive and complementary supply to extra-regional markets. Within the dominant paradigm, the opportunities, and also threats, of such international economic neighbourhood effects are typically ruled out, as a result of treating the world economy as structureless.

These are the five key areas of difference in policy emphasis between the dominant paradigm and East Asian approaches. They are rooted in the conflict between the global/national frames for explanation and evaluation, and between the specific policy objectives: the dominant paradigm's global objective to promote a LIEO and the late industrialisers' national objectives to promote national development through rapid industrialisation.

PART 2: THE ANATOMY OF MISUNDERSTANDING

The controversy about the East Asian development experience has focused on whether economic success can be attributed to markets *or* states.[12] But because

East Asian type policies are characterised by the government promoting national development through the activity of private enterprise, this focus is misdirected. Since the policies rely on private enterprise as the principal engine of growth they can be represented as 'market-based'; equally it is possible to call them 'state-led' because economic activity has been directed towards national goals. But each of these polarised descriptions is in some sense a misrepresentation of a system which relies on both markets *and* states, and which has been described, with reference to Japan, as 'a plan-oriented market economy system' [*Johnson, 1982: 10*]. As Shinohara [*1982: 23*], describing Japan during the post-war catch-up, puts it, 'the success of guidance from above was only made possible by dynamism from below'.

The argument that these policies diverge from the dominant paradigm by putting more reliance on state action actually strengthens the explanatory frame of the dominant policy paradigm. Constructing the East Asian debate in the terms of 'markets versus states' reinforces methodological nationalism because, whether it is more or less interventionist, national economic success is attributed mainly to national factors, and in particular to national policy.

To equate the misunderstanding of East Asian industrialisation with an underestimation of the role of the state in the development process is correct in some sense, for the promotion of a LIEO gives pride of place to market rationality. But whenever this estimation of the role of the state is grounded in methodological nationalism, it compounds misunderstanding.

The anatomy of the misunderstanding is better analysed as the misinterpretation of *how*, within a global frame of reference, states work with markets to promote national development. From this perspective, the five areas of policy difference identified in section III are the five main axes of misunderstanding. They are tension points around which confusion in the definition of key terms, misdescriptions and omissions and incoherence in the structure of arguments, are particularly likely to arise when East Asian development is interpreted in the terms of the dominant paradigm.

IV. 'OUTWARD-ORIENTED' AS A KEY WORD

A key word in the misunderstanding of East Asian development is the adjective 'outward-oriented'. This label, which is sometimes conflated with 'export-oriented', is widely used to describe the policies in successful East Asian economies and was the first way in which development success in East Asia was interpreted in the terms of the dominant paradigm. 'Become outward/export-oriented like them' probably remains ingrained in the general imagination as the most powerful lesson of what other developing countries can learn from East Asian success. But 'outward-oriented' is a very curious term. Its deployment in the analysis of East Asian industrialisation seriously distorts the logic of East Asian policies.

The Meaning of 'Outward-Orientation' – Keesing versus Balassa

The notion of 'outward-orientation' has a long history. The distinction between models of development oriented 'towards the outside' and others oriented 'towards the inside' was first put forward by ECLA in 1949. ECLA's model of 'development towards the inside' has served as the archetype of such a strategy. But what constitutes an outward-oriented strategy has been more difficult to specify.

A first attempt was made by Keesing [*1967*] in a paper which seeks to characterise the benefits of an '*outward-looking*' strategy of industrial development. He regarded Japan as the best exemplar of an 'outward-looking strategy', but actually what constituted this strategy was difficult for him to define. As he put it:

> I am not making a case against import substitution. That is a process that will occur whether policies are inward- or outward-looking, and whether import substitution is fostered deliberately or not. To some extent I *am* concerned with the intensity, breadth and frequency of government intervention. Reliance on the domestic market permits a high degree of government intervention, whether in Soviet or Latin American fashion. By contrast, an outward-looking strategy compels moderation ... An outward-looking like an inward-looking strategy, however, may be characterized by a distrust of *laissez-faire* and free trade.
>
> I do *not* mean by an outward-looking strategy that a country places heavy reliance on exports of manufacturing, either as an engine of growth or as a means of obtaining the imports essential to development. Rather, exports of manufactures are promoted at an early stage in the process of industrial growth for the sake of indirect benefits ... . Again, I am not suggesting that nations should contort themselves to export manufactures without regard to the paucity of local resources ... .
>
> *The phrase 'outward-looking' is deliberately chosen to signify a constant and deliberate attention to industrial and trade happenings outside the country.* One ingredient in the policy is a strong effort to remain in touch, absorb the latest technology, catch up and become competitive with the most advanced industrial countries. *The government subsidises activities serving these ends* [*Keesing, 1967: 304*; emphases added in the last paragraph].

This definition of an outward-looking strategy – 'a constant and deliberate attention to industrial and trade happenings outside the country' – is one way of articulating the notion that national economic policy is to be formulated within a global, rather than national, frame of reference. But, 'attention to happenings globally' is quite vague, and after this key insight, Keesing actually works with the more tangible definition that the essence of an outward-looking strategy is to promote export of manufactures 'at an early stage in the process of growth'.

Bela Balassa [*1970*] took over Keesing's arguments that an outward-looking strategy was superior to an inward-looking strategy, but he changed the meaning of the term, and later re-labelled it an '*outward-oriented*' strategy. For Balassa, an outward-looking strategy was distinct from an inward-looking one in terms of 'the attitudes taken toward participation in the international division of labour', and, in a critical move, these attitudes to participation were now said to be expressed in the system of incentives for efficient resource allocation between different industries and different markets. Thus as he puts it:

> An inward-looking strategy tends to minimize these benefits [of participating in the international division of labour] by fostering the expansion of production to serve domestic needs and favouring it over exports *and* imports. In so doing, discrimination is introduced among domestic activities since import-competing industries are benefited at the expense of export sectors. There is also discrimination in favour of domestic production as against imports, and in individual industries, production of domestic needs is encouraged as compared to exports. These three forms of discrimination are negligible under an outward-looking strategy. Such a strategy provides essentially the same opportunities for individual industries; it does not create a bias against imports; and it does not discriminate between the domestic and foreign sales of a given industry [*ibid.: 25*].

With this new definition, being outward-looking is reduced to participation in the international division of labour and such participation is equated with neutrality of the system of incentives. In a discursive move similar to the re-definition of the term 'structural adjustment', one particular way of being 'outward-looking' (Balassa's) is defined as what being 'outward-looking' (in Keesing's sense of a constant attention to global happenings) actually means.

This has serious adverse consequences for subsequent understanding of East Asian development. 'Neutrality of incentives' are substituted (and later wrongly assumed to be sufficient) for 'a strong effort to remain in touch, absorb the latest technology, catch up and become competitive with the most advanced countries'. Keesing's observations that an outward-looking strategy can entail *subsidising activities which enable a country to increase productivity and become competitive internationally*, and *can be characterised by a distrust of laissez-faire and free trade*, are lost. Moreover, Keesing's critical insight, that being 'outward-looking' entailed a global analytical framework for national policy design, is buried.

The Extension of its Domain of Application

Balassa's original formulation of the nature and value of outward-oriented strategies had specific reference to 'semi-industrial countries'. In his first exposition of the concept he focused on Argentina, Chile, Czechoslovakia and Hungary in the post-war period as examples of 'inward-looking strategies' and Denmark and Norway in the same period as examples of 'outward-looking strategies' [*Balassa, 1970*]. But just as with the term 'structural adjustment', the geographical domain in which the term was deployed changed between the 1970s and 1980s. The argument that outward-oriented policies are superior to inward-oriented was extended from 'semi-industrial countries' to all developing countries. An important example is World Bank [*1987*] which classifies the trade regimes of a large sample of developing economies as inward- or outward-oriented, including some 'semi-industrialised' countries but also Burundi, Tanzania, Ethiopia, Ghana and Sudan. After this move, lessons from semi-industrialised countries can be applied willy-nilly to less developed countries, a process which has been critical in promoting mistaken policy designs for Africa.

With such universalisation to all developing countries, it has become possible to view 'inward-orientation' and 'outward-orientation' as two 'archetypes' of development strategy, as Balassa [*1989*] himself put it. These are set out in Table 2.

TABLE 2

'INWARD-ORIENTATION' AND 'OUTWARD-ORIENTATION'
AS ARCHETYPAL DEVELOPMENT STRATEGIES

INWARD-ORIENTED	OUTWARD-ORIENTED
1. POLICIES	
More State-Directed	More Reliance on Market Mechanism
Promotion of Import-Substitution Industries	'Export Promotion'
Price Distortions	Limited Price Distortions
Anti-Agriculture Bias	Neutral Inter-Industry Incentive Structure
Overvalued Exchange Rates	Competitive Exchange Rates
Protection through Direct Import Controls and Licensing	'Liberalised' Trade Regime
Rigid Labour Markets	Flexible Labour Markets
2. PERFORMANCE	
Slow Economic Growth/Stagnation	Rapid Economic Growth
Slow Export Growth	Rapid Export Growth
Very Unequal Income Distribution	Increasing Income Equality
Weak Employment Growth	Strong Growth of Employment and Real Wages

Development policy can now be conceptualised, as it always has been, as facilitating a transition from one state of affairs to another. But whereas in the 1950s to the 1970s, transition was seen as a movement from an agricultural to an industrial society, a process of structural change, here the transition is from an inward-oriented to an outward-oriented economy, a process involving the closer integration of a national economy with the rest of the world.

Semantic Confusion and Semantic Flexibility

Although the dichotomy between 'inward-orientation' and 'outward-orientation' has been critical in persuading governments in developing countries to undertake unilateral liberalisation and integrate their economies more closely with the rest of the world, it is more complex than it first appears.

Firstly, it is not in reality a dichotomous choice, for there are degrees of being outward-oriented and inward-oriented. Moreover outward-orientation can refer to both the state of being outward-oriented and the process of making a transition to that state, a process which has been explicitly defined as 'trade liberalisation'.

Secondly, the terms 'outward-oriented' and 'inward-oriented' most usually refer to the nature of a country's trade regime, but they can be used to describe industrial policies or, more broadly, development strategy. With the use of these terms, there has been a tendency to make foreign trade policy reform the centre-piece of development strategy.

Thirdly, there is not a complete symmetry between 'inward-oriented' and 'outward-oriented' trade regimes. The former involves a bias of incentives in favour of production for the domestic market over production for exports, but the latter does not imply there is a bias in favour of production for exports over production for the domestic markets. Rather 'outward-orientation' is apparent in an *absence of bias* against exports. This is because, technically, a trade regime is said to be outward-oriented if, on average, incentives are neutral, biased neither for nor against exports.

This neutral trade regime could be in place in a situation of free trade, or alternatively it could be present in situations where import tariffs are combined with, and offset by, export subsidies. Thus, although outward-oriented strategies are often said to be 'export promotion' strategies, this does not *necessarily* mean the active promotion of exports [e.g. *Lal and Rajapatirana, 1987: 197*]. Moreover, although the process of outward orientation is described as a process of 'trade liberalisation', it is possible to have an 'outward-oriented', 'liberalised', economy with import protection! As Anne Krueger [*1978: 89*] puts it, 'a regime could be fully liberalized and yet employ exceedingly high tariffs in order to encourage import substitution'.

The last point could potentially weaken the role of the notion of outward-orientation in internalising adherence to a liberal international economic order.

But the literature projecting the benefits of outward-orientation has downplayed this possibility [e.g. *World Bank, 1987: 78*], thereby increasing the confusion over meanings. As Edwards [*1993: 1364–5*] argues: 'In the late 1980s the policy debate on the merits of alternative trade regimes has become increasingly confused and increasingly ideological. At the centre of these controversies was the inability to define clearly what was meant exactly by alternative policies and by *trade liberalization* reforms.'

Further semantic confusion has arisen because of the elision of the term 'outward-oriented' with 'export-oriented' (as in the quotation from Krueger above, p.87). This vulgarisation of the concept of 'outward-oriented' substitutes a description of a development pattern (namely, the proportion of domestic output which is exported) for a development strategy (namely a structure of incentives). But it has been supported by the assumptions often used to test the relationships between trade policy and economic growth, which have involved, as in Balassa [*1982: 51*], the use of 'the growth rate of exports as a proxy for policy orientation'. Moreover it reflects the fact that, for some observers, export growth rather than trade policy improves economic performance. For example, Krueger [*1978: 274*] found, in a multi-country comparative study of the effects of trade regimes on growth, that: '[F]actors associated with better export performance explain whatever systematic differences there are in growth rates under different phases of the regime; the fact that the regime is liberalized (or restricted) does not seem to have any additional influence.'

The semantic confusion surrounding the term 'outward-oriented' is not surprising. It is typical of key words in development policy discourse, which tend to be appraisive terms which both describe a state of affairs and express an evaluation of it (good or bad) at the same time. Such terms are usually 'essentially contested' [*Connolly, 1974*] (see also Gasper on 'Essentialism' in this collection). But nor is the confusion inconsequential. Through the conflation of 'outward-oriented' with 'export-oriented', and semantic slippage in which outward-orientation is equated with a neutral trade regime in East Asia whilst what it means elsewhere is a free trade regime, it remains possible to achieve a fairly faithful description of some aspects of the East Asian development experience, while at the same time projecting their outward-orientation as model which supports the norms and principles of a LIEO. Semantic confusion also offers semantic flexibility.

Shaky Empirical Foundations

The superior performance of the outward-oriented strategy over the inward-oriented strategy has been explained analytically and empirically. Analytically it has been argued that an outward-oriented strategy allows countries to reap the benefits of specialisation according to comparative advantage, permits the realisation of economies of scale, and provides the spur of competition which induces technological change. These benefits are not achieved in an inward-oriented strategy, which is also adversely affected by the negative effects on efficiency and equity of rent-seeking activities.

The empirical case for superior performance of 'outward-oriented' economies has relied on labelling successful East Asian economies as 'outward-oriented'. The first illustration given of the positive effects of a transition from inward-orientation to outward-orientation referred to Taiwan and Korea, with the argument at that time focused on industrial policy [Balassa, 1971]. During the 1970s, the two city-states – Hong Kong and Singapore – were also identified as being 'outward-oriented' and, ignoring their specificities as entrepôt economies, and the fact that a critical factor in their economic growth as cities has been their ability to control in-migration, they have been added to the two northeastern 'Tigers' as models of outward orientation.

An important empirical method used to claim that outward-oriented policies are superior has been correlation of national trade policies with country economic performance. Such work, founded on methodological nationalism, can easily fall into a number of traps, and the statistical exercises do not bear close scrutiny [Edwards, 1993]. They have adopted subjective classifications of trade policies which are questionable for individual countries, and have misidentified causal factors. Singer [1988: 233] shows how the associations between degrees of outward- and inward-orientation and economic performance in World Bank [1987] can equally be used to argue that 'poorer countries find it more difficult to progress than countries already further up the development ladder'. High correlations have been found between export growth and GDP growth. But it also has been shown that these high correlations occur not simply for exports but for *all* main components of GDP [Sheehey, 1990]. It is even possible to establish statistically significant relationships between baseball-playing and growth rate of real per capita income in a sample of 95 non-OPEC and non-communist countries between 1960 and 1990 [Wall, 1995].[13]

The Distortion of the Logic of East Asian Policies

The flexible definition of the term facilitates the labelling of East Asian economies as 'outward-oriented'. The successful East Asian economies have had very high rates of export growth, and it seems common sense to describe them as 'export-oriented'. Moreover, if, *at a single moment in time*, one examines the structure of incentives in a country seeking to promote sequentially sector-by-sector a series of transitions from import substitution to export expansion, just like Akamatsu's flying geese, one would observe a mix of import tariffs and export subsidies which conforms – *on the average* – to the neutral trade regime version of 'outward-orientation'. And if one examines the system of incentives *over time* in a country which uses protectionist measures selectively and for limited periods as productivity and international competitiveness by local firms increase, one would observe a sequence in which gradual trade liberalisation actually occurred.

Balassa's initial analysis of Taiwan and Korea in 1970 correctly identified one aspect in their flying-geese pattern of industrial development, namely the *first-stage* transition from import substitution to export expansion for *simple labour-intensive consumer goods*. But because of the timing of Balassa's analysis, it inevitably ignored the 'second-round' capital goods import substitution which began in the 1970s and which was followed by further sectoral transitions from import-substitution to export expansion. Thus a transition *at the industry level* was misdescribed as an *economy-wide transition*.

This misdescription has persisted. Moreover it has been reinforced through the misdescription of some East Asian trade regimes as an 'offsetting' mix which produces a neutral overall pattern of incentives. This cross-sectional view simply obscures the dynamic sequence of development at the industry level, and it renders incomprehensible the logic associated with elaborating different policies for different industries at different moments of time, including both import substitution and export promotion at the same time.

In substituting a description of a development pattern for a development strategy, the conflation of 'export-oriented' with 'outward-oriented' assumes that the latter is the cause of the former. The focus on exports hides the fact, already discussed in section III, that in East Asian-type policies national demand is taken to be a part of global demand (the global is not external). But the most damaging effect of identifying the East Asian economies as 'outward-oriented' (in Balassa's sense) is the misunderstanding of the development process and the role of public policy in it.

At the most basic level, misunderstanding is founded on the fact that the case for outward-orientation directs attention towards the incentives for efficient resource allocation and takes capital accumulation for granted. Balassa [*1982: 3*] even defines the term 'incentives' as 'governmental measures that affect the allocation of resources – land, labour, and capital – among industries, and that influence the orientation of economic activities between exportation and import substitution'. This excludes, by definition, the deployment of government incentive measures to accelerate capital accumulation and learning through raising the 'animal spirits' of entrepreneurs. But it is precisely these which have been at the heart of how governments accelerated industrialisation and growth over the long run in East Asia [*Akyüz and Gore, 1996*].

V. *THE EAST ASIAN MIRACLE* AS A KEY TEXT

The problem of explaining how outward-oriented policies are translated into long-term growth is addressed head-on in *The East Asian Miracle: Public Policy and Economic Growth* [*World Bank, 1993*]. This important text (henceforth 'the Report') extends discussion of the East Asian development experience, which had focused on the 'Four Tigers', northwards to Japan, and southwards to Indonesia, Malaysia, and Thailand.[14] It drops the fictions that there has been little government intervention in these economies and that policy was neutral between sectors. Moreover, it expands the focus of policy analysis by looking not simply at how far particular policies establish incentives for efficient resource allocation, but rather at how policies influence what it calls the *three* central functions of 'growth-oriented economic management' [*ibid.: 87*] – accumulation, efficient resource allocation, and productivity growth.

The Object of Analysis

The eight countries covered in the Report (which are described as 'high performing Asian economies' – HPAEs) are identified as being particularly successful in that they have sustained rapid economic growth *and* achieved low and declining inequality over the period 1960 to 1990. But the central thrust of the Report is to explain their *growth* performance.

This is discussed, in classic methodological nationalist fashion, as the outcome of a set of national factors which in turn reflect national policies. The international economic environment does not even enter the explanation, and is only considered in the Report when it argues that the problem of access to markets in industrial countries will depend on limited intervention in pushing exports. Regional factors are considered in two brief pages which discuss the extent to which high performance can be attributed to East Asian geography (ready access to common sea lanes, and relative geographical proximity encouraging regional linkages), culture (the common cultural heritage of the ethnic Chinese) and history ('massive U.S. economic assistance and military spending in the region throughout the cold war' [*World Bank, 1993: 80*]. These regional characteristics are admitted as potentially significant, but their importance is downplayed because 'economies that are part of the same matrix of geography, culture and history as the HPAEs but followed different policies ... have yet to share in the East Asian miracle' [*ibid.: 81*]. Thus, the Report turns to 'the policies that have shaped East Asia's success' [*ibid.*], arguing that 'the success of the East Asian economies stems partly from the policies they have adopted and partly from the institutional mechanisms used to implement them' [*ibid.: 352*].

Identifying the policies which produced the 'miracle' is difficult given the range of countries. The Report deals with the intra-regional differences by suggesting firstly that there were a variety of different ways in which the 'functions of growth' were attained: 'There is no single East Asian model' [*ibid.: 347*]. But secondly, it seeks the lowest common denominator amongst all the countries (a policy which they all can be said to share). It also focuses mainly, though not exclusively, on the period after 1960.

The selection of countries and the time frame are crucial in determining the policy conclusions reached. The lumping together of the northeastern and southeastern Asian economies and city-states serves to 'water down' the distinctive policy experience of Japan, Korea and Taiwan which is based on the promotion of national firms. Moreover by focusing on the period 1960-90, deep analysis of the development experience in the 1950s, which is crucial for understanding how rapid growth and industrialisation got started, is avoided.

The Message of the Report

The Report presents a more complex view of the role of public policy in East Asian development than accounts which focus solely on 'outward-orientation'. Modifying the injunction of the 1980s to 'Get the Prices Right', it argues that rapid growth was due to 'Getting the Fundamentals Right' – ensuring macroeconomic stability; building human capital; creating effective and secure financial systems; limiting price distortions by maintaining the relative prices of traded goods close to international prices; being open to foreign technology; and developing agriculture [*World Bank, 1993: 347–52*]. It is acknowledged that '[i]n most of the economies, in one form or another, the government intervened – systematically and through multiple channels – to foster development and in some cases the development of specific industries' [*ibid.: 5*]. But these interventions are said to have been of a certain nature and of a modest scope. In particular: (i) successful interventions were designed to correct market failures; (ii) interventions were consistent with macroeconomic stability; (iii) many interventions were implemented in a way which simulated market competition in that they were orchestrated through 'contest-based competitions' and subject to the competitive discipline of external markets as a performance test; and (iv) when interventions failed they were pragmatically abandoned.

An important admission of the Report (compared to earlier analyses from the standpoint of the dominant paradigm) is that '[o]ur judgement is that in a few economies, mainly in Northeast Asia, in some instances, government interventions resulted in higher and more equal growth than otherwise would have occurred' [*ibid.: 6*]. But this finding is immediately qualified by linking successful intervention to the presence of certain 'institutional prerequisites' whose absence in other developing economies renders the same forms of intervention inadvisable elsewhere.

Thus the Report reinforces the 'market-friendly' development consensus which is expounded in World Bank [*1991*]. It moves away from the view that both external and domestic economic relationships must be liberalised. But it strengthens the defence of openness in external relationships by *linking* the success of internal selective interventions to open external relationships which provide competitive discipline.

The Practices of Persuasion

The Report describes itself as 'an essay in persuasion' based on analytical and empirical judgement [*World Bank, 1993: 6*]. Its message is supported by various cross-economy regression analyses and tests of statistical significance. But in practice, the persuasive power of the Report depends on a logically dubious characterisation of policies.

(a) The False Authority of 'Fundamentals'

The discussion of policy is founded on the distinction between 'fundamentals' and 'interventions', and depends critically on how 'fundamentals' are defined. The answer which is given is that fundamentals are policies which make growth possible, whilst non-fundamentals can contribute to, or detract from, 'the rapid growth made possible by good fundamentals' [*World Bank, 1993: 354*]. The idea that there are some necessary policy conditions for growth to occur is quite logical. But the Report then *also* defines 'fundamentals' as policies which 'affect the attainment of growth functions primarily through market-based mechanisms of competitive discipline' [*ibid.: 89*]. Interventions are thereby, without any rationale, equated with non-fundamentals, and the key conclusion that 'widely-shared market-friendly policies are the foundation of East Asia's success' [*ibid.*]. is thus made true *by definition.*[15]

'Getting the fundamentals right' sounds like common-sense. But even ignoring the fact that the HPAEs did not always adhere to the 'fundamentals',[16] this statement is actually meaningless, for it is apparent from the text that the precise specification of the 'fundamentals' is somewhat arbitrary. At two points in the text [*ibid.: Figure 2.1 and 348–52*], six policies are listed as 'fundamentals'. But one of these six, agricultural development policies, is not discussed in the main chapters on policies and their impact, and in the discussion of Figure 2.1 it is actually omitted. As the text puts it:

> The *six* policies listed as fundamentals are so defined in the sense that they affect the attainment of growth functions primarily through market-based mechanisms of competitive discipline. *Three* – macroeconomic stability, effective financial systems and limited price distortions – assist markets. *The two others* – high investment in human capital and openness to foreign technology – require efficient markets to operate [*ibid.: 89*; emphasis added].

Later in the text, 'secure property rights and complementary public investments infrastructure', which are curiously missing in the main list, are mentioned in passing, along with 'low relative prices of investment goods' [*ibid.: 242*]. To the extent that the category is arbitrary, 'getting fundamentals right' is an empty slogan.

(b) Making Interventions 'Market-Friendly' and 'Market-Conforming'

The analysis of interventions in the Report ignores what the logic and rationale of these policies were to the policy-makers themselves, and rather explains why some succeeded, and demonstrates how others failed, within the terms of the dominant paradigm.

Within that framework, interventions are regarded as policy distortions which *should* stymie growth in most circumstances, and a focal question animating the narrative is to explain why this did *not* happen. This is in fact why the Report reaches the conclusion that much intervention was designed to correct market failure. As it puts it:

> We maintain as a guiding principle that for intervention that attempts to guide resource allocations to succeed, they must address failures in the working of markets. Otherwise, markets would perform the allocation function more efficiently. We identify a class of economic problems, coordination failures, which can lead markets to fail, especially in the early stages of development. We then interpret some of the interventionist policies in East Asia as responses to these problems ... [*ibid.: 11*].

Such an approach serves to render East Asian interventions 'market-friendly' from the outset, prior to analysis. It confirms the dominant paradigm in a circular way by asserting that what *did* happen was what logically *should* have happened *given the assumptions of the dominant paradigm.*

This analysis also masks the fact that what 'market failure' means within the frame of a goal-directed economic policy is different from what it means in the frame of the market-friendly paradigm. In the former case, the inability of the market to achieve industry-specific goals can be seen as market failure; or more broadly, market failures can be said to arise 'when the goods and services deemed necessary by society cannot be easily or adequately provided through dependence on only the free economic activities of private sectors motivated by private profit' [*JDB/JERI, 1993: 28*]. Moreover in a goal-oriented approach, action is taken in anticipation of market failure rather than *ex post.*[17]

Some interventions are said to have failed, but identifying them in the super-successful HPAEs presents a major challenge. The methodology adopted is not to estimate the effects of policies on growth (which *is* done in the case of countries with a poor economic performance), but rather to show that policies have not caused economic outcomes to be different from those which would have occurred if market forces had been given free play. Ironically, and in the familiar pattern of re-defining key terms, such failed policies are described as 'market-conforming'. This takes over a term, which as noted earlier, is pivotal in a classic analysis of industrial policy in Japan [*Johnson, 1982*]. With this transformation, the term 'market-conforming', which had been used to label a central problem confronting East Asian policy makers, whose successful resolution is a key lesson from this region for other developing countries – namely, how to design policies which harness markets and private enterprise to the achievement of national goals – is associated with the measurement of policy failure.

Both industrial policies and restrictions on capital movements are identified as 'market-conforming' interventions in this way. But for industrial policies, this judgement is founded on a narrow definition of industrial policy as 'government efforts to alter industrial structure to promote productivity-growth' [*World Bank, 1993: 304*] which predefines the terrain on which effectiveness should be evaluated. This focuses on the inter-sectoral pattern of growth within the manufacturing sector and ignores the critical issue of how industrial policy accelerated the rate, and sustained the momentum, of growth, which is vital in understanding the East Asian development experience.[18] With regard to capital export restrictions in Japan, Korea, and Taiwan, the Report states that 'the existence of restrictions at a time when these economies were achieving high and rising savings rates challenges the premise that free and open financial markets are always best for growth' [*ibid.: 285*]. But this challenge is quickly absorbed with a non-sequitur which renders the impact of these policies 'market-conforming':

> The obvious failure of such restrictions in economies prone to capital flight suggests that capital is too fluid to be retained when domestic conditions are inimicable to savings and investment. Therefore the simplest explanation for the seeming success of these restrictions in NE Asia is that the economies offered returns adequate to retain capital even without restrictions [*ibid.: 285*].

(c) The Artificial Separation of Interventions

The analysis of interventions focuses particularly on three types of intervention adopted in the successful East Asian economies, and argues that: (i) repressing interest rates and directing credit can work, but requires so much institutional capacity that its use is not recommended; (ii) industrial policies 'were largely ineffective' [*ibid.: 312*]; and (iii) 'the most successful selective intervention in the HPAEs' [*ibid.: 325*] was the broad commitment to manufactured exports, which it defines as an 'export push strategy'. But this splitting of policies into different types (more or less successful, more or less transferable) separates measures which are logically related. Directing credit is a tool of industrial policy, and one of the ends of that policy is to increase exports [*Rodrik, 1994*]. As a consequence, the Report sees the promotion of exports as a matter of trade policy *per se*, and not a matter of policies which promote capital accumulation and technological change to build up firm-level productive capabilities and thus compete internationally. Moreover the way in which industrial policies can play a pivotal role in managing the interplay between internal productive structure and the external economic environment in a way which can accelerate growth is simply put aside.

The Meaning of the 'Export-Push' Strategy

It is through such policy-splitting (together with seeking a lowest common denominator for all the HPAEs which describes what they have done over the whole period 1960–90) that the 'export-push' emerges as a central policy lesson for other developing economies. But the use of this term is also discursively significant. Once again, the Report redefines a term which has previously been elaborated to understand East Asian industrialisation and coopts it in support of a market-friendly LIEO.

An early usage of the term can be found in a study of how locally-owned firms in five East Asian countries develop as exporters [*Wortzel and Wortzel, 1981*]. Their analysis suggests that a critical shift at the firm level is from 'passive dependence on "importer pull"', in which the local firm sells low-cost production facilities to foreign customers who set product specifications and undertake marketing, to 'active pursuit of an "export push" strategy' [*ibid.: 52*], in which local firms, on the basis of acquired capabilities, undertake product design and marketing, even establishing their own brand names and becoming suppliers of know-how. But the notion of an export push strategy which the Report re-defines is not this firm-level strategy but rather Bradford's application of the term to define a trade regime in which the effective exchange rate for exports is greater than that for imports rather than roughly equal to it (as in 'outward-orientation') [*Bradford, 1986; 1990; 1994*].

Bradford's concept of the 'export-push strategy' is important because it breaks from the false dichotomy of inward-oriented/state intervention versus outward-oriented/market-based, and *names* an outward-looking strategy (in Keesing's sense of attention to global happenings) which is interventionist. Such a strategy does not simply remove bias against exports, but is actually biased towards them.[19] Its objective is to increase the market share of a country's exports rather than to establish a permissive state of openness which allows a country to be responsive to external demand. Moreover, according to Bradford, there are strong theoretical reasons for arguing that interventionist export-oriented strategies are more effective than neutral 'outward-oriented' strategies, and also some of the most successful East Asian economies used them.

The Report absorbs this challenge by taking over the term 'export push' and redefining it in a way which associates it more closely with a neutral trade regime. In contrast to Bradford's definition, the Report argues that there are three main variants of the export push strategy in East Asia: a free trade regime; a neutral trade regime which combines export incentives with substantial protection of the domestic market; and trade regimes which involve gradual reductions in import protection, coupled with institutional support of exporters and a duty-free regime for inputs into exports. In the only place in the Report where this key concept is precisely defined, a footnote, the export-push strategy is specified as 'sustained movement toward parity of incentives between export and import substitutes, combined with institutional support for exporters' [*World Bank, 1993: 156*].

The export push strategy is thus reduced to just a variant of Balassa's 'outward orientation'. And a key lesson which other developing countries are encouraged to draw from East Asian success is that 'economies making the transition from highly protectionist import-substituting regimes to more balanced incentives would benefit from combining import liberalization with a strong commitment to exports and active export promotion, especially in those cases in which the pace of liberalization is moderate' [*ibid.: 23*].

The Incoherence of the Narrative

The Report makes the East Asian development experience conform to the dominant paradigm, but the analysis of the effects of public policy on growth in East Asia can only make sense in the context of a particular understanding of the growth process. At this broader level the authors have to strain in order to make the whole text cohere.

(a) Equivocation on the Importance of Capital Accumulation

A principal difficulty of the Report is to construct an explanation of rapid capital accumulation in which public policy conforms to the tenets of a market-friendly LIEO with trade liberalisation and free capital movements. This is required by the functional growth framework, but is made more important as a key finding of the empirical analysis of the determinants of growth is that 'about two-thirds of East Asia's extraordinary growth is attributable to rapid accumulation' [*ibid.: 48*], and, according to one model, 'between 60 and 90 per cent of their output growth derives from accumulation of physical and human capital' [*ibid.: 58*].

An important feature of the Report is that, unlike the earlier work within the dominant paradigm on East Asia, it does not take accumulation for granted. But its account of the role of policy in promoting accumulation emphasises 'fundamentals' rather than 'interventions' (see, for example, the quotation above, page 107, on market failure), and is unconvincing with regard to the critical issue of how domestic savings and investment rose [*Akyüz and Gore, 1996*]. Moreover, despite the fact that most of the growth in the HPAEs can, according to the Report itself, be attributed to capital accumulation, more attention is actually paid in the text to efficient resource allocation and productivity change.

This shift of emphasis is achieved by making the basic question of the text not 'why have these economies grown rapidly?', but rather 'why have these economies grown more rapidly than other developing economies?'. Although the cross-economy regression equations show accumulation of physical and human capital can 'explain' a large proportion of the economic growth of the HPAEs themselves, the *differences* in actual growth rates between the HPAEs and Latin America and between the HPAEs and Africa are not well-explained by actual differences in investment rates and school enrolment rates. As the Report puts it:

> Controlling for their superior rates of accumulation, the HPAEs still outperform while Sub-Saharan Africa or Latin America underperform in the statistical relationship between accumulation and growth, leaving much of the regional difference in per capita income growth unexplained (even though a large fraction of HPAE success is explained). They have been apparently more successful in allocating resources they have accumulated to high-productivity activities and in adopting and mastering catch up technologies [*World Bank, 1993: 54*].

With this move, total factor productivity (TFP) growth is identified as pivotal in the performance of the HPAEs relative to other developing countries. TFP measures the portion of growth *not* attributable to growth in the quantity of factor inputs, and by stressing its role, the importance of physical capital accumulation in particular is marginalised, and emphasis shifted to the ways in which policies promoted efficient resource allocation and productivity growth.

(b) Making Openness and Exports Matter

This shift in emphasis is important for on this ground it is possible to make 'openness' and close integration to the world economy through exporting matter in the explanation of the East Asian 'miracle'. But this can only be achieved through a tenuous chain of logic which involves two *further* steps.

First, the Report attributes the TFP growth in the HPAEs largely to movement towards international technological best practice. This is a difficult task. TFP, as a residual variable, is a chaotic category whose sources, according to the Report, include 'better technology', 'better organization', 'gains from specialization', 'innovations on the shop floor' [*ibid.: 48*];

'allocative mistakes' [*ibid.: 56*]; and even 'intersectoral reallocation of labour from agriculture to industry' [*ibid.: 50*]. The proportion of TFP growth due to movement towards technological best practice is estimated through a statistical procedure which, even according to the Report, entails 'very restrictive assumptions' [*ibid.: 56*].[20]

Secondly, the Report links movement to best practice to the process of exporting, and re-introducing the importance of human capital, it identifies a central growth mechanism in the HPAEs: 'We believe rapid growth of exports, a result of the export-push policies of the HPAEs, combined with the superior performance of these economies in creating and allocating human capital, provided the means by which they attained high rates of productivity-based catching up and TFP growth' [*ibid.: 316*].

Through these tortuous moves, 'openness' emerges as an important explanatory variable as 'openness is consistently associated with superior TFP performance' [*ibid.: 322–3*]. A process mechanism linking export-oriented policies to long-run growth, one of the missing links in the analysis of outward-orientation, is thus identified. Moreover the logical gap which was opened up almost 25 years earlier when Balassa substituted 'neutrality of incentives' for Keesing's 'a strong effort to catch up and become competitive' as he re-defined the term 'outward-looking', is closed empirically by proving that policy neutrality and alignment of national with international prices actually promotes catching up. But the price of these moves, in terms of misunderstanding East Asian industrialisation, is high.

The equation of TFP growth with movement towards international best practice suppresses the role of intersectoral labour transfer from low-productivity agriculture to high-productivity manufacturing, and from low-productivity to high-productivity manufacturing sectors, in promoting productivity growth. Thus the Report represents what is happening in the East Asian economies as a process of closer integration with the world economy rather than a process of structural transformation and industrialisation in which relations with the rest of the world were of central significance and changed.[21]

Moreover, the attribution of productivity-based catching-up to exporting identifies one way in which technological capacities have been built up, and assumes that it adequately describes this process as a whole. The mechanism identified has certainly occurred in some sectors through a form of subcontracting known as OEM (original equipment manufacture) [*Hobday, 1995*]. But in the Report's formulation the complex dynamic connections between internal capability-building and export demand are simply assumed; other important channels of technology transfer, particularly licensing, which have been important in the region and which are not linked to exporting (sometimes deliberately so) are omitted; and the role of FDI, which raises many complex issues, is ignored. In short, the complex process by which learning and technological upgrading actually happens is grossly oversimplified.

Even with all this discursive work to make export orientation and openness decisive in the growth process, the argument can only be sustained with some statistical manipulation. The only direct indicator of trade strategy which is inserted into the cross-economy regressions to test the effects of trade policy on GDP and TFP growth, an indicator of 'openness' in terms of the relationship between domestic and international prices, is actually *not* significant in the regression equations explaining economic growth when it is introduced together with the variables of manufacturing export performance (see Table 6.17). The text manages to obscure this by mis-stating its results in the text [*ibid.: 321*]. And although it *is* statistically significant in the equations explaining TFP growth, this analysis involves explanation of TFP growth from 1960–89 by an indicator which measures 'openness' from 1976-85, an exercise which is conceptually contradictory in the terms of the Report for the export push strategy involves a shift over time towards greater parity in incentives between exports and import substitutes.

VI. THE LIBERALISATION OF THE FLYING GEESE

The emphasis which the World Bank's East Asian Miracle study places on exporting heightens one of the critical logical problems of methodological nationalism: the 'fallacy of composition'. If one country is advised to increase exports of a particular commodity, say coffee, it may reap benefits, but if all coffee-growing countries are thus advised, and further, some non-coffee-growing countries are advised to diversify in to coffee as a 'non-traditional' export, the likely outcome will be very different [*Cline, 1982*]. This fallacy is partly addressed in the Report by arguing that market access depends on the adoption of policies which are regarded as fair in the international community. But a second response provides a final example of the misunderstanding of the East Asian development experience: the redescription of Akamatsu's notion of the wild-geese-flying pattern of economic development as an example of the stages of comparative advantage.

The stages 'theory' proposes that the commodity composition of a country's exports will change according to its changing comparative advantage as it develops. The main stages are: (1) reliance on primary (agricultural or mining) product exports; (2) exports of products associated with available raw materials; (3) exports of simple labour intensive consumer goods; (4) exports of more sophisticated capital goods; and (5) exports of R & D and technology intensive goods. To transpose Akamatsu's development pattern into these terms, it is necessary to think of the 'geese' as countries rather than profiles of imports, production and exports for specific sectors. After transforming a thesis about *sectoral* development into a thesis about *spatial* development in this way, an analysis of *production* restructuring has to be reduced to an analysis of the changing composition of *exports*, and finally changes in the structure of exports must be attributed to changes in a country's comparative advantage.

With these moves two birds are killed with one stone. Firstly, it is possible to argue that a 'natural' process of upgrading will occur as physical and human capital endowment matures in a country. Therefore countries should not distort the system of incentives in favour of products in which the country does not have a comparative advantage at any given moment in time. Secondly, it is possible to dispel export pessimism. As Balassa [*1981: 165–7*] argues:

> With countries progressing on the comparative advantage scale, their exports can supplant the exports of countries that graduate to a higher level ... .
>
> A case in point is Japan whose comparative advantage has shifted towards highly capital intensive exports. In turn, developing countries with a relatively high human capital endowment, such as Korea and Taiwan, can take Japan's place in exporting relatively human capital intensive products, and countries with a relatively high physical capital endowment, such as Brazil and Mexico, can take Japan's place in exporting relatively physical capital-intensive products. Finally, countries at lower levels of development can supplant the middle-level countries in exporting unskilled labor-intensive commodities.

The transformation of Akamatsu's flying geese model into a stages of comparative advantage theory comes in two versions. The simpler ignores any direct linkages between leading and following countries. A more complex version relates the change in the composition of exports in the following countries to a process of industrial transfer from leaders to followers, as in the following example:

> The main mechanism underlying this increasing [economic] interdependence in the Asia Pacific region is the transfer of industries, particularly manufacturing industries, from early starters to late comers. In fact, there has been a shift in the countries which have comparative advantage in mature industries such as textiles and steel; namely, from the United States and Japan to the Asian NIEs, and from the Asian NIEs to ASEAN. This is known as the 'flying geese pattern' of industrial development ... [*Yamazawa, 1992: 1523*].

The flying geese model, in either of these transformations, is presently becoming central to discussion of sustained growth and industrialisation in southeast Asia. It has a common sense appeal because the inter-sectoral and inter-economy sequence of change conforms, to some degree, with the pattern of economic restructuring in the region. But as with the deployment of the term 'outward orientation' to represent a dynamic two-track industrial policy of infant industry protection and export promotion as a neutral trade regime, these transformations involve appropriating a term, changing its meaning, and using it in a way which actually misunderstands the mechanisms of change.

This is clearest for the simplest version for it attributes the dynamics of change simply to changes in national factor proportions within countries. The more complex version recognises the importance of international neighbour-hood effects, which could potentially act as a route out of methodological nationalism. But there has been a tendency to maintain the internal/external dichotomy in the explanation of growth, and to attribute rapid growth in follower countries to industrial re-structuring in leading countries [e.g. *Ozawa, 1991: 153*].

Both these free market versions of the flying geese model downplay the influence of industrial policy in both the more and the less industrialised countries within the region, and also the effects of protectionist measures in rich countries which target manufactured goods originating in particular countries. The simplest version also represents economic restructuring as a 'natural' process, assuming, in contrast to Akamatsu, that progression through the stages of export development is an automatic process. Arguing that Japan, Korea and Taiwan exemplify the stages thesis simply ignores a central thrust of their industrial policies which was to override the dictates of static comparative advantage at any moment in time and promote structural change and industrial upgrading in line with an expected dynamic trend in comparative advantage. Finally, the assumption that progression up the stages of comparative advantage will dispel the fallacy of composition is itself fallacious, as can be shown by simple calculations of the volume of clothing and footwear exports from Indonesia, Malaysia and Thailand which are required to reach the same levels of exports per capita of the four 'Tigers' in these commodities.[22]

There is no doubt that the idea of East Asian countries as a flock of flying geese has now become a potent metaphor which acts to coordinate investment expectations within the region. But perhaps the greatest cost arising from the liberalisation of the flying geese is the forgetting of Akamatsu's original formulation – an analysis based on a global frame of analysis and rich in consequent insights. As with other transformations in key words identified in this article, this forgetting forecloses policy options and ingrains the misunderstanding of East Asian industrialisation.

VII. CONCLUSION

This study has argued that the dominant development paradigm since the early

1980s has been characterised by a peculiar combination of global liberalism and methodological nationalism. The normative goal of development policy practice in the dominant paradigm is to reinforce a liberal international economic order (LIEO); the explanatory frame within which this goal is justified is analysis of how national factors, and in particular national policies, affect national economic performance. The main rhetorical form in the dominant paradigm is arguments which claim that national economic interests are best fulfilled through the adoption of a set of policies which conform to the principles and tenets of a LIEO. Shifts in policy emphasis during the 1980s and early 1990s reflect changes in content of the desired LIEO, from a laissez-faire to a 'market friendly' LIEO, and the addition of some concern to guarantee minimum levels of consumer welfare.

Methodological nationalism is not an optional feature of the dominant development discourse, but serves as the conceptual basis on which global liberalism is justified to individual developing countries. But methodological nationalism is only a coherent approach to explanation if national economies are completely isolated and closed from outside influences. The more that the norms of a LIEO are adhered to, the more that national economies become open to outside influences, and the less tenable methodological nationalism becomes as a form of explanation. The dominant paradigm is thus unstable and unsustainable.

This policy frame creates misunderstandings when used to interpret the East Asian development experience. East Asian type development policies have been elaborated within an explanatory framework which analyses trends and identifies policy options in a global context, and within a normative framework which has been economically nationalist, oriented to the goal of national development through industrialisation. The construction of the East Asia debate in terms of 'states versus markets' has reinforced methodological nationalism, and thus compounded misunderstanding. It prevents consideration of how, within a global frame of reference, states work with markets to promote national development.

The conflict between policy frames and objectives results in five main areas of difference in policy emphasis, which are also the major axes of misunderstanding in texts which interpret East Asian development experience in the terms of the dominant paradigm.

(i)   East Asian policies are not narrowly focused on the system of incentives for efficient resource allocation, but are broadly concerned with ways and means of accelerating capital accumulation.

(ii) East Asian policies are not simply export-oriented. A national policy formulated in a global context considers patterns of global demand and global supply; national demand is taken to be part of global demand (the global is not external).

(iii) Openness is not taken to be a good thing in itself in East Asian policies, rather the relationship of the national economy to the rest of the world is strategically and pragmatically managed in order to support national development objectives.

(iv) Industrial policy in the East Asian successes has been an essential means of articulating the relationships between internal and external factors in promoting development.

(v) Economic relationships with less developed countries within the region, including direct investment and trade linkages, and competitive and complementary supply to extra-regional markets, are developed as part of East Asian type national policies.

Attempts to interpret East Asian development in the terms of the dominant paradigm entail omissions and over-simplifications, semantic slippages and narrative incoherence on these five main axes. The cost is further delay in proper understanding of the important policy innovations which have been created in East Asia, innovations which, with adaptation, could do much to improve development policy design in poorer countries.

The process of re-naming terms which this study describes confirms the view that an innovating political agent needs to construct persuasive arguments with the available normative vocabulary: manipulating meanings, domains of application and the value attached to certain key terms [*Skinner, 1974*]. But it is also apparent that familiar structures of argument are mobilised to justify completely new policy designs. Thus the shift from a national to a global frame of reference for normative evaluation has been justified using methodological nationalism.

Policy frames are, by their nature, difficult to get out of. Some organisations which might play a lead in this, such as UNCTAD, face pressures to focus more of their work on policy options at the national rather than global level. But faced with logical problems and the empirical challenge of East Asian industrialisation, a paradigm shift in development policy discourse is inevitable. It may initially involve wider experimentation with East Asia type policies. But these are themselves evolving, with, in particular, increasing orientation to regional objectives. It also remains a moot point whether it is possible to realise the same results with simultaneous widespread adoption of this approach. The most likely paradigm shift is therefore the full globalisation of development discourse, the adoption of a global policy frame for both explanation and evaluation.

Discourse analysis is not an academic parlour game to identify the worst combination of current buzz-words [*Robertson, 1984*]. It is not an arcane archaeological search for original meanings. It is not another avenue for criticising developmentalism [*Sachs, 1992*]. It is an analysis of the discursive rules which constrain and enable particular kinds of action, and the practices through which those rules are negotiated. At a global level, those rules are an important dimension of international regimes; they are an ever-changing social institution which, at each moment in time, shapes possible moves which can be made to construct persuasive arguments in relation to social and economic development issues. This study has sought to illuminate such rules and practices in the areas of international trade and industrialisation, through analysis of policy frames. It is through reflection on the framing of policy that the inevitable task of re-framing can begin.

NOTES

1. For discussion of the importance of policy frames in policy practice, see Schön and Rein [*1994*], a book which only came to my attention as the final draft of this study was being completed.
2. Throughout this study the term 'global liberalism' is shorthand for various types of liberal international economic order.
3. For discussions of methodological individualism, see Lukes [*1973*]; Hodgson [*1988: Ch.3*].
4. 'Dependency theory' covers various approaches to explanation. Some are methodologically nationalist in the sense that they separate external and internal factors, attribute what has been happening in dependent countries exclusively to external factors, and then suggest how, with de-linking, a growth process solely founded on internal factors *can be made to occur*.
5. An example is work on global commodity chains [*Gereffi, 1995*].
6. See Toye [*1994*] for a measured history.
7. This built on the pioneering work of Little, Scitovsky and Scott [*1970*]; and Krueger [*1974*].
8. This compromise has been summarised as Keynes at home and Adam Smith abroad [*Maier, 1987: 121–52*]. According to Ruggie, it 'has never been fully extended to the developing countries', who 'have been disproportionately subject to the orthodox stabilization measures of the IMF' [*Ruggie, 1982: 413*].
9. Yanagihara characterises the difference between this goal-oriented approach and the approach of the dominant paradigm thus:

   Asian perspective on economic management is essentially 'developmental' in the true sense of the word. Asians tend to think of economic development in terms of fostering infant industries, building up intra- and inter-industry linkages, providing for infrastructure, promoting education and training, and extending necessary financial and technical assistance, rather than approach the question in terms of policy environment and incentive framework. The Asian perspective might be called an 'ingredients approach', while that of Anglo-American orthodoxy may be characterized as a 'framework approach' [*Yanagihara, 1993: 35*].

10. Johnson [*1982: 24*] argues that 'the very idea of the developmental state originated in the situational nationalism of the late industrializers … '. For a recent literature review and analysis, see Leftwich [*1995*].
11. For an assessment of the influence of Akamatsu's ideas, see Korhonen [*1994*], and of the importance of the sectoral development patterns which he identified in Japan within East Asia, see Yamazawa [*1990*]; ESCAP [*1990*].
12. Wade [*1990: 22–32*] summarises the main positions in the debate.
13. This reference was brought to my attention by Hans Singer.
14. The Report was actually financed by the Japanese government and had its origin in controversy

between the World Bank and Japan over aspects of Japanese aid policy which were not sectorally neutral [*Okubo, 1993*]. For an illuminating account of the origins and writing of the Report, see Wade [*1995a*].

15. Discussion with Ha-Joon Chang was particularly helpful in clarifying the points in this paragraph. For further discussion of the fallacies of the dichotomy between fundamentals and interventions see Amsden [*1994*].

16. For example, an index which measures the closeness of domestic prices to international prices shows that 'Japan, Korea, and Taiwan, China rank in the fifth deciles, below such developing-economy comparators as Brazil, India, Mexico, Pakistan and Venezuela' [*World Bank, 1993: 301*]. For further discussion of the extent to which the HPAEs did not adhere to the fundamentals, see Lall [*1994*] and Wade [*1995b*].

17. Okimoto [*1989: 11*] provides an interesting analysis of the difference between Japanese and American approaches to market failure.

18. Even on this narrow pre-defined terrain, various analysts have shown the deficiencies of the Report's findings that industrial policy failed, including misclassification of promoted sectors as unpromoted and analysis at a level of aggregation which is irrelevant to policy [*Chang, 1995; Lall, 1994; Kwon, 1994*].

19. In some parts of the literature this trade regime is described as an 'ultra-export promotion strategy' to distinguish it from the 'export promotion strategy' embodied in the neutral trade regime [*Bhagwati, 1988*].

20. Specifically: (i) dividing sources of TFP growth into technical progress (the movement of best practice), technical efficiency change (the movement towards best practice), and allocative efficiency change; (ii) assuming firstly, that the movement of best practice does not vary across countries and thus differences in rates of TFP change between countries can be attributed to movement towards best practice or allocative efficiency, and secondly, that high income economies are allocatively and technically efficient and so productivity growth in these countries is based on movement of best practice; and then (iii) calculating TFP change for the high-income economies only and subtracting the average rate of TFP change for the high economies from TFP change in low- and middle-income countries estimated using the elasticities of output with respect to both human and physical capital obtained in the high-income sample.

21. This impression is also conveyed by the labelling of the successful economies as HPAEs rather than 'newly industrialising economies', a term reserved for Indonesia, Malaysia and Thailand, and the list of the characteristics which differentiate these economies from other developing countries. This omits industrialisation and actually starts with 'more rapid output and productivity growth in agriculture' [*World Bank, 1993: 27*].

22. These points were made by Robert Rowthorn in the seminar on 'Development of East and South-East Asia and a New Development Strategy – Role of Government', held on 30–31 October 1995, in UNCTAD, Geneva.

REFERENCES

Akamatsu, K., 1961, 'A Theory of Unbalanced Growth in the World Economy', *Weltwirtschaftliches Archiv*, No.86, pp.196-215.

Akamatsu, K., 1962, 'A Historical Pattern of Economic Growth in Developing Countries', *The Developing Economies*, Vol.1, No.1, pp.3–25.

Akyüz, Y. and C. Gore, 1996, 'The Investment-Profits Nexus in East Asian Industrialization', *World Development*, Vol.24, No.3 (forthcoming).

Amsden, A., 1989, *Asia's Next Giant: South Korea and Late Industrialization*, New York: Oxford University Press.

Amsden, A. 1994, 'Why Isn't the Whole World Experimenting with the East Asian Model to Develop?: Review of The East Asian Miracle', *World Development*, Vol.22, No.4, pp.627–34.

Balassa, B., 1970, 'Growth Strategies in Semi-Industrial Countries', *Quarterly Journal of Economics*, Vol.84, pp.24–47.

Balassa, B., 1971, 'Industrial Policies in Taiwan and Korea', *Weltwirtschaftliches Archiv*, Band 106, pp.55–77.

Balassa, B., 1981, *The Newly Industrializing Countries in the World Economy*, New York: Pergamon Press.

Balassa, B., 1982, *Development Strategies in Semi-industrial Economies*, New York and London: Oxford University Press.

Balassa, B., 1989, 'Outward Orientation', in H. Chenery and T.N. Srinivisan (eds.), *Handbook in Development Economics*, Vol.II, Amsterdam: North Holland.

Bhagwati, J., 1988, 'Export-Promoting Trade Strategy: Issues and Evidence', *World Bank Research Observer*, Vol.3, No.1, pp.27–57.

Bradford, C.I., 1986, 'East Asian "Models": Myths and Lessons', in J.P. Lewis (ed.), *Development Strategies Reconsidered*, Washington, DC: Overseas Development Council.

Bradford, C.I., 1990, 'Policy Interventions and Markets: Development Strategy Typologies and Policy Options', in G. Gereffi and D.L. Wyman (eds.), *Manufacturing Miracles: Paths of Industrialization in Latin America and East Asia*, Princeton, NJ: Princeton University Press.

Bradford, C.I., 1994, *From Trade-driven Growth to Growth-driven Trade: Reappraising the East Asian Development Experience*, Paris: OECD.

Castells, M., Goh, L. and R.Y-W. Kwok, 1990, *The Ship Kip Mei Syndrome: Economic Development and Public Housing in Hong Kong and Singapore*, London: Pion Limited.

Chang, H.-J., 1995, 'Explaining "Flexible Rigidities" in East Asia', in T. Killick, *The Flexible Economy: Causes and Consequences of the Adaptability of National Economies*, London and New York: Routledge.

Chenery, H.B. and M. Syrquin, 1975, *Patterns of Development, 1950–70*, London: Oxford University Press.

Cline, W.R., 1982, 'Can the East Asia Model be Generalized?', *World Development*, Vol.10, No.2, pp.81–90.

Connolly, W. E., 1974, *The Terms of Political Discourse*, Oxford: Martin Robinson.

Cornia, G.A., Jolly, R. and F. Stewart, 1987, *Adjustment with a Human Face*, Oxford: Clarendon Press.

Edwards, S., 1993, 'Openness, Trade Liberalization, and Growth in Developing Countries', *Journal of Economic Literature*, Vol.31, No.3, pp.1358–93.

ESCAP, 1990, *Restructuring the Developing Economies of Asia and the Pacific in the 1990s*, New York: United Nations.

Foxley, A., 1983, *Latin American Experiments in Neoconservative Economics*, Berkeley, CA: University of California Press.

Gereffi, G., 1995, 'Contending Paradigms for Cross-Regional Comparison: Development Strategies and Commodity Chains in East Asia and Latin America', in P.H. Smith (ed.), *Latin America in Comparative Perspective: New Approaches to Methods and Analysis*, Boulder, CO: Westview Press.

Gibbon, P., 1993, 'The World Bank and the New Politics of Aid', *The European Journal of Development Research*, Vol.5, No.1, pp.35–62.

Giddens, A., 1984, *The Constitution of Society*, Cambridge: Polity Press.

Hobday, M., 1995, 'East Asian Latecomer Firms: Learning the Technology of Electronics', *World Development*, Vol.23, No.7, pp.1171–93.

Hodgson, G.M., 1988, *Economics and Institutions: A Manifesto for Modern Institutional Economics*, Cambridge: Polity Press.

ILO, 1976, *Employment, Growth and Basic Needs: A One World Problem*, Geneva: ILO.

JDB/JERI (The Japan Development Bank and Japan Economic Research Institute), 1993, *Policy-Based Finance: The Experience of Post-War Japan*, Final Report for the World Bank, Tokyo.

Johnson, C.A., 1982, *MITI and the Japanese Miracle: The Growth of Industrial Policy, 1925–75*, Stanford, CA: Stanford University Press.

Keesing, D.B., 1967, 'Outward-looking Policies and Economic Development', *Economic Journal*, Vol.77, No.306, pp.303–20.

Korhonen, P., 1994, 'The Theory of the Flying Geese Pattern of Development and its Interpretations', *Journal of Peace Research*, Vol.31, No.1, pp.93–108.

Krueger, A.O., 1974, 'The Political Economy of a Rent-seeking Society', *American Economic Review*, Vol.64, No.3, pp.291–303.

Krueger, A.O., 1978, *Foreign Trade Regimes and Economic Development: Liberalization Attempts* and Consequences, Cambridge, MA: Ballinger Pub. Co. for NBER.

Krueger, A.O., 1981, 'Loans to Assist the Transition to Outward-looking Policies', The World Economy, Vol.4, No.3, pp.271–82.

Krugman, P., 1995, 'Dutch Tulips and Emerging Markets', Foreign Affairs, Vol.74, No.4, pp.28-44.

Kwon, J., 1994, 'The East Asia Challenge to Neoclassical Orthodoxy', World Development, Vol.22, No.4, pp.635–44.

Lal, D., 1980, 'A Liberal International Economic Order: The International Monetary System and Economic Development', Princeton Essays in International Finance, No.129.

Lal, D. and S. Rajapatirana, 1987, 'Foreign Trade Regimes and Economic Growth in Developing Countries', World Bank Research Observer, Vol.2, No.2, pp.189–217.

Lall, S., 1994, 'The East Asian Miracle: Does the Bell Toll for Industrial Strategy?', World Development, Vol.22, No.4, pp.645–54.

Leftwich, A., 1995, 'Bringing Politics Back In: Towards a Model of the Developmental State', Journal of Development Studies, Vol.32, No.3, pp.400–27.

Little, I., Scitovsky, T. and M. Scott, 1970, Industry and Trade in Some Developing Countries, Oxford: Oxford University Press, for OECD Centre, Paris.

Lukes, S., 1973, Individualism, Oxford: Basil Blackwell.

Maier, C., 1987, In Search of Stability, Cambridge: Cambridge University Press.

Mosley, P., Harrigan, J. and J. Toye, 1991, Aid and Power: The World Bank and Policy-Based Lending in the 1980s, (2 vols.), London: Routledge.

Okimoto, D., 1989, Between MITI and the Market: Japanese Industrial Policy for High Technology, Stanford CA: Stanford, University Press.

Okubo, H., 1993, 'Japanese Two Step Loans: The Japanese Approach to Development Finance', Hitosubashi Journal of Economics, Vol.34, pp.67–85.

Ozawa, T., 1991, 'The Dynamics of Pacific Rim Industrialization: How Mexico Can Join the Asian Flock of "Flying Geese"', in R. Roett (ed.), Mexico's External Relations in the 1990s, Boulder, CO and London: Lynne Rienner Publishers.

Rein, M. and D. Schön, 1993, 'Reframing Policy Discourse', in F. Fischer and J. Forester (eds.), The Argumentative Turn in Policy Analysis and Planning, London: University College London Press.

Robertson, A.F., 1984, The People and the State: An Anthropology of Planned Development, Cambridge: Cambridge University Press.

Roche, M., 1992, Rethinking Citizenship: Welfare, Ideology and Change in Modern Society, Cambridge: Polity Press.

Rodrik, D., 1994, 'King Kong meets Godzilla: The World Bank and The East Asian Miracle', CEPR Discussion Paper, No.944.

Ruggie, J.G., 1982, 'International Regimes, Transactions and Change: Embedded Liberalism in the Post-War Economic Order', International Organization, Vol.36, No.2, pp.379–415.

Sachs, W. (ed.), 1992, The Development Dictionary: A Guide to Knowledge as Power, London: Zed Books.

Schön, D. and M. Rein, 1994, Frame Reflection: Toward the Resolution of Intractable Policy Controversies, New York: Basic Books.

Sheehey, E.J., 1990, 'Exports and Growth: A Flawed Framework', Journal of Development Studies, Vol.27, No.1, pp.111–16.

Shinohara, M., 1982, Industrial Growth, Trade and Dynamic Patterns in the Japanese Economy, Tokyo: University of Tokyo Press.

Singer, H.W., 1988, 'The World Development Report 1987 on the Blessings of "Outward Orientation": A Necessary Correction', Journal of Development Studies, Vol.24, No.2, pp.232–36.

Singh, A., 1994, 'Openness and the Market Friendly Approach to Development: Learning the Right Lessons from Development Experience', World Development, Vol.22, No.12, pp.1811–23.

Skinner, Q., 1974, 'Some Problems in the Analysis of Political Thought and Action', Political Theory, Vol.2, No.3, pp.277–303.

Smith, S., 1982, 'Class Analysis versus World Systems: Critique of Samir Amin's Typology of Underdevelopment', Journal of Contemporary Asia, Vol.12, No.1, pp.7–18.

Toye, J.F.J., 1994, 'Structural Adjustment: Context, Assumptions, Origin and Diversity', in R. van der Hoeven and F. van der Kraaij (eds.), Structural Adjustment and Beyond in Sub-Saharan

Africa: Research and Policy Issues, London and Portsmouth: James Currey and Heinemann.

Wade, R., 1990, *Governing the Market: Economic Theory and the Role of Government in East Asian Industrialization*, Princeton, NJ: Princeton University Press.

Wade, R., 1995a, 'The World Bank and the Art of Paradigm Maintenance: The East Asian Miracle as a Response to Japan's Challenge to the Development Consensus', mimeo.

Wade, R., 1995b, 'The East Asian Miracle: Why the Controversy Continues', International Monetary and Financial Issues for the 1990s, *Research Papers for the Group of Twenty-Four*, Vol.V, Geneva: UNCTAD.

Wall, H.J., 1995, 'Cricket v Baseball as an Engine of Growth', *Royal Economic Society Newsletter*, July, pp.2–3.

Williamson, J., 1993, 'Democracy and the "Washington Consensus"', *World Development*, Vol.21, No.8, pp.1329–36.

World Bank, 1981, *Accelerated Development in Sub-Saharan Africa: An Agenda for Action*, Washington, DC.

World Bank, 1983, *World Development Report 1983*, New York: Oxford University Press.

World Bank, 1986, *World Development Report 1986*, New York: Oxford University Press.

World Bank, 1987, *World Development Report 1987*, New York: Oxford University Press.

World Bank, 1990, *Report on Adjustment Lending II: Policies for Recovery of Growth*, Document R90-99, March.

World Bank, 1991, *World Development Report 1991*, New York: Oxford University Press.

World Bank, 1992, *World Bank Structural and Sectoral Adjustment Operations: The Second OED Overview*, Report No.10870, Washington, DC: World Bank.

World Bank, 1993, *The East Asian Miracle: Public Policy and Economic Growth*, New York: Oxford University Press.

Wortzel, L.H. and H.V. Wortzel, 1981, 'Export Marketing Strategies for NIC and LDC-Based Firms', *Colombia Journal of World Business*, Spring.

Yagci, F., Kamin, S. and V. Rosenblaum, 1985, 'Structural Adjustment Lending: An Evaluation of Program Design', *Staff Working Paper No.735*, Washington, DC: World Bank.

Yamazawa, I., 1990, *Economic Development and International Trade: The Japanese Model*, Honolulu, Hawaii: The East-West Centre.

Yamazawa, I., 1992, 'On Pacific Economic Integration', *The Economic Journal*, Vol.102, pp.1519–29.

Yanagihara, T., 1993, 'Asia-Pacific Zone: Its Emergence and Evolution', *Journal of International Economic Studies*, Vol.7, No.1, pp.23–40.

Yoshihara, T., 1962, 'Japan's Trade with Developing Countries: A Note Based on Foreign Trade of Japan 1961', *Developing Economies*, Vol.1, No.1, pp.106–20.

Reading Americans on Democracy in Africa: From the CIA to 'Good Governance'

DAVID MOORE

In spite of the cold war's end, American discourse on democracy in Africa has remained essentially unchanged from the decolonisation era. In this study, both early CIA assessments of the prospects for decolonisation and current 'good governance' discourse are situated within the peripheral manifestations (the 'modernisation' paradigm) of the contradictions of capitalist hegemonic discourse. The study demonstrates that little has changed in American views of African democratic prospects: 'guidance' and intervention remain. But since the geopolitical reasons for ostensible tutelage have now disappeared, when facing difficult 'transitions' the 'exit option' is more likely than before.

> [Democracy is coming] to America first,
> the cradle of the best and of the worst.
> It's here they got the range
> and the machinery for change
> and it's here they got the spiritual thirst.
> [*Leonard Cohen, 1993*]

Soon after the 1990 fall of Liberia's Samuel Doe, the government of the United States of America made plans to send its citizens home. A journalist, who happened to be the wife of the American ambassador, described the order of departure thus:

> The US Peace Corps programme closed, sending the 150 volunteers home. *The development experts left.* [Weeks later] 6 US Navy warships ... head[ed] towards Liberia in case the remaining Americans had to be evacuated ... The Americans were coming not to intervene, but to pluck their own people from the midst of impending tribal butchery and leave the country to its fate [*Schuster, 1994: 58, 67–8*] (emphasis added).

David Moore, Department of Politics, Flinders University, Adelaide, Australia. The author would like to thank Raymond Apthorpe for encouraging him to write this study and, together with Des Gasper, for editorial assistance and suggestions – not all of which he was able to follow. Thanks also to Mike Gismondi at Athabasca University, Alberta, for putting him on to the CIA Research Reports: Africa.

These words bear witness to the inextricable intertwining of politics and 'development assistance'. They put in cold relief recent American and World Bank policies, programmes and conditionalities concerned with issues of 'good governance' in their African client states. They serve to illustrate the 'common sense' behind western pleas to African governments to get their houses in order: if the quest fails 'development' and the experts assumed to direct it will disappear – replaced, at best, by food aid.[1] 'Good governance' is now touted as the way to avoid the Liberian fate. Its policies and conditionalities are seemingly as important as the economic structural adjustment programmes' emphases on 'getting the prices right'. It is as if the days of 'political' development and modernisation have returned to the international development agencies' agenda, with the same uncomfortable but inevitable mix of calls for democracy *and* order.[2] 'Get your governments right' is the advice, and development will follow. If the state can clear the path, the wonders of economic liberalism will be able to manifest themselves. Fail, and we will leave you to your 'tribal butchery'.

This study purports to suggest that the roots of this fragility of American commitment to democracy in Africa are long. They reach far back into the cold war era, when Americans were jostling for the allegiance of the newly emerging African independent states. Their strategy for the gaining of this fealty involved the promise of democratic tutelage, but their hopes for its achievement were slim. As the material taken from CIA documents will show, American perceptions of the process of 'detribalisation' of the Africans slated to rule the new states were ambiguous at best and racist at worst. Most of all, however, the roots of this uncertainty are grounded in the tenuousness of liberal theories of democracy themselves: market freedom is unreservedly linked to political freedom. When the two do not match in reality, American policy-makers have to turn either to 'order' or to 'exit'.

This contradiction is at the root of most American policy discourse on development and democracy, even as the cold war has ended and a resurgence of interest in 'political development' (in the guise of 'good governance') has swept through the apparatuses of development in the western world [*Schmitz: 1995*]. Concurrent with this revival of political modernisation praxis has been a proliferation of associated academic and consultancy-type analysis (there is even a 'senior governance expert' in the Washington consulting trade).[3] Few of these studies situate the discourse of good governance in the history of the first half-century of the age of neo-colonial 'development', or for that matter within the context of American imperial efforts. I will try, in a preliminary way, to remedy these oversights and to compare the contemporary ideology and practice of 'good governance' with that of the early days of the Central Intelligence Agency's analyses and actions in Africa. I will suggest that in the American realm of development discourse, *le plus ça change, le plus c'est la même chose.*

More broadly, this study will indicate that any study of contemporary development policy must take into account the contradictory 'meta-discourse' of American efforts to create economic, political and ideological hegemony on a global scale in the last fifty years.[4]

To understand development policy discourse one must be able to ascertain its basis in the ideological assumptions of the society in which it is rooted. Furthermore, one must be able to get to those roots by examining their changes in relation to shifts in the global political economy and the social movements in it which have made dominant powers alter their hegemonic strategies.[5] The bare-bone American views of democracy have not changed, even with the end of the cold war. In spite of the fact that an emphasis on the state or the market as the runway for 'takeoff' and cradle of modernisation has varied in the post-Second World War era, the essence of 'democracy' for those Americans who hope to 'recolonize' Africa [*Saul, 1993*] (before they give up and leave it) remains the same: that liberal markets and democratic politics go hand in hand.

I. THE CONTRADICTIONS OF EXPORTING LIBERAL CAPITALISM

There is a crucial and debilitating contradiction between political equality and market freedom; but the dominant American ideology holds that they are intrinsically compatible and mutually reinforcing. Contrary to that endearing belief, the freedom of the market usually creates economic and social inequalities which render political equality largely formal and subject to diminution. Capital can only concede up to a certain point when pressure from below threatens to move 'political' equality into the realm of economic power. As Hayek so eloquently put it, those who have economic power get worried when 'democracy' threatens to appear to them to be 'agreement by the majority on sharing the booty gained by overwhelmingly a minority ... or deciding how much is to be taken from them' [*Schwarzmantel: 1995: 213*], and will then pull back even limited forms of political democracy.

Capital can quickly pull back from liberal democracy. If collective politics from below threaten positions of privilege and the conditions for the reproduction of capitalism, they are labelled undemocratic and are thus curtailed. If democratic demands for economic and social reform arise in situations which capital sees as 'zero-sum' then they will not be granted and the system in which they are generated will be discredited and dismantled. Such reforms can only be worked out when capitalism is expanding so that some of its surplus can be distributed in *political* ways – rather than through vague promises and processes of 'trickling down' – in conditions in which the total economic pie is growing such that the population as a *whole* can benefit and be seen to benefit from negotiating within the confines of the capitalist order. In those sorts of times, the contradiction between economic and political freedoms can be ameliorated and hegemony maintained. This state of grace cannot last indefinitely, however. Conditions of economic crisis, stagnation and even slow growth can easily tear it asunder [*Bienefeld, 1994: 94–129*]. These conditions make up the norm for most countries in the 'third world'.

This generalisation, relevant since the rise of modern capitalism, does however tend to assume a political-economic system centred within borders of national states which were capable of mediating the capital–labour contradiction *and* the national-international one [*Cox, 1991: 337*] (see also Gore in this collection). It is Eurocentric and focused on concerns of hegemonic construction and maintenance *within* Europe. The situation is further complicated when one deals with the cases of *imperial* states and those of *peripheral* ones.

In the imperial states, the leading classes of the world combine the ambiguities of local hegemony with global *noblesse oblige* and other less altruistic attributes of conquest which come to the fore if the conquered's assumed consent wears thin. The characteristics of global rule become brutal when acquiescence turns to successful rebellion, and even more desperate when a once powerful international hegemon is in the decline. With every new imperialist epoch, of course, there are interesting variations on the theme: today, the extraordinary sway of unregulated global finance capital and the dispersion of national capitalist power, concurrent with the technologies of split-second global communications networks enabling the frenetic mobility of money, production and the cultural frameworks for hegemony and counter-hegemony, make the slipping of the current hegemon somewhat unique. However, the general rules of hegemonic decline are no doubt similar; confusion at the centre is multiplied into chaos on the periphery. This time around, the collapse of the one-time ideological 'counter-hegemon' adds noise to the din. The demise of Soviet-style socialism could mark the end of an (ideological) history many democratic socialists and Marxists are glad to see go. Yet it seems its passing has carried with it other alternatives to the increasingly one-dimensional dominant ideology, thus leaving struggles for the expansion of liberal democracy's promises on infertile ground [cf. *Escobar, 1995; 1992*].

In the peripheral states, hegemony is very rarely, and even then only contingently, national. This is simply because of the dominating presence of the metropole, be it centred in a state or decentred in global and 'multi-lateral' flows and institutions [*Campbell, forthcoming*]. No matter how skilful the local ruling classes are at exploiting 'the resources of a dependence', through their 'strategies of extraversion' [*Bayart, 1993: 26, 196–200*] an autonomous hegemony is largely out of the question in the periphery. The surplus necessary for the smoothing of the contradiction between liberal economics and political equality is most often just not there. Nor is there, in most cases, a 'civil society' organised enough to demand reforms from a state which sees itself acting in its own interests.

Before the recent demise of capitalism's golden age [*Marglin and Schor, 1990*] there was a particular aspect of the *noblesse oblige* side of the post-Second World War hegemonic effort which helped wash these contradictions away. The dream of easy 'development' was one of the new detergents for dirty imperialism. Its difference from some of the justifications for the previous, colonial, age of European imperialism was limited – because it still took for granted the superiority of the western, capitalist, way – but it was much grander in scale. It did not claim, as did Carlyle for his age, that the 'nigger's ... ugliness, idleness, [and] rebellion' doomed him to subhumanity and the 'beneficent whip' [*Said, 1993: 121–2*]. Nor did it restrict itself to the selection of a small class of third world rulers, native in 'blood and character, but English in opinion, morals, and intellect', as in Macaulay's discourse on the purported civilisational process [*Anderson, 1983: 86*]. Rather, the new and liberal ideology of development appeared to welcome *everybody* into the fold. It aspired to the westernisation of *all* 'natives' *all over* the world.

Such supreme confidence rested on the surety that American-style capitalism was boundless. In so far as this mirage has disappeared, the dry, sterile sand beneath the dream of development should be apparent to all. But while there is now less apparent optimism, the contradictions are said to reside only in the manner in which 'democracy' and 'the market' are *implemented* around the (third) world. As the justifications for liberal democracy are becoming more and more flawed, the calls for the betterment of its *techniques* become increasingly harsh – yet at the same time, strained [*Schmitter, 1995: 17–18*].

The contradictions of Robert McNamara's recent recantation of rampant imperialism in the Vietnamese war are typical of this rethinking. Most of his words ring true to his attestation that 'we made an error not of values and intentions but of judgement and capabilities... the USA fought in Vietnam for...good and honest reasons' [*McNamara, 1995: 21*]. For McNamara, one of the most important of these reasons was the promotion of 'individual freedom and political democracy'. Yet in other parts of his hindsight, he claims he and his colleagues misread and misjudged the characteristics of the South Vietnamese because they were viewed in 'terms of our own experience. We saw in them a thirst for – and a determination to fight for – freedom and democracy.' He claims also to be rethinking the delusions of omnipotence held by the American wagers of war: 'political order and stability ... must be forged by a people for themselves'. But while conceding 'we do not have the God-given right to shape every nation in our own image as we choose', he never clearly recants on his core values and the USA's duty to spread them around the world. Such uncomfortable oscillating among these fundamental moral visions reveals the limits of American liberalism. If in the end he must rest with the shallow admission that mistakes of 'judgement and capabilities' were the cause of failure, those boundaries are soon reached.

If McNamara reflects the angst among liberal Americans on the eve of their descent, it is no wonder that the policies of 'good governance' are so shaky. McNamara's words could easily be drawn from current reconsiderations in development discourse: do the words of the World Bank reviews of structural adjustment programmes which suggest that 'the policies are right, but those who implement them get it all wrong!' sound familiar? [*Bienefeld, 1995; Clay and Schaffer, 1984*] (see also Gasper on 'Essentialism' in this collection). If such discourse stops short of the realisation that 'the people' in small foreign countries might well wish to forge a 'political order and stability' based on principles other than the American version of 'individual freedom and political democracy', then many more Vietnams are in the offing and all the best 'judgement and capabilities' on the means of imposing American ideologies will not stop them. No wonder that in Africa – where the difference between local and imperial versions of democracy may be the largest [*Davidson, 1992*] – the various American-designed 'capacity building projects' to hasten the institutionalisation of good governance sound ever more hollow and ridiculous as they proliferate. One can predict that as their shallowness becomes apparent, we will witness a return to calls for 'order' much as we did in the wake of the early efforts to implement 'political modernization' [*O'Brien, 1971*]. With it will return either the imposed order of modernisation's (post)modern-day equivalent, including a revised CIA, or exit.

This study then, will continue to examine the contradictions of Africa-exportable American democracy by looking at the early thinking behind one of its most forceful agencies – the CIA in its youth – and comparing that to the presuppositions behind its more diplomatic and modern developmental cousin, 'good governance'. Before examining this relationship, however, some broad assertions about the nature of development discourse are in order. Following examination of the continuities between past CIA and present good governance policy discourses, the study will look at contradictions in the language and practice of constructing 'democracy' through the conditionalities of structural adjustment programmes.

II. AMERICAN DEVELOPMENT DISCOURSE AND AMERICAN HEGEMONY

The ideology and practice of American international development policy since 1945 can be understood as part of the concerted effort of the USA's state intellectuals to assert their country's hegemony over the rest of the world

[*Moore, 1995; Hoare and Nowell-Smith, 1971: 5–6, 59*]. Harry Truman's 1949 presidential inauguration marked one of the more significant components of the post-Second World War golden age of capitalism when he announced that he believed Americans should help poverty-stricken but 'peace-loving' peoples in the third world to 'realize their aspirations for a better life', that he envisaged 'a program of development based on the concepts of democratic fair dealing' and that 'greater production' through 'a wider and more vigorous application of modern scientific and technical knowledge' would constitute the base of this programme (cited in Escobar [*1995: 3*]). Those words in his inaugural Presidential speech signified the expansion of the American dream to the more than half of the world stage characterised by poverty instead of plenty. They embodied the hopes of happiness through the compounded increases in production and consumption that had marked American history, as well as the European past which had been transplanted and transformed in the 'new world'. Now that the USA had emerged from the Second World War as the leader of the capitalist world, its politicians, statesmen and business leaders felt it was their duty to spread the good word, as with the Marshall Plan in Europe: rebuilding political economies to keep markets and minds open to American-dominated international capital and culture. It seemed logical to expect that some of the good life could now be extended to the majority of the world's people who lived 'in conditions approaching misery' [*ibid.*]. There was no doubt that Americans would benefit too, but it was assumed that the expansion of markets, and if necessary a moderate dose of state planning, would ensure the mutuality of benefits to all concerned. Utopia was just over the horizon.

There was one problem, indicated clearly, if elliptically, in the Truman declaration. Truman said that Americans should 'make available ... the benefits of our store of technical knowledge' in order to help poverty stricken but 'peace-loving peoples' realise their hopes for a better life. Their future would be improved by a 'program of development based on the concepts of democratic fair dealing'. The questions begged by these phrases are quite basic: who were *not* 'peace-loving peoples?' and, what *were* Truman's notions of democracy and fair dealing? People who do not love peace can range from 'savages' in the third world to 'communists' in the second, and from fascists in Europe to feminists on the home front. Notions of democratic fair dealing run the gamut from pure *laissez-faire* economics, seeing the evil hand of totalitarianism behind the mildest modes of welfare capitalism, to radical notions that democracy can only exist with workers' control of the field, the shop-floor *and* the commanding heights of the political economy. It is not hard to see who Truman judged as dedicated to peace and 'playing fair' for democracy: in the cold war context of his words, those to the left of US Democrats were more than likely warrior-like and prone to cheat the rules of American democracy. So what to do about those who have differing ideas of democracy, and who may be prepared to be less than 'peace-loving' in their advocacy? Against them, the defenders of 'peace and democracy' were entitled to break the rules. The interpretation of 'peace-loving' and 'democratic' thus defined those outside the pale. The iron fist of coercion hidden under the velvet glove of consensual hegemony could soon be revealed to enforce such prerogatives of definition.

Such were the defining ambiguities of the early and mostly optimistic moments of the new hegemonic era. Its confidence was strong, but it was tinged, however slightly, by the fears suggested by the far sides of the common notions of fair and peaceful play. These concerns were tied to other, more concrete, ones. The first was the Communist Menace. That discoloration in the global picture enabled the construction of the Central Intelligence Agency with a constitutional vagueness allowing covert actions of any sort [*Church, 1977: xxii*]. A second disquiet was a broader one, not unconnected with the first. This was 'disorder'. Truman's choice of the word 'program' when he announced his public vision of 'development' surely indicated a hope to *plan* development, and when the penners of World Bank missions said they could not rely on 'natural forces' (World Bank cited in Escobar [*1993: 134*]) to manufacture capitalism they were admitting that *laissez faire* would not do the trick, just as much as asserting that primitive and naturalistic social forms could not usher in the new era. A *plan* would have to order the transformational project. Further beyond that, however, was fear of the mob, for itself but also for what it could turn into: the anarchy and chaos of the untrammelled masses could soon be transformed into the first fear – Communism [*Campbell: 1992, 28*]. Disorder – lack of peace – could turn into the sort of order most despised by the American advocates of freedom.

This emphasis on ordered economics and politics produced a developmental mindset conducive to capitalism through indicative planning and democracy by tried and true representative ritual. If the latter process proved too messy, a dose of authoritarianism was warranted. Thus in its first post-war era – roughly from the end of the Second World War to the end of the 1970s – mainstream development discourse was constituted by a belief in state capitalism. Admittedly much more entrenched on the European than the American side of the Atlantic, this belief was strong enough to last until the end of the 1970s. Then, buffeted by the debt crisis, the near excesses of 'basic needs', the pressures from dependency theory and political and economic threats such as the New International Economic Order which led to them [*Cox, 1979*]), and the waves of Thatcherite and Reaganist neo-liberalism, the mainstream developmental bottom-line became that of 'structural adjustment'. The belief (unfounded but routine, given the rise in anti-state ideologies) that state mismanagement was the cause of the post-1970s African crisis gave the international managers of credit and credibility the excuse they needed to launch an experiment to create capitalism out of the blue – *sans* state and almost *sans* society ('society does not exist', said one of their leaders) – and out of the blueprints of *laisser-fairiste* visionaries.

It is this second era in which we are now ensconced. In spite of the buzzwords of sustainability, equity, participation, and now 'good governance', the dominant discourse is that of getting the 'monster state' off the backs of the 'masses' [*Bernstein et al., 1990; Bernstein, 1990*]. There is little evidence that the policies have broken the back of the state *or* ushered in the utopia of an entrepreneurial capitalism [*Gibbon et al., 1992*], but the debt crisis and the policies of adjustment in its wake have given the multilateral financial institutions all the excuses they might have needed to get a seat at the tables of governance. Some of their main agenda setters admit as much: an internal World Bank document partly written by Elliot Berg, the intellectual architect of structural adjustment, claims that one of the main motivations behind SALs (structural adjustment loans) was to 'win access to the most senior policy makers, thereby permitting Bank staff to accelerate reform and to influence its character ... to buy a place at the policy table' [*Berg and Batchelder, 1985: 11, 27*]. Given that the World Bank seems to have consensus that most of these 'senior policy makers' are part of a 'whole ruling class or ruling élite [which] may be at issue' – and Berg cites Paul Baran, Frantz Fanon and René Dumont in support of such a proposition! – it seems clear that a great part of its agenda is to change the behaviour of such 'rent-seekers' or persuade them to leave the political scene [*ibid.: 24*]. This sort of macroeconomics merges with politics: it would seem that 'good governance' was thus never far from structural adjustment.

Neither the politics or economics of developmentalism is very far removed from the academic realm of development discourse. The institutions and language of policy-making have always been intertwined with dominant discourses in the universities. From the first World Bank missions, made up of young academic economists, through liberal modernisation to conservative 'order,' from Latin American structuralism to dependency theory, from orthodox Marxism to the political economy of rational and public choice, to the political scientists writing background papers on 'good governance' [*Williams and Young, 1994: 91*] there have always been linkages between ivory towers and bureaucracies and policy-makers. To say that is not reductionist, nor is the claim of a clear link between both agency and academic forms of development discourse and the shifts in the global political economy a call for determinism; but it is to retreat from sheer idealism. Can it be mere chance that both conservative and radical critiques of liberal development theory came to the fore in the wake of revolutions in Cuba and Vietnam, and that the academic forms of economic 'rationalism' were concurrent with the deregulation of global finance capital?

The relative autonomy of academia and the sophistication of development discourse have insured that the relationship with the 'real world' of bureaucratised aid is not one to one. After 50 years, there *is* a relatively coherent, yet flexible and ideologically diverse, body of knowledge that can be worked upon by scholars. Intellectual resources can be drawn upon that are not controlled by national and international policy making apparatuses, which in themselves now reflect some of the diversity within the academy and may even reinforce it. The work of Canada's International Development Research Centre (IDRC), for example, partly reflects some more radical moments in the history of development discourse and can draw on the intellectual labour of unorthodox scholars to buttress these tendencies. But dominant agencies and intellectual apparatuses will always seek to co-opt or else remove such tendencies: witness the World Bank's invitations to subordinate agencies to buy into 'slices' of sectoral programmes in its worthy-sounding *Sub-Saharan Africa: From Crisis to Sustainable Growth* [*1989: 193*]; and imagine the negotiations as the IDRC, Swedish agencies, NGOs with radical aspirations and the imperious Americans battle over how to share the ground under housing and health programmes in the new South Africa [*Bond, 1995*]. As Björn Beckman [*1933: 33*] makes clear, all the buzzwords of the new development language can too easily support the hegemonic drive of neo-liberalism (see also Apthorpe in this collection).

In sum, the framework of this first half-century of developmentalist discourse has been bounded by the language and practice of late capitalism, its main shifts have been conditioned by the move from the state-assisted economic forms of the first 30 years to the current doctrine (if not reality) of *laisser faire*, and these shifts are distinctively related to the success and crisis of capital's golden age.

The *political* discourse around developmentalism may have a less clear relationship to the vicissitudes of the global economy, however. The battle between political liberalism and conservatism may not be as temporally related to the rise and fall of the post-war boom as the struggle between economic liberalism and *dirigisme*. Part of the reason is because neither economic or political theorists have really decided whether the best state for capitalism is an authoritarian or libertarian one. Another part may be that the rise of such threats as the Vietcong or the possibility of southern Africa taking a distinctive turn to the left in the mid-1970s have no direct relationship to shifts in high finance and the contradictions in western capitalism. Indeed, there may even be cases of reverse flow: as Hirschman notes, Samuel Huntington's dour pessimism about development, democracy, and decay in the third world made its way through the Trilateral Commission and into a denunciation of 'too much democracy' in the United States [*Hirschman, 1991: 118–21*].

Whatever the reasons for the contradictions within the political side of development discourse, there is plenty of room even within its most expansive variant for coercive tendencies. Truman's words about democracy's relation-ship to the love of peace, planning, programmes and production make it clear that for those beyond the pale foreign intervention is required. For those outside of the charmed circle, American liberalism – like all forms of righteous-ness – can easily turn into various hues of authoritarian thought and practice.

Leonard Binder describes liberal modernisation theory as 'essentially an academic, and pseudoscientific, transfer of the dominant, and ideologically significant' pragmatic-pluralist paradigm attempting to explain American politics. Its problem was not in its defence of American imperialism, but in its extension as a misconstrued universal 'science' to the new field of development. This pseudo-theory extends:

> an image of ourselves as some liberals would like us to be to the potentiality of other, quite different countries. In fact, liberal development theory is a radical call for virtually unlimited expansion of political participation in developing countries, and it is a radical assault on all established institutions, traditional elite and religious structures, corporate arrangements, distributive coalitions, and the like. As such it was a gross distortion of what the United States was actually like and it was viewed increasingly as an irresponsible academic construction [Binder, 1986: 11–12].

'It is easy', Binder observes, to understand why such misconstrued theory 'aroused considerable opposition among conservative scholars long before the Marxist opposition got its act together' [ibid.: 11–12]. His comments on the fate of this pseudo-theory serve as a good lead-in to a review of early CIA thinking on the applicability of liberal theory to Africa.

III. THE CIA ON AFRICA: THE EARLY YEARS

Given Truman's words about the relationship between American aid and the peace-loving clients waiting for democratic fair play, it is appropriate to have some insight into the thinking of the agency responsible for discovering such people in the turbulent days of Africa's decolonisation. Such a remit would not have been easy, especially since most American observers were unprepared for the emergence of African nationalism. Even so, the CIA recognised the difficult balancing act it had to perform in order to keep aspiring nationalists on the right side of the capitalist/communist divide. It had to persuade the colonial powers to let go of their underlings, lest the colonised become too upset and look to the East; yet it also had to go slowly in this persuasive task lest the Europeans became alienated. A 1948 report stated that:

> The colonial powers must fully recognize the irresistible force of

nationalism in their dependencies and take leadership in guiding these dependencies gradually toward eventual self-government or indepen- dence, if they are to retain their favoured position in these areas. A policy of far-reaching colonial reforms, designed to foster colonial political, economic, and social development, would do much to neutralize the more violent aspects of native nationalisms and to substitute orderly evolution toward the inevitable goal of independence for the violent upheavals characteristic of the present situation. Only through such a new cooperative relationship can the colonial powers in the long run hope to retain their close ties with these areas and the maximum of political and economic advantage. Unless the colonial powers can be induced to recognize this necessity for satisfying the aspirations of their dependencies and can devise formulae which will retain their good will as emergent independent states, both those powers and the US will be placed at a serious disadvantage in the new power situation ... [*CIA, 1948: 14*].

The 'new power situation' was, of course, the competition with the Union of Soviet Socialist Republics (USSR). The competition for Africa was recognised as crucial. The document reminds its readers that the United States was directly reliant on some of the colonies for strategic and critical materials, and 'new nations arising in these areas, jealous of their sovereignty, may well be reluctant to lend such assistance to the United States' [*ibid.: 12*]. The dilemma was what kind of imperialism to avoid: too much pushing of decolonisation would 'run the risk of alienating the colonial power', but too little would 'alienate the dependent peoples' thus laying the 'groundwork for future disruption' and over the long term weaken both Western Europe and the USA '*vis-à-vis* the USSR'.

Yet aside from the worries about the global balance of power, there is also concern with 'gradual' movement to 'eventual' self-government through 'orderly evolution' instead of the 'violent' (and that word is often repeated) upheavals which were common to 'native nationalism'. It is clear that the liberal belief in the possibility of non-revolutionary social and political change is paramount here – if only the right 'formulae' can be found and if the crusty old European powers can be persuaded to act in their own best interests.

The search for 'native nationalists' who would be able to take their people down the evolutionary road to capitalism was part of the effort to avoid violence and its apparently inherent connections with 'extremism' and 'Communism'. For the National Security Council report in 1957 (long enough after 1948 to warrant taking African nationalism seriously) it was clear that such nastiness could be avoided if the right kind of nationalism was allowed to flourish: 'We wish to avoid in Africa a situation where thwarted nationalism and self-determinant aspirations are turned to the advantage of extremist elements, particularly Communists' [*National Security Council, 1957: 2–3*]. Nationalism was seen to have no *necessary* linkage to extremism and its logical companion, but it might well turn into such irregularities if it was not allowed to run its course. If that natural evolution would work its way out, 'the deprivation of African markets and sources of supply to Western Europe' could be avoided, too. The advice of this report was to encourage 'orderly development' by 'welcoming and extending political support to new states, such as Ghana, as they emerge' and 'supporting and encouraging constructive nationalism and reform movements ... when convinced they are likely to become powerful and grow in influence' [*ibid.: 6–7*].

American policy-makers were advised to support *moderate* nationalist movements – not just any type. The question whether to support a 'non-constructive' nationalist movement which seems likely to be powerful and influential was not directly answered. Morality was not yet balanced against Machiavelli. The query is, however, addressed in an indirect manner. At the bottom of the analysis is the suggestion that 'the African' is really incapable of making up his or her own mind.

> [T]he African is still immature and unsophisticated with respect to his attitudes towards the issues that divide the world today. The African's mind is not made up and he is being subjected to a number of contradictory forces. This pressure will increase in the future. The African is a target for the advocation [sic] of Communism, old-fashioned colonialism, xeno-phobic nationalism, and Egyptian 'Islamic' propaganda, as well as for the proponents of an orderly development of the various political entities in the area in question, closely tied to the West [*ibid.: 7–8*].

If the Africans were childlike, the good American parents could be allowed to make up their minds for them. Yet in spite of the purported innocence of 'the African', the National Security Council report also presumed relatively clear answers to 'where the leaders and the peoples feel their best interest [sic] lie' [*ibid.: 7*].

> The eventual political orientation of the emerging African states will probably be determined by what the leaders and peoples conceive best serves their own interests measured primarily in terms of 'independence' and of 'equality' with the white man. Our policies therefore must be designed to convince the African that by association with the West he can best achieve his goals in a manner which in the long run will be most to his advantage [*ibid.: 8*].

The quotation marks around *independence* and *equality* may have been mocking the applicability of such concepts to people considered so immature and unsophisticated. Nevertheless, the American policy-makers concerned believed that they had a fair idea of what *everybody's* needs were – and feared that they might not be met through flag independence and formal equality. If the basic American desire was an insatiable appetite for consumption, then that is the gap that had to be filled within the souls of African brethren. If the latter were feeling a bit unsettled and disoriented during the long transition to modernity – the 'shock of westernization' as a 1956 report put it [*Department of State, 1956: 4*] – the answer to their problems lay in the assurance that 'the good things in life' inherent with that project would come in due course [*ibid.:* 6]. In the meantime, however, there would be some problems. The same report's special section on the 'detribalized African' (subtitled 'His Lot is Social and Economic Insecurity') opined that due to lack of employable skills the individualised epitome of this insecure social group 'cannot yet command sufficient income to provide enough of the good things of life to offset the loss of security incurred in breaking away from the tribal environment'. The project of modernity, assumed here to involve the smashing of security for the sake of the consumable pleasures of 'the good things in life', is assumed to be attainable with the gaining of marketable 'skills'. There is nary a word about the distortions of the colonial – soon to be neo-colonial – society and global economy which have made such pious hopes a nonsense.

One wonders, too, just what is meant by the 'good things in life'. If those which come with American-style modernisation are good, is the 'security' of the tribal life thereby 'bad'? Is the uncertainty inherent with the ripping away of one's means of production, so that there is only labour power or petty commodities left to sell, thereby 'good'? Is being torn away from a pre-capitalist mode of social reproduction, and replacing its satisfactions of social and kinship solidarity with the individual calculations of pleasure in the world in which all that is solid melts into air, also the best of all possible worlds? If this report is at all representative, such were the missionary truths in the minds of modernisation's purveyors and surveyors.

One would hardly expect the early American proselytisers to have doubts about the intrinsic worth of their mission. They did, however, have second thoughts about how easy it would be to export it, given the insecure lot of those to whom it was sold. The insecurity of 'the native', born of lack of skills and the alienation inherent on de-tribalisation, left the social and political situation volatile; the 1957 policy report prophesied that 'the detribalized African will be an easy target for elements eager to exploit his traditional need for leadership and guidance' [*National Security Council, 1957: 18*]. Paternalistic platitudes like these helped justify the elimination of 'exploitative elements'; the assassination of Patrice Lumumba, no doubt by 'moderates', was soon to happen.

The search for such moderates, in spite of the difficulties in dealing with child-like interlopers into modernity and their penchant for the leadership of extremists, would nonetheless have to go on – for the good of the African and the pursuit of development. What made such a task even more tricky was the additional fact that 'these policies cannot be effective if the African feels he is merely a pawn in a power struggle' [*ibid.: 8*]. Read in another way, these words could mean 'although the African is a pawn in the power struggle between the Soviets and us, we must try to hide that fact from him'. Why else let the phrase slip into the discourse? It appears that the talk about the de-tribalised African needing 'guidance' into the angst-ridden age of modernity serves as a preemptive justification for intervention. The paternalist patter about protection from unsavoury characters ready to pounce on the unsuspecting, tentatively progressing innocent – perhaps studying at night school to gain the 'skills' needed to earn the cash to buy into the 'good life' – serves as an excuse to stop the other side in the global power struggle. The proposed difficulties involved in the African making up his mind while being subjected to a number of 'contradictory influences' reflected American uncertainty whether to pressure the colonial powers to speed up the decolonisation process or to slow it down in the hopes that a little bit more breathing space would allow them to help the nationalists come to a moderate conclusion about how to best attain the good life.

There is little doubt that the ivory-towered kin to the CIA felt much the same way. Edward Shils was one of the more notable of the modernisation theorists who focused on the nationalists and dared to call them by their name: 'intellectuals'. His hopes for the moderate among them and fears about the extremists mirror those of the CIA, although his rhetoric about their role may well exaggerate their importance. With words like these, however, it is little wonder that this new 'class' may have been the most watched in the world:

> The gestation, birth, and continuing life of the new states of Asia and Africa, through all of their vicissitudes, are in large measure the work of intellectuals. In no state-formations in all of human history have intellectuals played such as role as they have in these events of the present century ... The prominence of intellectuals in the politics of the[se] new states ... arises in part from the special affinity which exists between the modern intellectual orientation and the practice of revolutionary or unconstitutional politics, of politics which are uncivil in their nature [*Shils, 1971 (1960): 249–50*].

Such analysis seems to suggest that these ill-paid and underemployed young men, living in cultures craving for 'charismatic' leadership, should be watched. They crave authority (equated with a 'need for incorporation into a new, alternative collectivity' [*ibid.: 256*]) – even though they claim to desire emancipation. Such characteristics make for a volatile situation, but because it

is intellectuals who are the only 'political' group in the societies under
analysis, Shils' analysis comes very close to that of the CIA: the contest is
between 'those intellectuals who speak for civility in a modern society', whose
'radicalism ... need not however be revolutionary or ideological', and 'the
dense incivility of their fellow-intellectuals' [*ibid.: 275-6*]. Given that even
these stalwart heroes of moderation have to struggle against their 'own
inhibitions' as well as 'the rocky obduracy of the traditional order' [*loc. cit.*]
their chances did not seem too good. However, it is part of the subtext that
people like Professor Shils would be there to add to their 'talents, virtue and
good fortune' [*ibid.: 276*] – as would be the talents of the CIA.

It is not this paper's purpose to chronicle the realities of CIA action in
Africa as it attempted to hasten the progress of its choice of democratic
stalwarts. Most students of that continent's history are aware of what happened
to 'extremist elements' such as Patrice Lumumba, who the CIA did not bless
with its good fortune, and the virtuous intellectuals which it did (for example,
Holden Roberto). Here we will instead investigate the similarities – cold war
or not – between the perspectives on democracy held by the CIA and other
intelligence gatherers in the 1950s and those held by development discoursers
who see 'good governance' as the new hegemonic guarantor.

IV. THE GROUNDINGS OF 'GOOD GOVERNANCE'

Susan George and Fabrizio Sabelli [*1994: 142–61*] claim that 'good
governance' is the World Bank/IMF consortium's last refuge. If structural
adjustment policies do not work to bring Africa into the fold of modernisation-
for-all – and it is unlikely they will [*Bienefeld, 1995*] – then the unfulfilled
conditionalities of good governance will provide a good way to 'blame-the-
victim'. Failure can be laid at the steps of those who were not simultaneously
accountable, transparent, efficient and democratic. 'Good governance' offers a
double opportunity: another route 'to instil Western values in borrowing
countries' and the option to fault them 'if things go wrong' [*George and
Sabelli, 1994: 142*].

One might think that if western values had not been instilled among the
African intelligentsia after so many decades of the colonial commissioners and
the post-colonial practitioners of modernisation, then the cause might be lost.[6]
It may be that George and Sabelli are wrong to think that the Bank is hedging
its bets on the future; they might not pay enough credence to the inherent
optimism of the development ideologists. In the Bank's new guise of
missionaries for good governance, they can simply lay the blame on an age of
misperception, marked they would say by the mistaken belief that the job of
development could be done through state-led capitalism. For them the new
dawn of development and democracy can begin with the strident assertion that

free markets and liberal democracy are synergistic: structural adjustment was wrong only in that it underrated the latter. Now, the building of a strong capitalist-oriented 'civil society' will help Africa lift itself up by the bootstraps. Teach them properly, say the reinvigorated modernisationists, and there still might be a chance.

Indeed, to talk of a 'new' policy of good governance is somewhat misleading. It appears that the key players are similar. Elliot Berg, the main author of *Accelerated Development in Sub-Saharan Africa* [*World Bank, 1981*] the report which signposted structural adjustment (and which informally bears his name) zeroed in on the state less than five years after structural adjustment loans (SALs) were first implemented [*Berg and Batchelder, 1985*].[7] After admitting that 'the criteria for selection of SALs are not clear', that 'the theory of reform on which the SAL rests is not clearly spelled out', and that the 'SALs are often too complex, and embody too much fictional conditionality' [*ibid.: 7*], his 'critical' report to the World Bank then went on to suggest that the 'whole ruling class or ruling elite may be at issue' [*ibid.: 24*]. This is an extreme sociological simplification for something Berg and Batchelder have admitted is a convoluted 'economic' problem. They resort to citing radical scholars such as Baran and Fanon and go on to suggest how to create the sort of national bourgeoisie Fanon would have hated, unless he had been part of the stageist school of Marxism which posited the need for a classical bourgeoisie to precede a socialist revolution. Berg and Batchelder claim that SAL conditionality has enabled the bank to 'get to the policy table' and to elevate 'the level of policy dialogue; its macroeconomic, trans-sectoral character [now] elicits attention at cabinet level or above' [*ibid.: 27*]. Yet this may not be enough: 'it can be argued that most of the "real" progress in reform occurs – if and when it occurs – at lower political and bureaucratic levels' [*ibid.: 31*]. Thus, the whole state, from top to bottom, must be cleansed of the bad attitudes of the 'detribalized man' of the 1956 Department of State report.

However, the two World Bank advisers caution against the Bank including 'institutional change … [which is] long-term in nature … not readily quantifiable … [and the] monitoring [of which] is in most cases subjective' [*ibid.: 34*], in their conditionalities as if they are operating on the same 'time track' as policy reforms.

> The intractability of institutional problems seems to be a permanent source of surprise and disappointment. The Bank staff involved know the lesson: that these problems are deeply rooted in the environment of underdevelopment, require much more thoughtful attention and will change slowly even with the most intelligent and sustained assistance. But the lesson does not seem to be adequately institutionalized [*ibid.: 36*].

Rather than tackle the big problem, these advisors suggest 'greater simplicity and focus, [and] a more modest set of reform goals'. One is tempted to add: 'and if SALs worsen "the environment of underdevelopment", well, that is not our fault or our problem'. The paper seems to proceed on two different planes: one recognises, at least at the level of symptoms, the intractable nature of underdevelopment; but the other goes on as if the technical fixes of SALs will do something to change those symptoms and in a modest and incremental way even alter the trajectory of the disease. The two modern-day Machiavellian princes caution the Bank against trying to do too much *and* simultaneously suggest that there is a whole lot to be done.

It now seems that the Bank disregarded the words of restraint and has decided to go the whole route of 'institutional change'. Only four years after the in-house warning, the Bank released its *Sub-Saharan Africa: From Crisis to Sustainable Growth* [*World Bank, 1989*]. With its admonishment for not only less government but *better* government, it seemed to throw all caution to the wind and accept the fact that 'in the final analysis, everything is connected to everything else' [*George and Sabelli, 1994: 155*]. In spite of its constitutional requirement to be apolitical, the Bank has moved from technocracy to statecraft. Extending beyond tax reform and getting the prices right, to social sector review, accountability, transparency and the rule of law, it has entered the murky realm of 'institutional change' with the bulldozing optimism of its dam-building days. One should not be surprised at such social engineering: manipulating a country's foreign exchange regime was never an apolitical act. What is different and almost incredible is the increased shamelessness of this new intervention.

The contradictions in the new agenda are blatant too. The Bank is riding the waves of the current fascination with 'civil society' in the hopes of building up an effective counterfoil to the rapacious state, but aims also to increase the state's capacity to create the proper playing field for such flourishing. 'Capacity-building' is seen as necessary for the creation of the consent for the new order which structural adjustment could not usher in; and, unsaid, is also needed to implement a sufficient quota of repression as the still unchanged policies of neo-liberalism are implemented [*Bernstein, 1990: 23*]. The architects of such wide-reaching reform must certainly realise that declaring the political doors shall be opened will allow the articulation of broader social demands, not only the atomised ones of the market. When the former are expressed to a state forced into austerity, measures for diminishing expectations must be found. 'Participation' – the democratic tie-in to 'good governance' – is thus the velvet glove shrouding the iron fist of enforced scarcity.

There is much enthusiasm for the politics of participation in Africa at the United States Agency for International Development (USAID), traditionally imbued with a Peace Corps type of ethos and with Congressional approval to talk 'Politics' to its African clients. It carries the torch for this ideology more forthrightly than the World Bank, its big multilateral brother. Robert Charlick, the aforementioned 'Senior Governance Expert' is one of the louder voices criticising the World Bank's technocratic approach to governance and emphasising the normative aspects of the task [*Charlick, 1992*]. He advocates replacing the 'good' in 'good governance' with 'democratic' and suggests that the fostering of Weberian 'publics' will lead to the development of African societies imbued with rules and norms de Tocqueville would have been proud of. Civil society's liberalisation will, for Charlick, benefit 'local level actors, and productive economic actors, such as business associations and farmer groups [which] have frequently been excluded from the policy process in the past' [*ibid.: 16*]. Assisting them will lead to better economic decisions as well as strengthen governance: letting a hundred flowers bloom on the capitalist side of the civil society will help establish the rules and norms enabling societies to run themselves along the lines required by capital.

In this view, the Leviathan state envisaged by the 'order'-oriented modernisers will not be necessary. Capitalism will become organic. No one need worry that the 'publics' take advantage of this increased participation to lobby for the consumption of state services instead of 'investment, savings and sound fiscal management' because preferences for state spending on such services as clean water, education, and health 'stem from structures of authoritarian, often illegitimate, states which have excluded most social interests from participation in public policy making, rather than from excessively participatory states' [*ibid.: 12*]. Aside from a degree of historical inaccuracy and the underhanded association of social spending with state socialism, such a statement implies that the potentiality of rentier-like behaviour on the part of the masses will disappear with the advent of American-style democracy: the pleasure of participation will wipe out the desire for affordable health and housing. Charlick is aware that his prophecy may not fulfil itself so he advocates 'strengthening the advocacy and analytic capabilities of non-governmental organizations ... associated with production' [*ibid.: 16*]. In short, USAID should fund pro-business lobbyists and consultancies.

This is just what USAID is doing, except that these lobbyists and consultancies are more than likely to be in the United States than in an African country. USAID advertises widely on the Internet. Of the more prominent postings are announcements of the closure of offices in scores of African countries, advice for potential American contractors, and lists of projects performed through freelance consultancy. For those who have access to Internet, and possess the requisite neo-classical economic theory or public choice political economy, a score or more of plane-trips around Africa makes the global village a reality. In such a world, offices in Africa are superfluous.

One of the USAID-funded institutions in this brave new world is called the

International Foundation for Electoral Systems (IFES). Its mission is to

> support a program of research to identify conceptual frameworks,
> historical, theoretical and analytical material, and practical case material
> ... to broaden the Agency's understanding of the institutional, legal and
> behavioral bases of democratic and pluralistic orders to provide a
> stronger underpinning for Agency and regional policy and strategy, and
> for country programming [*USAID, 1995*].

One of its many projects, entitled 'Macro and International Economic
Analysis' is directed by the consultancy group 'Development Alternatives'. It
promises to recruit American and third world 'scholars and/or practitioners to
apply the approaches and methods developed by the project's research in the
design, implementation and evaluation of democratization development
projects'[*ibid.*].

The project's specific agenda, though seems to have more to do with Dr.
Berg's 1980 goals than with democracy *per se.* Indeed, it seems that the original
agenda has not even been replaced by 'good governance'. The project's
'description of services' includes 'to provide AID Bureaus and Missions with
quick response short-term technical and advisory services in the following areas:
macroeconomic, fiscal, and monetary policy; national budgets; public sector-
private sector roles; and international trade and finance', and that it may provide
these in the 'context of program or project planning, design, evaluation or
implementation'. Keywords such as 'international debt and debt payments ...
integration agreements ... denationalization and privatization ... and measures to
increase competition and the scope of market forces' pepper the list of the
project's 'delivery orders' [*ibid*].

If the 1985 Berg and Batchelder report to the World Bank suggested 'the
ruling class was at issue', and implied that it should either be transformed or
be encouraged to go, this USAID proposal indicates what should be done if the
ruling class has been relieved of its power. 'Development Alternatives' will
run Africa's economy – with some help from 'Transparency International',
'Management Systems International', and 'Nathan Associates' – and any other
Beltway entrepreneurs rallying to the cause [*ibid*].

In the end, this is part of an attempted recolonisation project. It is unlikely
it will work, both because Africa is closer to Bayart's [*1993*] world of shadow
theatre than to the economic rationalism of the Bates's and Diamonds [*Gibbon
et al., 1992: 9–18; Saul, 1994; 1996*] and because the neo-liberal policies still
underpinning these programmes tear away any chance of reconstruction before
it starts. Perhaps, however, the Berg proposal to the USAID is part of a battle
between the cold-hearted econocrats of the World Bank circa 1980 and on the
other side a new, softer Clintonesque school in USAID coming out of the
Peace Corps nostalgia plus a World Bank faction influenced by the likes of

Herman Daly [*Hellinger and Hammond, 1994*].[9] A return to the relatively benevolent and optimistic modernisation approach is not impossible in American aid policy. However, there are two immediate reasons not to hold one's breath for a rosy future. First, in spite of nostalgia for a pre-Reaganist world, classical modernisation theory in practice did very little to assist Africa to a sustainable path: indeed, it may well have left it vulnerable to the ravages of SAP solutions. African state capitalism did not work that much better than the neo-liberal solution which came in to clean it up. Secondly, the Gingrich revolution may well stop such moderation in its tracks, and American aid programmes may be retrenched ever more.

There is another reason why any optimism should be tempered. Very little has changed in the underlying assumptions of the American role in Africa since it took it upon itself to replace the colonial powers. Washington's analysis of the articulation of modes of production and culture does not seem to have improved significantly since the 1950s CIA's focus on the problems of 'detribalization' for African elites, or Edward Shils' fears about state-bound intellectuals and the eternal conflict between 'tradition and the modern' [*Shils, 1960; CIA, 1948*]. The new words on 'tradition' seem to absorb notions from participatory development and to suggest new forms of democracy taking the old into account [e.g. *Landell-Mills, 1992*]; but the re-invigoration of 'indigenous institutions' is only to be encouraged if they are 'compatible with modernization and development' [*ibid.: 544–5*]. Through structural adjustment the vexed nexus between 'tradition' and the state can be cut; the tendency for nepotism, patron-client relations and corruption can only be erased with vigorous privatisation programmes and the like. It is only thus that 'African managers' can 'set aside their loyalties to their community ... [and] the heavy obligations that take up a large proportion of their time' (Landell-Mills quoted in Williams and Young [*1994: 95*]). Landell-Mills does not consider a new kind of state which could blend such community obligations with a reworked democracy, but instead almost openly suggests that external agencies go beyond the state to strengthen 'civil society' [*Landell-Mills, 1992: 566*]. In any case 'components of civil society ... will be ... strengthened by the economic liberalisation and privatisation measures that typically form a key part of the on-going structural adjustments being undertaken in most countries' [*ibid., 567*]. This might nicely weaken any possibility of a democratised state being able to challenge the social engineers from the IMF and the World Bank – and such consulting agencies as 'Development Alternatives' – with their places in the shade of the village tree as well as their ever more prominent seats at the tables of state.

As Furedi indicates, similar discourses on 'traditionalism' can be thinly veiled attacks against *any* post-colonial African state; not just a badly managed one. They are easily blended in with an attack on nationalism *per se*.

> The main political legacy of celebrating traditional culture is to transform Third World nationalism into an all-purpose monster responsible for every disaster that has afflicted post-colonial societies ... the starting point of anti-colonial nationalism, the liberatory impulse of the oppressed, has now been confused with its final outcome – the collapse of post-colonial nations. This confusion is the intellectual precondition for the rehabilitation of imperialism [*Furedi, 1994: 103-6; cf. Davidson, 1992*].

In this way, any action taken by the American democracy-exporters can be justified. If the state is portrayed as evil, then any means can be used to get around it. If western 'democracy' (tied up with the market as it is) is seen as the way to eradicate this evil, and if neo-liberal views of western democracy see it as a product of *elite* culture [*Diamond, 1993: 4*], but the African elite is seen as incapable of producing the required political culture, then it is necessary to create a new elite from below (within African society). To buttress that process, the new elite can also be fashioned from above, imposed by and developed within 'international civil society', or in Robert Cox's words 'a transnational managerial elite' [*Cox, 1987: 359*]. The African state can be transcended, it is believed, if an alliance can be struck between the emerging bourgeoisie and the wandering political culture consultants. The state can be employed in this process, but only through closely monitored 'capacity building programmes'.

The revival of academic interest in 'political culture' is no doubt linked to this global project. It was, after all, a realisation that the culture of trucking, bartering and trading was not a given that led to the early days of political modernisation discourse. According to Gabriel Almond, the re-emergence of these concerns may spell the death-knell of public choice theory (Almond in Diamond [*1993: xi*]). The psychologists, sociologists and political scientists who have maintained the faith in the cultural transferability of the 'achievement motive' are encouraged to muster their resources in order to wean the majority of the African masses from their supposed tendencies to production for self-sustenance or – worse – rentierdom.

The same interventionist attitude prevails in the language of participation. Thus a USAID report on how to 'expand civil society' asserts that just as there is no natural *homo oeconomicus* neither is there a ready and waiting mass of participators. The process leading to this is one 'requiring complex interventions ... ' [*Shoemaker, 1995*].

> It is critically important to create appropriate rules and incentives that discipline governments long practiced in poor governance behavior, and that encourage civil society to play a larger role in promoting good governance. Africa is in the early stages of democratization, and some

rules have been changed, but many old rules are still on the books, creating incentive incompatibilities that, unless changed, will constrain the improvement of governance [*loc. cit*].

'The early stages' and 'many old rules': such language evokes the sentiments of the CIA man of the 1950s. Whether the 'old rules' derive from the pre-colonial days of tribal primitivism, the colonial days of benevolent authoritarianism, or the rapacious corruption of the post-colonial epoch, we can be sure that the Americans must come in with the broom and sweep in the new order. The 'incentive incompatibilities' must be removed for democratic governance as well as for the marketeers. It is a big job.

CONCLUSION

If there is a difference between American official development discourse on democracy at the end of the Second World War and the end of the cold war, it is only a subtle one. Perhaps the hope now is that economic and political 'science' can replace the CIA: but the military hand is never far from the glove of the American way, be it clothed in the rhetoric of science or of consumable dreams. No matter what the sheen of the discourse, the inequalities produced by most of these strategies will continue to be devastating. There is one more difference though: with the end of the Cold War and of benevolent liberalism, the USA may become more and more prone to the 'exit option'. If that option had been taken earlier, we might have more optimism about Africa's fate.

NOTES

1. According to Schuster [*1994: 95*], food aid is the best that foreigners can do in Liberia now and it is the only source of sustenance for more than two-thirds of its citizens.
2. See Binder [*1986: 3–33*] for an appreciation of the subtle contradictions of early democratic modernisation theory.
3. See Charlick [*1992*] and the comments in Moore [*1995*].
4. To differentiate 'meta-discourse' from 'policy discourse', I take the latter to mean the admixture of theory and practice found in governmental apparatuses, and the former to mean the deeper and underlying hegemonic beliefs and actions surrounding and informing what transpires in policy (and other) circles.
5. Moore [*1995*] attempts to perform this task in regard to the shifting content of the 'buzzwords' in post-Second World War development discourse.
6. One could ask what *sort* of western values? If consumerism is the aim (and for the CIA reporters above it seemed to be just that) then these values have sunk into the consciousness of the African governing class. If the supposed Protestant ideal of self-denying productivism is the goal, it may not have permeated quite as well.
7. Berg is director of the 'Development Alternatives' consultancy whose project on macroeconomics and democracy will be discussed later.
8. Hellinger and Hammond report that the US Treasury is unhappy with the Bank's handling of poverty in Africa, and sees its 1994 report, *Adjustment in Africa: Reforms, Results and the Road Ahead*, as an unconscionable cover-up.

REFERENCES

Anderson, Benedict, 1983, *Imagined Communities: Reflections on the Origin and Spread of Nationalism*, London: Verso.

Bayart, Jean-François, 1993 (1989), *The State of Africa: The Politics of the Belly*, London: Longman.

Beckman, Björn, 1993, 'The Liberation of Civil Society: Neo-Liberal Ideology and Political Theory', *Review of African Political Economy*, Vol.58, pp.29–34.

Berg, Elliot and A. Batchelder, 1985, 'Structural Adjustment Lending a Critical View', Washington, DC: World Bank Country Policy Department.

Bernstein, Henry, 1990, 'Agricultural Modernisation and the era of Structural Adjustment: Observations on Sub-Saharan Africa', *Journal of Peasant Studies*, Vol.18, No.1, pp.3–35.

Bernstein, Henry, Crow, B., Mackintosh, M. and C. Martin (eds.), 1990, *The Food Question: Profits versus People?*, New York: Monthly Review Press.

Bienefeld, M., 1994, 'Capitalism and the Nation State in the Dog Days of the Twentieth Century', in R. Miliband and L. Panitch (eds.), *Socialist Register 1994*, London: Merlin Press, pp.94–129.

Bienefeld, M., 1995, 'Structural Adjustment and Prospects for Democracy in Southern Africa', in Moore and Schmitz [1995: 91–128].

Binder, Leonard, 1986, 'The Natural History of Development Theory', *Comparative Studies in Society and History*, Vol.28, No.1, pp.3–33.

Bond, Patrick, 1995, 'Urban Social Movements in the Housing Question and Development Discourse in South Africa', in Moore and Schmitz [1995: 149–77].

Bratton, Michael and G. Hyden (eds.), 1992, *Governance and Politics in Africa*, Boulder, CO: Lynne Rienner.

Campbell, David, 1992, *Writing Security: United States Foreign Policy and the Politics of Identity*, Minneapolis, MN: University of Minnesota Press.

Campbell, David, forthcoming, 'Political Prosaics, Transversal Politics and the Anarchical World', in M.J. Schapiro and H. Alker (eds.), *Territorial Identities and Global Flows*, Minneapolis, MN: University of Minnesota Press.

Central Intelligence Agency (CIA), 1948, 'The Breakup of the Colonial Empires and its Implications for US Security', ORE 25-48, Washington, DC.

Charlick, Robert (Senior Governance Expert), 1992, 'The Concept of Governance and Its Implications for AID's Development Assistance Program in Africa', prepared for the AID Africa Research Bureau under the Africa Bureau Democracy and Governance Program, Washington, DC: Associates in Rural Development Inc.

Church, Frank, 1977, 'Introduction', in Tyrus G. Fain (ed.), *The Intelligence Community: History, Organization, and Issues*, New York: Bowker.

Clay, E. and B.B. Schaffer (eds.), 1984, *Room for Manoeuvre*, London: Heinemann.

Cohen, Leonard, 1993, *Stranger Music: Selected Poems and Songs*, Toronto: McClelland & Stewart, and on the album, 'The Future'.

Cox, Robert, 1979, 'Ideologies and the New International Economic Order: Reflections on some Recent Literature', *International Organization*, Vol.33, No.2, pp.257–302.

Cox, Robert, 1987, *Production, Power and World Order: Social Forces in the Making of History*, New York: Columbia University Press.

Cox, Robert, 1991, 'The Global Political Economy and Social Choice', in D. Drache and M.S. Gertler (eds.), *The New Era of Global Competition: State Policy and Market Power*, Montreal and Kingston: McGill-Queens University Press, pp.335–49.

Davidson, Basil, 1992, *Black Man's Burden: Africa and the Curse of the Nation-State*, London: James Currey.

Department of State, Office of Intelligence Research, 1956, 'Africa: A Special Assessment', Washington, DC.

Diamond, Larry (ed.), 1993, *Political Culture and Democracy in Developing Countries*, Boulder, CO: Lynne Rienner.

Escobar, Arturo, 1984, 'Discourse and Power in Development: Michel Foucault and the Relevance of his Work to the Third World', *Alternatives*, Vol.10, No.3, pp.377–400.

Escobar, Arturo, 1992, 'Imagining a Post-Development Era? Critical Thought, Development and Social Movements', *Social Text*, Vol.31/32, pp.20–56.

Escobar, Arturo, 1993, 'Planning', in Wolfgang Sachs (ed.), *The Development Dictionary: A Guide to Knowledge as Power*, London: Zed Books.

Escobar, Arturo, 1995, *Encountering Development: The Making and Unmaking of the Third World*, Princeton, NJ: Princeton University Press.

Furedi, Frank, 1994, *The New Ideology of Imperialism, Renewing the Moral Imperative*, London: Pluto Press.

George, Susan and F. Sabelli, 1994, *Faith and Credit: The World Bank's Secular Empire*, London: Penguin.

Gibbon, Peter, Bangura, Y. and A. Ofstad, 1992, *Authoritarianism, Democracy and Adjustment: The Politics of Economic Reform in Africa*, Uppsala: The Scandinavian Institute of African Studies.

Hellinger, Doug and R. Hammond, 1994, 'Debunking the Myth', *Africa Report*, December.

Hirschman, Albert O., 1991, *The Rhetoric of Reaction: Perversity, Futility, Jeopardy*, Cambridge, MA: Belknap Harvard.

Hoare, Quinton and Geoffrey Nowell-Smith (eds.), 1971, *Selections from the Prison Notebooks of Antonio Gramsci*, New York: International Publishers.

International Bank for Reconstruction and Development, 1950, *The Basis of a Development Program for Colombia*, Baltimore, MD: Johns Hopkins University Press.

Klitgaard, Robert, 1990, *Tropical Gangsters: One Man's Experience with Development and Decadence in Deepest Africa*, New York: Basic Books.

Landell-Mills, Pierre, 1992, 'Governance, Cultural Change, and Empowerment', *Journal of Modern African Studies*, Vol.30, No.4, pp.543–67.

Leys, Colin, 1994, 'Confronting the African Tragedy', *New Left Review*, Vol. 204, pp.33–47.

McNamara, Robert, 1995, *In Retrospect: The Tragedy and Lessons of Vietnam*, New York: Times Books (excerpts in *The Weekend Australian, 22–3* April), p.21.

Marglin, Stephen and J. Schor (eds.), 1990, *The Golden Age of Capitalism: Reinterpreting the Postwar Experience*, Oxford: Clarendon Press.

Moore, David, 1995, 'Development Discourse as Hegemony: Towards an Ideological History – 1945–1995', in Moore and Schmitz [*1995: 1–53*].

Moore, David and G.J. Schmitz (eds.), 1995, *Debating Development Discourse: Institutional and Popular Perspectives*, London: Macmillan.

Murphy, Craig and E. Augelli, 1993, 'International Institutions, Decolonization, and Development', *International Political Science Review*, Vol.14, No.1, pp.71–85.

National Security Council, 1957, 'US Policy toward Africa South of the Sahara prior to Calendar Year 1960', Washington, DC (NSC) 5719.

O'Brien, Donal Cruise, 1971, 'Modernization, Order and the Erosion of a Democratic Ideal', *Journal of Development Studies*, Vol.8, No.4, pp.351–78.

Said, Edward, 1993, *Culture and Imperialism*, London: Vintage.

Saul, John S., 1993, *Recolonization and Resistance in Southern Africa in the 1990s*, Toronto and Trenton, NJ: Between the Lines Press and Africa World Press.

Saul, John S., 1994, 'Globalism, Socialism and Democracy in the South African Transition', in Ralph Miliband and Leo Panitch (eds.), *Socialist Register 1994*, London: Merlin Press, pp.171–202.

Saul, John S., 1996, 'For Fear of Being Condemned as Old-Fashioned: Liberal Democracy vs. Popular Democracy in Sub-Saharan Africa', in *Socialist Register 1996*, London: Merlin Press.

Schmitter, Phillippe C., 1995, 'Democracy's Future: More Liberal, Preliberal, or Postliberal?', *Journal of Democracy*, Vol.6, No.1, pp.15–22.

Schmitz, G.J., 1995, 'Democratization and Demystification: Deconstructing "Governance" as Development Paradigm', in Moore and Schmitz [1995: 54–90].

Schuster, Linda, 1994, 'The Final Days of Dr Doe', *Granta*, Vol.48, pp.39–95.

Schwarzmantel, John, 1995, 'Capitalist Democracy Revisited', in L. Panitch (ed.), *Socialist Register 1995*, London: Merlin Press.

Shils, Edward, 1971 (1960), 'The Intellectuals in the Political Development of the New States', in Jason L. Finkle and Richard W. Gable (eds.), *Political Development and Social Change* (Second Edition), New York: John Wiley.

Shoemaker, Robert, 1995, 'Assessing Democratic Governance: Expanding Civil Society and Participation in the Political Process', *African Voices: A Newsletter on Democratization and*

Governance in Africa, Vol.4, No.1, Spring (available on the USAID World Wide Web Site, published by the Africa Bureau Information Center, operated by the Academy for Educational Development under contract to the USAID).

USAID, 1995, USAID World Wide Web Site.

Williams, David and T. Young, 1994, 'Governance, the World Bank and Liberal Theory', *Political Studies*, Vol.42, No.1, pp.84–100.

World Bank, 1981, *Accelerated Development in Sub-Saharan Africa,* Washington, DC: World Bank.

World Bank, 1989, *Sub-Saharan Africa: From Crisis to Sustainable Growth. A Long-Term Perspective Study*, Washington, DC: World Bank.

Essentialism In and About Development Discourse

DES GASPER

Several types of essentialism form potential dangers in policy and development discourse. First, essentialism in defining terms, including in claims that a term referring to a broad and multi-dimensional category means 'essentially' and exclusively such-and-such and is not 'essentially contestable'. Second, essentialism about the performance and desirability of policies and policy means, including: the treatment of a means or strategy as having 'inherent' performance attributes (strengths/weaknesses); and the treatment of a means as inherently (or 'basically') appropriate and 'proper'. Illustrations come from debates on rural centres, co-operatives, and collectivisation. Thirdly, essentialism in descriptions of schools of development thought and practice, discussed with reference to work by Kitching, Ferguson, Escobar and others on development discourse, and the stream of 'anti-development discourse'.

I. THE BASIC DEFECTS OF YOUR ESSENTIAL VISION OF DEVELOPMENT AND THE INHERENT STRENGTHS OF MY FAVOURED POLICY MEANS

Various authors propose lists of basic features of development discourse or of some mainstream in it. One central proposed feature is a frequent usage of the term 'development' as simultaneously descriptive and evaluative: as referring to specific empirical features or processes and at the same time as inherently good, good by definition. James Ferguson, like some earlier authors, describes this as a tacit oscillation between two definitions of development, one meaning modernisation, industrialisation and/or transition to capitalism, and the other meaning improvement of quality of life or increase of well-being [*1990: 15, 55*]. Negative experiences of industrialisation or capitalism or whatever then become excused as not real examples, not 'real development'; and the concept of 'development' can live on as at the same time a definite programme and an untarnishable promise. The programme becomes treated as essentially good, and the negative experiences as excusable misfortunes.

Des Gasper, Institute of Social Studies, PO Box 29776, 2502 LT The Hague, The Netherlands (e-mail: gasper@iss.nl).

The same syndrome of oscillation and untarnishability occurs commonly with other topics in development discourse like 'decentralisation', 'participation', or 'co-operation'. A policy means or approach is deemed inherently effective and desirable, although its good qualities may, it is said, often be disguised by other factors for which it is 'not to blame'. The means or approach has virtues but not failings. We can call this the 'beyond criticism' gambit.

Consider one example. Duelfer, amongst others, felt he must deny that service cooperatives have any inherent weaknesses.

> The failures of cooperatives in some instances are often attributed to a 'structural weakness' of the cooperative society as compared with other organizational forms. Detailed study of these cases shows however that failure was *in every instance* conditioned by a lack of preparation, planning and 'take-off' in the newly created cooperative [*Duelfer, 1974: 164*] (emphasis added).[1]

The failings are always merely contingent, never structural. Yet Duelfer does not exclude notions of structural weaknesses elsewhere. He vigorously alleges them for collective farming and holds that service co-operatives have structural strengths, in that they allow fulfilment of some (purported) social prerequisites for economic development [*ibid.: 189*]. Having structural strengths and no structural weaknesses, service cooperatives are deemed essentially appropriate policy means.

I hope to counter these and some related oversimplifications in and about development (policy) discourse(s). This study focuses critically on a number of types of essentialism, including claims that a widely used term referring to a complex general category means ('essentially') exclusively such-and-such, and claims that a policy means or strategy is inherently (or 'basically') appropriate, desirable or 'proper'.

'Development discourse' (DD) as a field has no clear boundaries, since development and development studies have none either; further, the types of discourse in them are not all of one type. Since we face not one type of nail, no single type of hammer will suffice. Here are some alternative delineations of DD, beginning with the broadest: (i) discourse that centrally uses the term (social/economic/political) development; (ii) discourse in development studies; (iii) discourse that uses 'developmentalist' presumptions (discussed in Sachs [*1992*]); (iv) discourse of development policy (see Apthorpe [*1986*]); (v) discourse of leading international development donors (see Ferguson [*1990*], Porter [*1995*]).[2] We are interested in all of these, but especially the last three, which are somewhat more coherent. They overlap and have much in common; where necessary we will distinguish them.

From the descriptive/evaluative ambiguity of the term 'development' and its acquisition of a status beyond criticism, we sense DD's interconnections and overlaps with policy discourse. My prime interest here is development policy discourse; but like any policy discourse it is not sharply distinct from descriptive and explanatory discourse in the same subject areas [*Stretton, 1969*]. Development discourse (or discourses; we will return to this point later) is perhaps especially intimately related to policy, given too some of its common roles: to mobilise, to reassure, and to manipulate, through concealment of divisive issues. Indeed some authors treat DD as a policy discourse, by using develop as a transitive verb: A develops B. None of these roles though, nor the corresponding discursive manoeuvres such as positive-normative ambiguities or overlaps, is unique to DD. Much policy discourse shares what Ferguson proposes as characteristic of DD: the attempt to depoliticise, to present disputed matters which affect people differently and on which they have different perspectives as being technical issues with technical solutions including, not least, solutions of the sorts which the purveyor of the discourse is able to provide [*Fischer, 1990*]. Further, not all development policy discourse, let alone all policy discourse, has this feature. We have to study many patterns, not a few.

In section II we look at essentialism in defining terms, and William Connolly's work on the functioning of 'essentially contestable concepts' in political discourse. Section III proceeds to essentialism in representations of the performance and desirability of policies and policy means, including two linked dangers: performative essentialism, the treatment of a policy-means as having 'inherent' performance attributes, particularly inherent strengths or weaknesses; and prescriptive essentialism, the treatment of a means as being inherently appropriate or inappropriate. It takes a set of development policy illustrations: rural centres, agricultural co-operatives, and collectivisation. Section IV considers essentialism in descriptions of schools of development thought and practice, with reference to the work of Gavin Kitching, more recent writings by James Ferguson and others explicitly on 'development discourse', and the stream of 'anti-development discourse'. Section V sums up.

II. ESSENTIALISM AND THE TERMS OF POLITICAL DISCOURSE

One often encounters the defence that indicated examples of failure of a policy were not 'real' or 'true' exemplars of the approach. This 'not one of ours' gambit can be valid, but it is a warning light: investigate-with-care. In the absence of awareness of the imperfection of terms and the pitfalls associated with performative concepts, much confusion can arise. We must look first at essentialism in defining any single concept; in Section III we can then go on to forms of essentialism in broader policy discourses.

Essentialism in definition holds that there are precise and obligatory definitions.[3] In a strong variant it holds that one can attain the ideal definition: a set of necessary conditions which together are a sufficient condition for use of a term [Scriven, 1976]. In practice we find we cannot do this, except for some new or rarely used terms, particularly those in specialised fields.[4] This inability reflects the fact that we cannot envisage all possible conditions in which terms are or will be used. Usually we can state some necessary conditions, plus other 'criteria' which individually are not necessary but of which one or other sufficient combination is necessary. The set of such sufficient combinations is unlikely to be completely definable. 'Criteria' fade off into 'connotations', properties which happen to often occur in practice; there is no hard dividing line between the two. Connotations carry important information and it is unreasonable to try to excise them. And that is all there is: not any 'buried secret formula which encapsulates the meaning in a more precise way' [ibid.: 130]. Much of our perception and application of categories is through reference to concrete examples and unstated and incomplete patterns that are imputed from them. A range of imputations are possible, not just one; and they further evolve in use and as new examples arise. The evolution is aided by their remaining partly implicit.

Attempts to enforce ideally precise definitions will rapidly fail, because they can neither capture present-day nuances nor anticipate all future demands. A new term in a specialist field can be free of connotations, and so it has a temporary apparent perfection of definition. But, once it is put to use, it soon 'develops a life of its own', even in mathematics [ibid.: 131]. The history of its applications colours the inevitable gaps left by its defining conditions and criteria, and in effect modifies them.

This incompleteness of definition is also called 'open texture'.[5] Incomplete definitions still have important content, for they exclude many things; this is the contrast theory of meaning [Scriven, 1976].[6] We instead refine a definition only as far as is required to establish a relevant difference in a particular use-situation. Openness is of course a matter of degree, and is usually greater for generalised and abstracted theoretical concepts.

One can illustrate these points for many a focus of discussion: 'ownership', 'socialism', 'class', 'equality', 'co-operatives', 'development', and so on. Commonly such terms span multi-dimensional activities or entities, for which general labels will be 'loose concepts' [Kamarck, 1983], that is, implicitly weighted indexes which aggregate and simplify and are unlikely to support strong behavioural generalisations. For example production systems usually involve numerous activities and inputs, for each of which the ownership, management and operation may then each in turn be private or collective (of various types); we thus need more than the two aggregate categories 'private' and 'collective'.[7] Connolly [1993] speaks similarly of 'cluster concepts'. The notion figures crucially in his theory of political discourse, which we will look at in a moment.

In administration and law, ordinary terms are given more restricted meanings in order to reduce their openness of definition [*Brennan, 1977: 96ff*]. In contrast, proverbs in unrestricted everyday language, and many political declarations, trade on the gnomic force of brevity. For short statements can be read with whatever contextual conditions, refinements or qualifications one likes or finds convenient. Precision of language should not, however, be judged according to an unattainable perfection, but by reference to what is needed in a particular context. Ability to make such judgements is the mark of expertise in a situation. Proverbs are often on the surface mutually contradictory, but this need not make them false or vacuous. It is worth saying both 'look before you leap' and 'he who hesitates is lost', if there are not too infrequent circumstances where there is real danger of leaping too soon, and others with real danger of hesitating too long. Proverbs can thus have value as pitfall markers. They can have negative value if treated as laws; for example, the adages seen in traditional theories of planning and administration – 'Coordinate! Collect information! Clearly specify objectives!' and so on – which have been systematically criticised by Simon [*1976*] and Caiden and Wildavsky [*1980*].

Following Gallie [*1956*], Connolly holds that many central political terms, such as 'interests', 'freedom', or 'politics' itself, are 'essentially contestable'. Conflicting interpretations of them exist which reflect differences on many matters, which (probably) cannot fully be rationally resolved in practice and for the foreseeable future. Contributory elements include the following. (i) The terms concern cluster concepts whose various criteria are numerous and partly in dispute. (ii) These criteria use other concepts of which some are themselves essentially contestable; for example, many definitions of 'freedom' use the concept of 'constraint' [*Connolly, 1993: 166*]; definitions of 'development' may refer to 'opportunities', 'needs', 'autonomy' and so on. (iii) The disputes on meaning reflect not only factual and theoretical differences that are in principle resolvable one day, but also less tractable matters such as the conception of human agents. Thus the contestability of the concepts reflects the disputability of many basic political issues. Debate over the concepts is part of politics and is, in part, political [*ibid.: 39–40*].

Connolly suggests these central political terms are typically also partly descriptive and partly evaluative in character; or, better put (given that all descriptions are from some viewpoint), many of them describe from a moral viewpoint [*1993: 39, 222ff*]. Their evaluative content cannot be excluded: there is no necessary-and-sufficient set of neutrally descriptive criteria to determine correct use, because evaluation is part of the very point of such a concept (for example, the concept of freedom, or of what is in an agent's 'interest'). Without the evaluative point or purpose of the concept, one could not say which neutrally descriptive criteria were relevant, nor apply it sensibly in new cases. These cases have typically unique features and may raise issues that the concept's definition does not cover, and which therefore require intelligent judgement in light of the evaluative purpose of the concept. However, the nature and implications of the evaluative content are themselves partly in dispute. The concepts are thus truly essentially contested.

'Development' of societies is an essentially contested cluster concept, employing a metaphor derived from biology in particular. In attempting judgements about overall change or overall improvement, not of single organisms but of organisations or entire societies, the problem of subsuming multiple competing trends typically becomes severe. Compared to biology or child development or kindred fields, in development studies any obfuscation of descriptive and evaluative usages of 'development' is more problematic, for the very values involved in judgements of improvement are disputed more, not just their relative weights.

Connolly has given us an account of political concepts which presents simultaneously the scope and limits to political discourse. The theory is not about limits only, and cannot be read as justifying one in whatever political conclusion one likes. It asserts partial not unlimited contestability (otherwise, why would the theory itself have weight?), and not a Foucauldian conclusion of the primacy of power [*Connolly, 1993: Ch.6*]. For understanding essentially contested political concepts in full-blooded daily use, Connolly advises that we cannot satisfactorily divide them into descriptive and evaluative versions. To do so would miss the point of how people actually conceive and use these notions. But it does not mean that distinguishing descriptive and evaluative versions cannot help in clarifying ideas about major terms in policy discourse – such as 'development', 'needs', 'entitlements', 'decentralisation', and more[8] – and in identifying some pitfalls and confusions in argumentation, as we see in the following section.

III. ESSENTIALISM IN TALKING ABOUT POLICY-MEANS AND
     POLICY-ENDS

Performative Essentialism

Commonly and naturally enough, some of a concept's conditions, criteria or connotations can be behavioural/performance features. Some concepts *are* behavioural (for example, 'an energetic man'). Yet behaviour is much more contingent than are, say, material attributes (for example, a person's eye colour). When talking of policy-means we especially wish to avoid performance features in their definitions, as these could become prejudgments of actual performance. Yet they may seem a normal part of everyday language; for example, if a co-operative is not functioning co-operatively, it feels natural to call it 'not a real co-operative', and to view co-operative functioning as part of the core of the term 'co-operative'. But 'co-operatives' would then be defined in such a way that 'co-operatives function co-operatively' holds for all cases, not merely most or some. 'Real' decentralisation of government is similarly supposed to necessarily advance popular participation. An asserted attribute is felt to be an empirical truth and yet is placed beyond empirical test.[9]

A corollary of this is that different groups may assert different behavioural attributes, linked to different definitions. For example, Schumpeter claimed as 'an historical observation [what] to his critics ... seems a childish trick of definition' [*Stretton, 1969: 120*], namely that capitalism tended to generate liberty and peace. In contrast 'Lenin was the first to discover that capitalism "inevitably" caused war' [*A.J.P. Taylor, 1963*].[10] One can similarly note the welter of views on humans' essential nature.

Since behaviour is contingent on many things, it becomes important which contingencies are taken as the universe of observation when making claims of essential or general character. For pet policy-means, favoured tame settings are usually taken. It is then argued that undesirable effects are not *inherent* in the approach, but are only seen in 'distorting' settings; although if we took the range of *actual* settings these might suggest that some undesirable effects are presently *inevitable*. Persuasive descriptions emphasise as 'essential' those potentials of favoured systems which are liked, but for non-favoured systems emphasise those potentials which are disliked. Non-favoured systems get considered in wild settings, or at least in actual settings; here their essence is held to be revealed, unlike that of a pet system (for example, structural adjustment) which is held to be concealed by distorting factors.

Differing views on the impacts of official foreign aid may in the same way reflect views on its settings, specifically views on whether the (recipient) state is essentially promotional or essentially parasitic. For example, Peter Bauer repeatedly attacked the very term 'aid', which 'prejudges the results [and ensures] that there is an automatic case for further and increased aid'. He complained that examples of damage caused by 'aid' are dismissed by reference to the corrections and 'reforms which are always promised' [*Bauer and Yamey, 1981: 2*]. The irony is that Bauer himself shied away from systematic survey of effects, preferring the safe haven of an a priori logic of negative impact: (i) specific results are held to be untraceable because of 'shunting', that is, aid in effect releases domestic resources for purposes other than the donors intended and which cannot be known for sure; but what can be known is (ii) that it channels resources through governments, which are (supposedly) inherently indolent and pernicious as resource-mobilisers and spenders, and 'so' (iii) aid must be deemed pernicious itself.

The tame/wild settings chosen for analysis may even be purely artificial, as in much economic theorising. Since there is an immense range of choice amongst specifications of variables and assumptions, the temptation arises to use those which seem to show the strength of liked systems or weakness of disliked systems, and to call on observations only when convenient to back pre-formed conclusions. Other systems' actual performance is often compared with a preferred system's abstract charms; and the preferred system's actual performance is then assessed only after the other systems have been ruled out on grounds of their a priori 'inherent' defects or their actual imperfect performance.

'Inherent Virtues'

Positive (or negative) valuations can be incorporated into the intuited or declared essence of a policy-means. The valuations tend to be strong: no half measures. Belief in an essential virtuousness may, non-coincidentally, be combined with belief in essential definitions; both stances give reassurance.

It is in order that some concepts are valuative, and that independent/ intrinsic value is attached to particular things. For example, a major but finite value may be placed on freedom of the press in its own right, that is, regardless of its effects; and a limited – even if great – instrumental value may also be attached to it insofar as the freedom helps bring good products. If we go further than that, prescriptive questions become settled in advance of any evidence.[11] Problems arise when valuations are introduced without clarity and limit, and in the conceptualisation of a policy-means. Proclamations of *overriding* value figure in attempts to gain not just reassurance but also resources and privileges.

Sometimes policy-means are given an extreme positive valuation because the goals they represent are felt to be so good or even felt as objectively binding; but sometimes because they are felt to be so effective in advancing accepted goals. This last case, of instrumental worth, will be considered further here.

The notions of 'inherent strengths' and 'inherent weaknesses' combine these performative and valuative essentialisms: entities are held to have inherent behavioural features which are also valued as good or bad. We saw this earlier, in Duelfer's defence of service co-operatives and Bauer's attack on aid-recipient governments. Comparable points arise in assessing planning techniques. Complicated systems of cost-benefit analysis, for example, have various impacts, many of them good, but also some biases towards persons and sectors more suited for manipulation of the categories and procedures involved [*Gasper, 1987*]. Such biases could, in theory, be countered by case-by-case adjustments and supervision. Thus Alan Williams [*1972: 529*] claims that biases are 'not inherent in the method of analysis, but only in the way in which it may be used by some practitioners'. This underplays the scarcity of resources for planning and supervision; thus there are inevitable biases given the constraints that are everywhere current and will long remain in force. I do not argue that cost-benefit is 'on balance' *inherently* bad; only that it *inevitably* has some bad effects, and that, contrary to Williams, it is not inherently and thus always desirable.[12]

If one is to use the language of inherent features one must accept both structural weaknesses and structural strengths, that stem from an approach's particularities. Any feature could be the source of both. Better still would be to see all strengths and weaknesses as conditional: they are manifested in certain circumstances but not others. A feature may on balance be a strength in some circumstances but a weakness in others. Contrary to Duelfer, this conditionality does not imply that failings which are in principle counteractable are not real failings and that they cannot affect the overall ranking of the policy-means. How strong the effect is depends on the likelihood and cost of fulfilling the conditions for achieving strengths while avoiding weaknesses. Overall rankings should reflect these patterns of conditional appropriateness, not an alleged inherent general appropriateness or inappropriateness.

Prescriptive Essentialism; Rural Centres, Cooperatives, and Collectivisation

'Prescriptive essentialism' means to hold that a policy measure is inherently appropriate. I have already implied how common this is, given the fairly natural inclusion of valuative and performance features into concepts, and given also organisations' and professions' needs for self-belief. A weaker variant involves the presumption of appropriateness in broad but unspecified 'normal' circumstances; arguments on those lines are sometimes acceptable, as not too untrue.[13] But something is clearly wrong when policies with very high requirements are considered as in no way inappropriate or flawed, but merely as let down by contingent weaknesses, which somehow exist in an inferior and separate realm from that of the virtuous policy concept.

Illustration 1 – Rondinelli on policies to promote urban centres for agricultural development

> The disappointing results in Kenya and Panama were due largely to problems of implementation and insufficient political commitment to the strategies, rather than to the soundness of the concepts underlying them [*Rondinelli, 1986: 243*].

In Kenya:

> [e]ven critics recognize that the shortcomings of the strategy lie primarily in implementation rather than in the appropriateness of the policies' ... [such a strategy] will require stronger political commitment, new and more serious efforts to coordinate the work of *the dozen or more major ministries and agencies responsible for various aspects of the*

> *programme* and expanded administrative capacity at the local level ...
> [etc. etc.] [*ibid.:244, 245–6*] (emphasis added).

And concerning those implementation problems:

> As in Kenya, [in Panama] *the problems of implementation arose not so much from the concept underlying this approach to regional development as from the complexity of the projects and the inability or unwillingness of national ministries and agencies to coordinate their activities* [*ibid: 250*] (emphasis added).

This is not a manufactured example in a Schafferian text to illustrate excuses and 'escape-hatches' in policy evaluation. It is from an article by the perhaps most published and most influential regional development planning author of the 1970s and 80s. Extremer forms of defensive dissociation from problems experienced are found in the annals of state socialism.

Illustration 2 – Sharing the credit and shifting the blame in collectivisation campaigns

> The thoughts of the Chairman are always correct. If we encounter any problem, any difficulty, it is because we have not followed the instructions of the Chairman closely enough (Lin Biao, cited in Wilson [*1995*]).

One important policy pattern is the unforeseen avalanche, illustrated by collectivisation/communisation/villagisation in the USSR in 1930, China in 1955/56 and 1958, and Tanzania in 1974/75. Programmes originally envisaged to take years raced ahead to fulfil most of their targets within months, that is, in a time span leaving no possibility of serious evaluation and feedback. Apologists rightly note the role of local initiatives here, but not their context. The vanguard centre does not and cannot know exactly what is the situation and what is possible in each locality, but it has some broad picture and wants to lean in a particular direction at a particular time. So it holds up selected examples for emulation and tells local cadres and officials: 'Don't fear to press ahead with policy X'. At the same time it covers itself by also saying 'Follow the mass line'. While the vagueness in instructions is partly unavoidable – for decisions must be made on the spot – it conveniently allows the centre to criticise cadres after they have acted, for having 'misinterpreted' instructions and lapsed into 'commandism' or 'tailism' (whichever suits the centre's convenience). Alternatively, the local cadres will be left sharing the credit for any success, and in second place to the farseeing centre, for they 'only' correctly interpreted its wise instructions [*Frank, 1958/59*].

The centre pays a price too. Local cadres do not know how valid are the centre's examples. Nor may the centre itself, but it needs to have some. Even if the examples are completely true, little may be known about how generalisable they are. Jack Gray [*1974*] was careful for these reasons to call the internally brandished Chinese examples 'myths'. Local cadres no doubt still give some credence to what the centre tells them is possible. They also wish to perform and not be open to the accusations of 'tailism' which others could use against them at this stage of the policy cycle (that is, prior to feedback from experience). The centre can start receiving reports from areas where conditions have proved easier for pressing ahead, plus some optimistically slanted reports; overgeneralise from them; decide it has underestimated mass enthusiasm, and redouble its pressure. Excesses and problems are later held to have 'resulted not so much from senseless directives from bureaucrats at the centre but rather from over-enthusiastic local cadres, many of whom took the prevailing rhetoric ... too literally', that is, literally [*Sklair, 1979: 324*]. The policy is still held to be essentially correct, when divorced from its 'contingent excesses' [*ibid.: 313*].

Belief in the inherent suitability of a policy-means can thus endanger the conduct of assessments in nearly all stages. In framing the assessment there is a tendency to neglect possible alternatives. In specifying objectives there are dangers of the favoured means coming to dominate more general ends, through endorsement of its specific form and traditions. In identifying performance, failures may be disowned (as not involving 'real' cases) and successes adopted, by switching between definitions (as in some defences of economic liberalisation); and successes may be unduly brandished, since success is assumed to be the representative case, found whenever the means is 'given a fair chance'. Next, in explaining performance, including failures, there is selective attention to seeking mitigation for the favoured approach, not for others; and (as we saw in the collectivisation and regional centres cases) a transfer of blame and responsibility to other forces and alleged misfortune. In sum, the danger is of self-reinforcing prejudgements, with criteria applied and evidence selected and interpreted in ways which endorse the initial stance. Such apologetics appear for many a problematic or controversial policy. Our third illustration shows most of these features.

Illustration 3 – Evaluation of Rural Co-operatives

> The absence of the conditions necessary for successful cooperatives was erroneously identified with failures of the cooperatives themselves [International Cooperative Alliance, quoted in (UNRISD [*1975*]).

In an earlier study Apthorpe and I noted the following features of a large body of co-operativist literature: (i) persistent neglect of important alternatives to co-operatives; (ii) a permissive extension of the definition of co-operatives, to include certain alternatives when those were successful; (iii) in contrast, a rigorous exclusion of many officially-established and recognised cooperatives that failed, as not being 'real' cooperatives, the definition of which in practice leans towards exclusion of the possibility of failure; or, whose failure is never their fault, but instead (iv) the fault of absent 'prerequisites' for success; leading to (v) a policy recommendation of 'fulfil the missing prerequisites' [*Apthorpe and Gasper, 1979; 1982*]. To claim that the 'prerequisites' for success were not provided, and that this is no fault of the policy, is one classic overall excuse. The worthy essence of co-operatives thus survives unscathed – but only through an implicit admission of limited powers and relevance, which stands in contrast to talk of inherent strengths and the claims to credit in those cases where the prerequisites were present.

The essentialist style in prescription is thus to call not just for the virtuous policy-means but for provision of its prerequisites for success, with little reference to cost and opportunity-cost. The World Bank [*1981: 131–2*] warns of the syndrome of arguing that 'the policy was good, only its management was bad; so we must provide more and better management' as if management was a non-scarce resource. Yet it argues in similar ways itself regarding structural adjustment.

In one way we can be indulgent; excuses ('anyone can make a mistake') and giving and taking credit are socially and psychologically required. Institutions and people seek to survive and go on. This does not remove the need in some instances to make summative assessments and choices. Policies cannot be judged primarily by their good intentions or supposed inherent worthiness regardless of actual performance. Problems arise when 'fideistic' motives become central, with needs for meaning being heavily expressed through attachments to particular policy-means. Criticism becomes perceived as impugning the essential worthiness of the policy-means and triggers across-the-board defence. There is even danger of disappointments intensifying the attachment, as past sacrifices cry out to be vindicated.

IV. ESSENTIALISM IN TALKING ABOUT DEVELOPMENT DISCOURSE

Essentialism in Labelling: Kitching on Populism and Neo-Populism

We have looked at essentialism in definition and in discourses about policy-means. In this section we extend our attention to representations of whole theoretical and policy positions and even of development discourse in general.

When criticising a particular real discourse a central problem is that the positions to be analysed are themselves not perfectly defined. They are frequently vague, complex and marked by internal tensions. One part seems to say one thing, and another part to say something different.

The tricky thing about reconstructions of any theory cum methodology is that they are unavoidably artificial. The aim is to show and to clarify the basic essentials of a particular view, but this can only be done by abstracting from the many particulars, in the fact the richness of that view. [So] [i]n a way, [Henry Bernstein and Howard Nicholas's] reconstruction of [Gunder] Frank's work is a caricature, but that amounts to saying that ice is cold [*Coppens, 1984: 301*].

The broader the position being characterised – for example, a 'paradigm' or 'orthodoxy' – the greater the difficulties. Some reconstructions are acceptable simplifications; others are unacceptable, such as assertions about the 'basic essentials' of other views which implicitly refer only to 'the bits convenient to my argument' or 'the parts that I have not ignored'. How could Dudley Seers [*1983: 42*] conclude that '[t]he 21st century visions of Herman Kahn and those of the Soviet futurologists are in essence the same'?

Several reviewers identify Peter Bauer as a mis-'labeller' in development economics [*Thirlwall, 1985; Riddell, 1985*], even after making allowances for the problems when attempting his type of broad critique. An arguable position suffers from excess. Similar points apply to Gavin Kitching's [1989] discussion of populism in development studies, in his widely-used and in many ways admirable textbook *Development and Underdevelopment in Historical Perspective.*[14]

Kitching claims that one mainstream in development studies shares a certain '*essential* populist' vision of development [*1989: 179*] (emphasis added). Thus: 'None the less, even when all [the] discontinuities have been recognized … the *essential* populist "vision"', as discerned by him in various thinkers from the 1810s to the 1930s, is still held by leading current developmentalists, including in the International Labour Office (ILO) [*ibid.: 101*] (emphasis added). Claims to know the 'essentials' of others' positions, better than they do themselves, ease his difficulties in fitting ILO, for example, into his neo-populist category. While 'in its recommendations on agriculture as on everything else, the ILO shows firmness about the general objective (maximizing productive employment) with a marked pragmatism about the means to be used' [*1989: 73*]; hey presto, 'despite all these differences we should note that the *essential* vision of development remains unchanged … A world of small enterprise…of small towns and cities arranged in ordered hierarchy … etc.' [*1989: 83*; emphasis added]. In reality ILO advocated *more* small enterprise, *more* emphasis on small towns and so on, than at present, within a *mixed* approach (walking-on-many-legs); but the invaluable word 'essential' – used similarly by Kitching at various points as we shall see – helps one to downgrade those parts of a position that are inconvenient for one's interpretation.

What concerns us here is the method of criticism, rather than whether

Kitching's policy views are better or worse than those he attacks. In his usage the label of populism is a negative evaluation, given for example his judgement that contemporary 'neo-populism' does not work. A semi-pejorative label is then taken and applied according to convenience, with claims to know the 'essentials' of others' views, even if these contradict what the people referred to say themselves (a stratagem favoured also by Bauer).

The earlier thinkers whom Kitching discusses are presented as arguing that material progress 'can come about without large-scale industrialization and urbanization' [*1989: 2*], but instead by small-scale individual enterprise [*1989: 19*] and cooperative marketing. For inter-war 'neo-populism', the proposed '*essential* features' [*1989: 59*; emphasis added] are different: now it was only held that 'large-scale industry ... must be *supplemented* by cooperative rural industrialization' [*loc. cit.*; emphasis added]. Elsewhere Kitching gives a cruder definition: that neo-populism 'opposes all forms of large-scale industrialization' [*1989: 42*]. Defining an easily demolished neo-populism allows Kitching to 'show' that China is not neo-populist, 'so' its areas of success do not in any way support arguments from writers whom he has stipulated as neo-populist.

Kitching claims that 'both populism and neo-populism share an overriding concern with problems of inequality in distribution' [*1989: 99*], a claim made also by Byres [*Kitching, 1989: 92*]. However, the examples that Kitching gives treat this concern as one to be balanced against others, not as overriding. The examples include Nyerere, who is quoted to that very effect [*1989: 70*] – but then disbelieved.

Selective belief is applied to Lipton too. 'I have presented Lipton as an anti-industrialist [*sic*]; though he goes out of his way to deny this' [*Kitching, 1989: 90*]. Similarly, 'Byres simply disbelieves the sincerity of Lipton's protestations'; and Kitching and Byres claim that neo-populist theories have 'vague time horizons' in which industrialisation is reserved for 'some distant future' [*1989: 91*]. It would be more accurate to suggest that Lipton was impressed by the patterns of dramatic industrial and national development on a small-farm basis that have been seen in East Asia, contrary to Kitching's suggestion that 'there is no historical or contemporary example of this combination' [*1989: 136*]. Lipton is one of several authors who argued for a particular sort of path to interdependent industrial-agricultural development.

Kitching repeatedly asserts that Tanzania after 1967 adopted a 'neo-populist' anti-industrialism. The claim is in tension with studies that indicated the presence of disincentive agricultural pricing and a strong weighting to industrial investment through the 1970s [*Ellis, 1980; Bienefeld, 1982; ILO, 1982; Dolman et al., 1984*]. Kitching also attacks neo-populist dissipation of resources across the whole country [*1989: 121*], although he notes elsewhere that 'a very conventional' concentration of much state agricultural investment was resumed from 1974 [*1989: 118*]. He concludes that: 'there is no doubt that overall results have been very disappointing' in Tanzania (p.108). The sources just cited note that economic and social results were in fact substantially better than the African average in the period to 1978, in a country rather poorly placed at independence.[15] It was on the basis of such results that in 1976–8 'decisions were ... taken, which either ignored foreign exchange implications, or considered them on the basis of absurdly favourable assumptions' [*Bienefeld, 1982: 309*], and stepped up import-intensive industrialisation plans while continuing the relative neglect of agricultural production and marketing. The warning from the balance-of-payments and food-supply crisis of 1973–5 was not taken, and Tanzania entered a major crisis initiated by external shocks from 1979.

This picture of an impetuous push for industrialisation is far from Kitching's. He defends his thesis of anti-industrialism by claiming that producer goods industries were neglected, and quotes Plan rhetoric of putting 'particular emphasis' on basic-needs related industries [*1989: 123, 139*]. One should note that these industries included even construction materials, and that few sectors will in practice fail to receive such epithets. The record of the several major 'basic' producer goods projects which were in fact started was very disappointing [*Coulson, 1979; 1982*]. While Kitching quotes Nyerere from 1965, calling for many small factories dispersed around the country rather than a single large factory [*1989: 67*], in industry after industry the studies of investment choices show the selection of the single large factory, often taken 'off-the-shelf' from a foreign supplier. So Kitching's criticism becomes 'not ... simply of an inadequate investment in industry but rather of investment in the wrong sort of industry and of the very inefficient manner in which all Tanzanian industries...are managed and operated' [*1989: 122*] – just the sort of ILO commentary he elsewhere labels neo-populist![16]

Kitching tries to distinguish his position as follows. He claims that ILO and Lipton grasp only the importance of 'static efficiency' not 'dynamic efficiency'; and states of the latter: 'In its most developed form this idea is known as the 'Dobb–Sen' thesis on choice of techniques' [*1989: 138*]. That thesis [*Sen, 1960*] was superseded by more general formulations of investment choice (including by Sen; for example, UNIDO [*1972*]) that were drawn on by ILO (including through Sen's participation – for example, Sen [*1975*]) and others. These formulations do refer to possible future trends, as do market choices and East Asian strategies. The cases made by ILO, Lipton *et al.* clearly go beyond static efficiency.

Without Kitching's 'essential vision' one might not lump together Nyerere with Lipton and the ILO. Kitching's Chapter 4 quotes Nyerere from the 1960s, and summarises his view of Tanzania's future as '*essentially* an agricultural one ... [with] a mass of self-reliant rural villages ... producing and consuming co-operatively, and dependent on agriculture at least for the foreseeable future'

[*1989: 66*]; '*essentially* rural and agricultural' [*1989: 122*; emphases added]. But in practice Nyerere – despite an alleged 'hostility to industrialization … [which] strengthened over time [*1989: 66*] – also supported policies for state farms, large parastatals, including in industry, priority to industrial and infrastructural investment and so on; and this (inexplicitly) is the policy whose record is criticised in Kitching's Chapter 5. So Kitching's characterisation of Nyerere's intentions is outdated or too simple, and/or his assessment of 1970s' Tanzanian policy as having followed Nyerere's 1960s' intentions is wrong. He does later note that 'Nyerere has had … considerable latitude to make state policy … [but less to] have that policy implemented' [*1989: 119*]. For 'policy' one should instead read 'official statements of national ideals'. Nyerere also fails to fit in a populist slot which (as characterised on pages 137 and 175) excludes both an interest in collectivisation of agriculture and a stress on ownership of the means of production as a source of exploitation.[17]

I have queried Kitching's statements on essential features of populism and neo-populism, as too various and inconsistent; and his usage of the terms, including claims as to the essential features of certain authors' ideas, as again inconsistent, both internally and with other evidence. A wish to be emphatic motivates choice of essentialist language; but emphasis could be obtained in other ways and essentialistic usage leads to many difficulties. One does not have to be a defender of all policies of the post-independence elites in Tanzania and similar countries in order to query the swingeing, often somewhat lordly, yet partly inaccurate attacks by Northern *fundis* from both Left and Right (such as *The Economist*). These grandiose attacks have contributed to the present hostility of many in the African intelligentsia towards social scientists from the North.

Kitching wrote his book partly as a text for students. One has to attract their attention, locate issues historically, and make clear that there are contending positions. Can this justify 'cartoon' simplifications? – 'Development for Beginners'. One wants to trigger students to think logically, as well as empirically, creatively, realistically, fairly, broadly – and not just to be stimulated to have, or accept, views, or just stimulated. One can then feel uncomfortable with some 'paradigms in social science' textbooks, while accepting several of them as an advance on the traditional 'mainstream-only' variety. Presentation of contending views can be done without an overly manipulative authorial voice; Corbridge's [*1993*] 'Debt and Development' comes to mind. One can let other authors speak for themselves where possible, and follow a 'Maxim of Presumed Seriousness' [*Klamer and McCloskey, 1989*]. We must presume, until sound evidence contradicts it, that others are serious too, and have thought seriously. To disbelieve authors' own claims of where they stand on major issues may be a way of avoiding the labour of understanding their positions, and is also in the long run probably not effective in 'winning hearts *and* minds'.[18]

Overgeneralisation on Development Discourse? Ferguson on Depoliticisation

James Ferguson's incisive and influential *The Anti-Politics Machine* stipulates development discourse as something distinct from academic discourse on development [*1990: 28*]. Matching the focus of his doctoral research on a foreign-aided project in Lesotho, he treats development discourse as international agency/donor/adviser discourse [*1990: 70–71*]. The book floats some general theses on the basis of this single, somewhat extreme [*1990: 73, 257*] case. The theses deserve both attention and critique.

We should note first that many countries not dominated by aid still use development as a central term; by population these cover most of the South, plus perhaps the former Soviet bloc. And there are in most countries major influences on development discourses other than donors and their organisational convenience. Countries are not passive or discourse-less. If one believes, however, that the ideas, norms, blueprints and personnel determining 'development' come in large part from the North, notably from a few donor organisations, and even set most of whatever unity 'development' has, then one must indeed study those organisations as closely as possible (see the contributions by Gore and Moore in this collection; and Williams and Young [*1994*]).

One of Ferguson's theses concerns agency survival and growth. It holds that development discourse (DD) involves conceptualising recipient countries 'in such a way as to maximize the potential role of "development" agencies' [*1990: 71*]. Would this fit, for example, 1990s' agency and donor discourses in Eastern Europe? Ferguson states the thesis more broadly:

> 'development' discourse typically involves not only special terms, but a distinctive style of reasoning, implicitly (and perhaps unconsciously) reasoning backwards from the necessary conclusions – more 'development' projects are needed – to the premises required to generate those conclusions [*Ferguson, 1990: 259*].

Now, total foreign development aid declined substantially from some major donors in the 1980s, and project aid declined much more and for nearly all donors; the trends continue in the 1990s. This sharp relative decline of project aid does not disprove but raises questions about Ferguson's thesis.

The thesis implies that the forms of development discourse would vary country-by-country, in order to arrive from very different conditions to the above 'necessary conclusions'; for 'the South' is dramatically diverse. As a country-specific corollary, Ferguson posits four components of 'the' DD representation of Lesotho: (1) aboriginal; (2) agricultural; (3) a national economy; and (4) subject to governmentality. He does consider the last two to have universal relevance in DD: ' ... "development" requires a bounded, coherent "national economy", responsive to the principle of "governmentality"' [*1990: 257*]. But like (1) and (2), (3) (a 'national economy') seems demonstrably non-universal, for example in donor discourses of the 1990s which can with open eyes consider Russia, Somalia, the Gaza strip or, indeed, Colombia. And (4) is formulated in such a way – 'the idea that societies, economies, and government bureaucracies respond in a more or less reflexive, straightforward way to policies and plans' [*1990: 194*] – as to be inapplicable in *any* country and unlikely to be assumed in many; not, for example, in Lesotho's neighbours, South Africa and Mozambique. The development discourse that Ferguson identifies for Lesotho is far from universal.

Many projects fail in terms of their stated objectives while being more successful in terms of unstated agendas. Ferguson's second thesis is reminiscent of Bauer: development and aid promote bureaucratic state control, as distinct from development agency goals. He introduces it by criticising 'political economy' writers who leap beyond the evidence to assert that development activities are fully determined by economic or 'objective interests' [*1990: 16*]. Even if actors choose according to their 'interests', events may not further these, due to unforeseen factors and effects, including the agency of others. Ferguson arrives at a version in which development projects diverge from the intentions of planners and donors but in practice further the agendas of national elites who control the state. Projects are instrumental towards 'expanding the exercise of a particular sort of state power while simultaneously exerting a powerful de-politicizing effect' [*1990: 21*]; and 'technical "development" interventions [could be] ... systematically intelligible as part of a two-sided process of depoliticization and expansion of bureaucratic state control' [*1990: 267*]. But we can note that while aid programmes through a recipient State are likely to serve its purposes, aid agencies do not operate only through aid. Aid can be a lever to obtain broader influence over policies, so we can indeed find discourses from international donors which have furthered, not just espoused, reduction of the local State.

Since interests are perceived in large part through ideologies and belief-systems which are discursively constructed then, as Escobar [*1995: 210*] puts it, there cannot be a materialist analysis that is not at the same time an analysis of discourses. Ferguson implies this in a chapter on 'The Bovine Mystique', when deconstructing technocrats' notions concerning why Basotho prefer to acquire cattle.[19] While emphasising for Basotho cattle-owners both ideologies and interests and their interrelation, he seems independently to emphasise interests when discussing the spread of bureaucratic state power, and when deriving development agency ideology (the conceptualisation of Lesotho) from interests (agencies want more projects). Some other authors go deeper in the analysis of the interplay and tensions between interests and ideologies.[20]

Spanning and supporting the two theses mentioned is a third, concerning depoliticisation, stated at first for Lesotho but later posited world-wide [*1990: 256*]. It holds that 'development' discourse represents the depoliticisation of poverty issues, whereby the above two effects (reproduction of development agencies and spread of bureaucratic state power) are effected through a conceptual apparatus which translates a reality of non-technical problems into 'simple, technical problems' for which the 'apolitical, technical, "development"' intervention which "development" agencies are in the business of making' is then seen as appropriate [*1990: 87*]. This translation can involve both highlighting/ignoring selected aspects, and sheer inventing of problems 'solely for the purpose of being able to propose technical solutions to them' [*1990: 88*]. It hides 'extremely sensitive political operations' [*1990: 256*].

What Ferguson adds thus is a forceful extension of the theme of depoliticisation, stimulated by, as he says, a striking though extreme case. Some of his more specific claims or assumptions may be overdone or unsustainable if applied more widely: for example, that DD is non-academic donor-discourse (except if true by definition), presumes a national economy and governmentality, and is always structured around a veiled promotion of development agency activity and of bureaucratic state power. The book is marked by a tension between its single case and a tendency to hint about DD in general. On page 257 it first claims to have 'avoid[ed] making grand or general claims about the way the "development" apparatus functions in other settings' than Lesotho, yet also secondly that 'the exaggeration [his extreme case] produces, if properly interpreted, may be seen not simply as a distortion of the 'typical' case, but as a clarification ...'. The reasons offered – the standardisation and circulation of donor personnel and of donor thought/ideology – would apply at best only to donor-discourse. However, *The Anti-Politics Machine* seems to have filled a need within alternative-development and anti-development discourses (see below), and the qualifying statements to its theses typically disappear when they are summarised elsewhere.[21]

If one is to have a single hammer for 'nailing' development discourse, then depoliticisation does quite well, up to a point. It fits the 'nails' of much donor discourse (as in Mitchell's [*1995*] devastating commentary on USAID) and considerable non-donor discourse too (see Tapscott [*1995*], on discussions within South Africa). But a description such as 'the technocratic depoliticized language of international development' [*Crush, 1995a: xii*] does not fit the language of political conditionality or human rights, or much of the discourse of many donors, notably numerous NGOs. Similarly Mitchell [*1995: 149*] asserts: 'Development is a discourse of rational planning'. Yet in some cases 'it' is instead more a discourse of national salvation, struggle and military-style campaign, in which costs are to be joyously borne rather than rationally weighed; sometimes a 'cargo-cult' discourse; and so on.

No single hammer can do the job. Better put, no single type of tool will suffice, for we do not face only nails. Consider three other contenders; they naturally partly overlap. Moore [*1995: 7*] offers another important focus: 'development discourse will be conceived as an integral part of capitalism's organizers' ongoing attempts to gain and maintain hegemony...all over the world'. Those attempts are not always through depoliticisation. And we must not overlook non-capitalist development discourses. Drinkwater [*1991*] outlines an equally plausible and equally limited claimant, this time of more Habermasian descent: a belief by policy makers and development agencies in their overwhelmingly superior knowledge, justifying their determination and imposition of policy. This better fits Stalinist or Maoist development discourse than does Ferguson's alternative. It also fits much other policy discourse (for example, Thatcherite); and it hardly fits progressive NGO or some Scandinavian donor discourse. Lastly, Kitching, Watts and others get good mileage out of the theme of populism in development discourse which we touched on earlier. Watts [*1993: 267*] speaks of attempts thereby to disguise differences and manufacture a national will; but populism can neither be equated to depoliticisation nor cover all of development discourse.[22]

Reflections on 'The Development Discourse', Anti Development-Discourse and Anti-Development Discourses

> a new revelation from a prophet none other than the discourse of development itself [*Escobar, 1995: 131*].

I suggested at the outset that 'development discourse' (DD) as a field lacks clear boundaries, since development and development studies have none either, and further that the types of discourse in them are not all of one type. We can also see large overlaps not just between DDs and historical and contemporary political discourses, but in addition with administrative discourses [*Hood and Jackson, 1994*], bureaucratic discourse (a variant of the former), donative discourse (Schaffer, cited by Apthorpe [*1986: 387–8*]) and so on, each of which overlaps with the others. Ferguson's donor discourse unsurprisingly matches some other donative discourse, the discourse of institutional givers. Since there is so much that is non-distinctive in DD(s), attempts to define it/them by what is distinctive could become misleading.

For many authors a wish to specify 'the development discourse' or 'the discourse of development' in some singular fashion remains irresistible.[23] They posit a fundamentally, essentially, unified practice and mind-set called 'development', expressed in 'the development discourse'. Authors who draw their approach for identifying this from theorists like Foucault or Schaffer (for example, *Escobar, 1995: 41, 110*] may find it hard to show that such discourse is distinctive, since those theorists claimed wider relevance. The claim, however, is that styles of group categorisation and labelling that are widespread in the modern world take on one special content in 'the' sphere of development.

Arturo Escobar claims to have identified '*the basic* tenets of *the* development discourse', and 'the *basic* set of elements and relations that hold together *the* discourse ... the *basic* system of categories and relations' [*Escobar, 1995: 151, 17*] (emphasis added). Yet unlike Ferguson he does not limit himself to international donor discourse; his work has instead a strong Latin American emphasis. The content of the set of basic tenets, elements, categories and relations is not quite so clear but, for example, 'it must be emphasized that bureaucratic control is an *essential component* of the deployment of development' [*ibid.: 145*] (emphasis added). This 'development' seems then to exclude free-marketeers and important approaches prominent in the 1980s and 1990s. Elsewhere he assures us that: 'although the discourse has gone through a series of structural changes, the architecture of the discursive formation laid down in the period 1945–55 has remained unchanged' [*1995: 42*]. The tree model of intellectual systems here receives steelframe-language: surface switches such as between bureaucratic control and laisser-faire may conceal an unchanging underlying architecture. Porter [*1995: 84*] too sees just 'one modernist project' of development since 1945.

Without denying some of the profound continuities proposed by these and other authors, my concern is that they give to an ideal type of one part of development discourse (often a different ideal type per author) the status of a real description of the whole. Kitching was more modest, claiming only to discern one (populist) mainstream. From pieces rich in other insights, we take two examples of overgeneralisation. Moore [*1995: 2*] holds that: 'Equity, democracy and sustainability have emerged during the last fifty years as *the core triad* of ideological concepts within development discourse'. These terms do demand attention, and re-claiming; but are terms like growth, modernity, independence, liberation, autonomy, and security less 'core'? Next, for Manzo [*1995: 237*] '(t)he idea of the modern West as a model of achievement and the rest of the world as an inferior derivative, remains *integral* to the concept of "development"'. To whom? The Japanese, Chinese or Koreans? Iraqis and Iranians? To Robert Mugabe or Nelson Mandela or Julius Nyerere? Manzo herself talks of the quest for a counter-modernist 'development', no doubt stripped of this supposedly 'integral' feature.[24]

Categorising 'a' type of discourse – 'DD' or 'anti-development discourse' or whatever – has both potential virtues and dangers. The general danger is oversimplification and misrepresentation of complex discursive fields; for example, if one presumes that discourses which have one or some features in common (such as use of the concept 'development') will and even must have all major features in common. We have seen assertions about 'essential' elements of a discourse such that even if the 'essentials' are not avowed by an author, in fact clearly disavowed, they are still attributed to him/her by the commentator as a result of an assigned membership of that stream of discourse. Commentators can also homogenise through expanded use of key terms. In some writing on 'the development discourse', 'development' seems to become on occasion like the dancing Shiva, many but one, omnipresent: 'development can be seen as an apparatus', 'development as a form of story telling' [*Crush, 1995b: 6, 14*], 'Development proceeded by creating "abnormalities" ...', 'Development ... [employed] the premise of the Third World as inferior' [*Escobar, 1995: 41, 54*], and so on.

Moving beyond 'anti development-discourse', which seeks to characterise, explain, criticise, demolish and displace a DD, some writers enter 'anti-development' discourse [*Watts, 1995: 45*], A-DD. Practitioners of A-DD operate a reverse form of the 'beyond criticism' gambit. For them, 'development', in some partly elusive descriptive sense, seems to be presumptively and essentially bad. A-DD deserves attention as a genre in itself, with its own conventional foci and practices, patterns of mutual quoting and endorsement, and stylised 'facts', such as the oft-repeated and questionable claims that 'development', created in the 1940s, has impoverished most people in the South. Such examination requires another occasion. Some A-DD claims 'do not look too different from the totalizing and essentialist visions of the old sort' [*Watts, 1995: 60*].

Crush [*1995b: 22*] explicates the title of his book as follows: 'The power of development is the power to generalize, homogenize, objectify'. Trying to build counter-churches, as perhaps in A-DD, runs the danger of reproducing major features of Rome, such as overgeneralisation itself. Whilst Escobar gives an interesting discussion of cultural hybridisation globally, he seems not to acknowledge that hybridisation has happened to 'development' too. Yet as he notes on his penultimate page: 'If one were to look for an image that describes the production of development knowledge today, one would use not epistemological centers and peripheries but a decentralized network of nodes...' [*Escobar, 1995: 225*]. This diversity of development discourses concerns not only sites of production but also what is produced, how, about what, and to what end.

V. CONCLUDING REMARKS

I suggested that 'development discourse' includes various types of discourse; we have to study many patterns, not a few. A plurality of practices requires a plurality of concepts. A title of 'Essentialisms in and about development discourses' would thus have been more accurate, if perhaps overly fastidious. When should one emphasise diversity and when instead elements of unity, declaring a dominant trend and downgrading the rest as 'exceptions'? Taking essentialisms, overemphatic and often oversimplified conceptualisations, as the common theme here reflects a judgement that work on development policy and development discourse requires more concepts and more careful attention to concepts. The study proceeded with this in four stages: starting with common examples from various fields; next examining underlying difficulties with all concepts and with attempts at essential definitions; then examining a series of abuses in policy discourse; and finally assessing a set of recent descriptions of development discourse.

We began with examples: the frequent positive/normative ambiguity of the term 'development' itself; and the 'beyond criticism' and 'not one of ours' gambits. These and similar manoeuvres can sometimes be valid, but must be treated as warning signs, to be investigated critically. The terms 'basic', 'proper' and 'essentially' likewise all require a second look, and often a third and critical one. We paid particular attention later to assertions about the '(basic) essentials' of others' positions, which at times refer only to 'the bits convenient to my argument'.

In Section II we saw the problematic base of claims of essential content: concepts are not and cannot be totally defined (they have 'open texture'); and they evolve, which provides cover for tacit evolution of positions (see Gasper, in this collection). Many important concepts in social science and political discourse – 'development' no doubt included – are 'loose/cluster concepts'. Related to this, many concepts in political discourse are 'essentially contestable', because of disagreements over their boundaries and the weighting of different recognition criteria, and over the content of their evaluative and appraisive criteria.

Section III noted that some concepts incorporate valuative and performance claims. We saw how these understandable features of everyday language can become sources of pervasive confusion in policy argument, especially when socio-political identities are being sought and defended. Different groups often include different behavioural features in the definition of a policy means/ approach and make different tacit assumptions about settings. A purported essence containing both behavioural features and favourable valuations of them will have an alleged inherent desirability, whose unconditionality provides a focus for commitment. Such prescriptive essentialism – claims that a policy means is inherently appropriate – leads in turn to calls of 'fulfil the prerequisites for success', regardless of costs, alternatives, constraints. Deep problems arise when these fideistic motives become central in policy discourse; new learning is stifled, as we saw for example in cases of authoritarian agricultural collectivisation.

When describing intellectual positions, not single concepts, we face further problems, for the positions are often vague, complex, and inconsistent, especially so for whole schools of thought and practice (Section IV). We took three cases. First, we queried Kitching's statements on 'essential' features of populism and neo-populism in development studies; and criticised his usage of the terms, including claims as to the 'essential' features of certain authors' ideas. Second, we outlined Ferguson's forceful statement of tendencies to depoliticisation in development discourse, stimulated by a Lesotho case. We saw that some of his more specific claims or assumptions can be overdone or unsustainable if applied more widely. If one is to have a single theme for capturing development discourse, then depoliticisation does well up to a point; but it fails to fit language on, for example, political conditionality or human rights, or much of the discourse of many donors. No single theme can capture the territory, as we saw too for a few other contenders. Third, for various authors a wish to specify 'the development discourse' in a singular fashion remains irresistible. Without denying some of the profound continuities they suggest, I argued that they give to an ideal type (often a different one per author) of one part of development discourse the status of a real description of the whole. While recent work on 'development discourse' has been stimulating, often fruitful, sometimes even revelatory, it would benefit from less concern to find a single stylish hammer that will deal with development discourse in just one blow.

NOTES

1. Duelfer's study was the main background document for the 1972 FAO Rome conference on co-operatives and development.
2. Thus for the 1950s Porter equates 'development practitioners' and 'technical assistance experts' [*1995: 75*].
3. The Collins English Dictionary gives these meanings. (A) Essence: 1. the characteristic or intrinsic feature of a thing, which determines its identity; fundamental nature. 2. the most distinctive element of a thing. 3. a perfect or complete form of something; for example, he was the essence of gentility. 4. [Phily.] The unchanging inward nature of something as opposed to its attributes and existence. 5. [Theol.] an immaterial or spiritual entity. (B) Essential: 1. vitally important, absolutely necessary. 2. basic; fundamental. 3. completely realized; absolute; perfect; for example, essential beauty. [4–6. from biology and music]. 7. something fundamental or indispensable.
4. In Lacey's [*1976*] words, whereas nominalism at most asserts the existence of nominal essences – complete stipulations of a term's meaning, as for the newly created term – essentialism asserts real essences, holding that only one of the possible stipulations is correct and reflects reality.
5. Brennan defines 'open texture' as the inability to state necessary and sufficient conditions for use [*1977: 104*]. The phrase was introduced by Waismann in the 1940s. 'It is not, he explained [for reasons similar to the contrast theory of meaning] to be confused with vagueness, being rather the possibility of vagueness. It characterizes most though not all empirical concepts. Take any material object statement. [For the] terms which occur in it … we cannot foresee completely all possible conditions in which they are used …' [*Pan, 1979: 238*].
6. To deny perfection of definition is not to assert a universal sameness. That would be the 'no bald men fallacy': that if all agree that a man with x hairs is not bald, then surely a man with (x – 1) hairs is also not bald; and so on, until 'surely' a bald man is not bald. Instead we operate with a

meaningful if fuzzy contrast between baldness and non-baldness.

7. See Rae et al. [*1981*] on the many dimensions of equality; Apthorpe and Gasper [*1982*] on definitions of 'co-operatives'; Blecher [*1985*] on production systems; and Wiles [*1977*] on property. We must go beyond 'the Victorian and Marxist [and Nozickian] oversimplification that ownership is an unambiguous, all-embracing, absolute power to dispose of something'; it is 'on the contrary ... a bundle of particular rights' which may be dispersed between many persons and institutions [*Wiles, 1977: 35*].

8. On decentralisation see Ferguson [*1990: 205, 225*], Gasper [*1991*], Slater [*1989*] and a special section in *Development and Change*, July 1990; on entitlements see Gasper [*1993a*]; on needs see Gasper [*1996*].

9. This syndrome involves definition of means in such a way as to be beyond criticism. A related syndrome is to impute ends from the specified means. A third type is imputation of ends from outcomes. A fourth, weaker, prejudgement is imputation of ends from one's approach more generally. 'Empirical tests are not very relevant, anyway, because the objectives ... are derived from the theories', claimed the late Dudley Seers [*1983: 33*]; but one can still be assessed by those objectives. Besides such prejudgements there are other types of bias, for example, from particular techniques; and other types of failing besides bias, like random inaccuracies.

10. Taylor continued: '[Lenin] discovered this only when the First World War was already being fought. Of course he was right. Since every great state was capitalist in 1914, capitalism obviously "caused" the First World War – but just as obviously it had "caused" the previous generation of peace'. Stretton [*1969*] and Apthorpe and Gasper [*1979*] analyse Schumpeter's contortions to defend ('true') capitalism against claims of any undesirable behavioural tendencies. The latter article further analyses concepts of essentialism. See also the literature summarised in Booth [*1993*] that has criticised essentialistic analyses by some Marxists and neo-Marxists of supposedly inexorable trends of capitalist systems, and their use of over-aggregated categories.

11. Consider the following. 'The censored press remains bad, even if it brings forth good products, for these products are good only insofar as they represent the free press within the censored press ... The free press remains good, even if it brings forth bad products, for these products are apostates from the character of the free press' (Marx, quoted by Kamenka [*1962: 27*]).

12. Williams partly defends cost-benefit analysis in terms of its good intentions rather than its practice. His adoption bid for Wildavskyian policy analysis thus claims it is just 'cost-benefit analysis writ large' [*1972: 533*]. Fromm [*1957*] and Schumacher [*1977*] comment on a possible narcissism in assessing oneself by different standards (one's good intentions, which may justify one's resort to any means) than one applies to most others (whom one judges by their actions). Enemies can even be judged by what one presumes are their bad intentions, and their good actions be seen as devilish deception.

13. Henderson [*1985*] resisted this when discussing essentialism in economic policy. For him, the variety of 'policy soap operatics' that he calls 'essentialism' is the presumption that some industries – 'clear to any experienced person' – are essential; these are typically 'basic' industries, for example, energy. While he is rightly sceptical of such a simple investment criterion, there is a serious though not overriding case for national autarchy in such industries, in an uncertain, often conflict-ridden, world.

14. The 1982 and 1989 editions are identical for the sections I discuss; the second edition adds a postscript. See Foster-Carter [*1985*] for another comment on the looseness of Kitching's use of 'populism'.

15. Kitching [*1989: 189*] argues that pre-1979 Tanzanian data exaggerate. Was this more than in other countries? And the main issue here is not how well 1970s' Tanzanian policies performed, but whether they were anti-industry; the answer is not.

16. See Kitching's Chapter 4 on ILO's 'sophisticated critique of large-scale capital-intensive industrialization as this has occurred ... in developing countries' [*1989: 82*].

17. Kitching finds it 'significant that [Nyerere's 1960s'] discussion of nationalisation and of peasant co-operatives occurs in the context of distribution, not production' [*1990: 70*]. Tanzania in the 60s had little manufacturing to speak of, but the existing agricultural estates were subjected to nationalisation and production co-operatives were officially promoted in a later phase.

18. Gavin Kitching has expounded his approach as follows (personal communication). Introductory

textbooks must in the first place generate reader interest. Where possible they should do this by: having a clear narrative or plot line; treating different topics in relation to a unifying theme, such as the critique of 'populism'; and deliberately adopting a somewhat simplified and coloured manner of presenting arguments, with the novice student invited to choose between mutually exclusive alternatives, not to synthesise, and with the author's own views to the fore. Checking on the meaning of terms and their consistent usage, on the accuracy of the alternatives presented, and so on, can be left to a later stage of learning, after students have first become involved in the subject-matter by a vividly judgemental intellectual saga. The degree of precision appropriate in characterising intellectual positions depends on context and audience; so if some students have absorbed *and* been favourably impressed by a caricature version of Lipton, the author's task is to make an effective counter-attack, which given the level of the audience must itself inevitably remain somewhat of a caricature. I differ on a number of points, and perhaps also on what is the acceptable level of simplification. First, can one only involve students through an emphatically judgemental presentation? I suggest not. Second, one should comment on both the caricature of Lipton *and* his own views, and distinguish them; otherwise transactions become 'crossed'. Third, what does one primarily want students to learn? – an approved view, or a sensitivity to different views and to logic and evidence? I would stress the latter. Finally, is advocacy via major simplifications an effective long-term way of advancing a viewpoint, in contexts where people have access to counter-evidence and counter-presentations for other viewpoints? Again I would suggest not.

19. ' ... cultural rules structuring property can never be accounted for by appealing to individuals and their rationality (or their "values"), for individual choices only occur within and in terms of a cultural order which is invisible to utilitarian theory (cf. Sahlins 1976)' [*Ferguson, 1990: 137*].

20. Similar comments may apply to Moore [*1995*]. Like Ferguson he separates development agency discourse and academic development discourse, but (i) gives better labels (development agency discourse and academic development discourse respectively), rather than defining development discourse as agency discourse, and (ii) examines their interrelation. However, his diagrammatic model [*ibid.: 12*] excludes non-agency, non-academic, discourse; and presents academic discourse as mainly acted on by agency discourse, much more than vice versa, and not directly acted on by nor influencing social realities beyond the agencies.

21. For example, 'James Ferguson (1990) has shown that the construction in development literature of Third World societies as less developed countries – similar to the WB mission's construction of Colombia as underdeveloped in 1949 – is an essential feature of the development apparatus' [*Escobar, 1995: 47*], though Ferguson only examined Lesotho. Escobar also accepts the second thesis, on development projects' unforeseen 'instrument-effect' of 'governmentalizing social life' [*1995: 146*], and tries to repeat the analysis for Colombia, but with limited evidence.

22. I have sketched elsewhere a discursive field of 'development studies as a frequently moralizing generalizing policy discipline', including nine or ten loosely articulated tendencies, not a single fixed package [*Gasper, 1993b: 5*]; that picture too simplifies and is incomplete.

23. For a few examples of the use of these phrases, see Sachs [*1992: 4*]; Mitchell [*1995: 150, 156*]; Shrestha [*1995: 266*]; Escobar [*1995: 12, 154–6, 213–4*].

24. The corresponding definition of 'integral' is 'being an essential part (of); intrinsic (to)' [*Collins Dictionary*].

REFERENCES

Apthorpe, R., 1986, 'Development Policy Discourse', *Public Administration and Development*, Vol.6, No.4, pp.377–89.

Apthorpe, R. and D. Gasper, 1979, 'Public Policy, Meta-Evaluation and Essentialism', *Occasional Paper No.75*, Institute of Social Studies, The Hague.

Apthorpe, R. and D. Gasper, 1982, 'Policy Evaluation and Meta-Evaluation: The Case of Rural Cooperatives', *World Development*, Vol.10, No.8, pp.651–69.

Bauer, P. and B. Yamey, 1981, 'The Political Economy of Foreign Aid', *Lloyds Bank Review*, Oct., pp.1–14.

Bienefeld, M., 1982, 'Tanzania: Model or Anti-Model?', in M. Bienefeld and M. Godfrey (eds.), *The*

Struggle for Development, Chichester: Wiley, pp.293–332.

Blecher, M., 1985, 'Inequality and Socialism in Rural China', *World Development*, Vol.13, No.1, pp.115–21.

Booth, D., 1993, 'Development Research: From Impasse to a New Agenda', in F. Schuurman (ed.), *Beyond the Impasse – New Directions in Development Theory*, London: Zed, pp.49-76.

Brennan, J.M., 1977, *The Open Texture of Moral Concepts*, London: Macmillan.

Caiden, N. and A. Wildavsky, 1980, *Planning and Budgeting in Poor Countries*, New Brunswick, NJ: Transaction Books.

Connolly, W.E., 1993, *The Terms of Political Discourse*, 3rd Edition, Oxford: Blackwell.

Coppens, H., 1984, 'Frank's Crisis', *Development and Change*, Vol.15, No.2, pp.301–18.

Corbridge, S., 1993, *Debt and Development*, Oxford: Blackwell.

Coulson, A., 1982, *Tanzania: A Political Economy*, Oxford: Oxford University Press.

Coulson, A. (ed.), 1979, *African Socialism in Practice*, Nottingham: Spokesman.

Crush, J., 1995a, 'Preface', in Crush (ed.) [*1995:* xi–xiv].

Crush, J., 1995b, 'Introduction: Imaging Development', in Crush (ed.) [*1995: 1–23*].

Crush, J. (ed.), 1995, *Power of Development*, London: Routledge.

Dolman, A. *et al.*, 1984, *Development Strategy and Transformation in Tanzania*, The Hague: RIO Foundation.

Drinkwater, M., 1991, *The State and Agrarian Change in Zimbabwe*, London: Macmillan.

Duelfer, E., 1974, *The Operational Efficiency of Agricultural Cooperatives*, Rome: FAO.

Ellis, F., 1980, 'Agricultural Pricing Policy in Tanzania 1970-1979', Economic Research Bureau, University of Dar es Salaam.

Escobar, A., 1995, *Encountering Development*, Princeton, NJ: Princeton University Press.

Ferguson, J., 1990, *The Anti-Politics Machine: 'Development', Depoliticization and Bureaucratic Power in Lesotho*, Cambridge: Cambridge University Press.

Fischer, F., 1990, *Technocracy and the Politics of Expertise*, Newbury Park, CA: Sage.

Foster-Carter, A., 1985, Book review, *Journal of Development Studies*, Vol.21, No.2, pp.294–6.

Frank, A.G., 1958/59, 'Goal Ambiguity and Conflicting Standards', *Human Organization*, Vol.17, No.4, Winter.

Fromm, Erich, 1957, *The Art Of Loving*, London: Allen & Unwin.

Gallie, W., 1956, 'Essentially Contested Concepts', *Proceedings of the Aristotelian Society*, Vol.56.

Gasper, D., 1987, 'Motivations and Manipulations: Some Practices of Project Appraisal and Evaluation', *Manchester Papers on Development*, Vol.3, No.1, pp.24–70.

Gasper, D., 1991, 'Decentralization of Planning and Administration in Zimbabwe – International Perspectives and 1980s Experiences', in *The Limits of Decentralization in Zimbabwe*, Institute of Social Studies, The Hague, pp.7–50, and *Working Paper No. 64*, Institute of Social Studies, The Hague.

Gasper, D., 1993a, 'Entitlements Analysis – Relating Concepts and Contexts', *Development and Change*, Vol.24, No.4, pp.679–718.

Gasper, D., 1993b, 'Policy Analysis and Evaluation – An Agenda for Education and Research', *Working Paper No.140*, Institute of Social Studies, The Hague.

Gasper, D., 1996, 'Needs and Basic Needs', *Working Paper* No.210, Institute of Social Studies, The Hague, and forthcoming in G. Koehler *et al.* (eds.), *Questioning Development*, Marburg: Metropolis Verlag.

Gray, J., 1974, 'Mao's Strategy for the Collectivization of Chinese Agriculture', in E. de Kadt and G. Williams (eds.), *Sociology and Development*, London: Tavistock, pp.39–65.

Henderson, P.D., 1985, *Innocence and Design*, Oxford: Blackwell.

Hood, C. and M. Jackson, 1994, 'Keys for Locks in Administrative Argument', *Administration and Society*, Vol.25, No.4, pp.467–88.

ILO, 1982, *Tanzania: Basic Needs in Danger*, Geneva: International Labour Office.

Kamarck, A.M., 1983, *Economics and the Real World*, Oxford: Blackwell.

Kamenka, E., 1962, *The Ethical Foundations of Marxism*, London: Routledge & Kegan Paul.

Kitching, G., 1989, *Development and Underdevelopment in Historical Perspective*, London: Routledge (2nd Edition); London: Methuen (1st Edition, 1982).

Klamer, A. and D. McCloskey, 1989, 'The Rhetoric of Disagreement', *Rethinking Marxism*, Vol.2, No.3, pp.140–61.

Lacey, A. R., 1976, *A Dictionary of Philosophy*, London: Routledge & Kegan Paul.

Manzo, K., 1995, 'Black Consciousness and the Quest for a Counter-Modernist Development', in Crush (ed.) [*1995: 228–52*].

Mitchell, T., 1995, 'The Object of Development - America's Egypt', in Crush (ed.) [*1995: 129–57*].

Moore, D., 1995, 'Development Discourse as Hegemony', in D. Moore and G. Schmitz (eds.), *Debating Development Discourse*, London: Macmillan, pp.1-53.

Pan, 1979, *Pan Dictionary of Philosophy*, London: Pan.

Porter, D., 1995, 'Scenes from Childhood – the homesickness of development discourses', in Crush (ed.) [*1995: 63–86*].

Rae, D. *et al.*, 1981, *Equalities*, Cambridge, MA: Harvard University Press.

Riddell, R., 1985, 'Bauer on Aid', *Development Policy Review*, Vol.3, No.1, pp.103–8.

Rondinelli, D., 1986, 'The Urban Transition and Agricultural Development', *Development and Change*, Vol.17, No.2, pp.231–63.

Sachs, W. (ed.), 1992, *The Development Dictionary*, London: Zed.

Sahlins, M., 1976, *Culture and Practical Reason*, Chicago, IL: University of Chicago Press.

Schumacher, E., 1977, *A Guide for the Perplexed*, London: Sphere.

Scriven, M., 1976, *Reasoning*, New York: McGraw-Hill.

Seers, D., 1983, *The Political Economy of Nationalism*, Oxford: Oxford University Press.

Sen, A., 1960, *Choice of Techniques*, Oxford: Blackwell.

Sen, A., 1975, *Employment, Technology and Development*, Oxford: Oxford University Press.

Shrestha, N., 1995, 'Becoming a Development Category', in J. Crush (ed.), *op.cit.*, pp.266–77.

Simon, H., 1976, *Administrative Behaviour*, 3rd edition, New York: Free Press.

Sklair, L., 1979, 'Relations of Production, Productive Forces and the Mass Line in the Formation of the Rural People's Communes in China', *Journal of Peasant Studies*, Vol.6, No.3, pp.311–41.

Slater, D., 1989, 'Territorial Power and the Peripheral State: the Issue of Decentralization', *Development and Change*, Vol.21, No.3, pp.501–31.

Stretton, H., 1969, *The Political Sciences*, London: Routledge & Kegan Paul.

Tapscott, C., 1995, 'Changing Discourses of Development in South Africa', in Crush (ed.) [*1995: 176–9*].

Taylor, A.J.P., 1963, *The Origins of the Second World War*, Harmondsworth: Penguin.

Thirlwall, A., 1985, Book review, *Journal of Development Studies*, pp.479–80.

UNIDO, 1972, *Guidelines for Project Evaluation*, prepared by P. Dasgupta, S. Marglin and A. Sen, Vienna: UNIDO.

UNRISD, 1975, *Rural Institutions and Planned Change*, Vol.VIII, Geneva: UN Research Institute for Social Development.

Watts, M., 1993, 'Development I: Power, Knowledge, Discursive Practice', *Progress in Human Geography*, Vol.17, No.2, pp.257–72.

Watts, M., 1995, '"A New Deal in Emotions" – Theory and Practice and the Crisis of Development', in Crush (ed.) [*1995: 63–86*].

Wiles, P.J., 1977, *Economic Institutions Compared*, Oxford: Blackwell.

Williams, A., 1972, 'Cost-Benefit Analysis: Bastard Science and/or Insidious Poison in the Body Politick?', in R. Haveman and J. Margolis (eds.), *Public Expenditure & Policy Analysis*, 2nd Edition, Chicago, IL: Rand McNally, 1977, pp.519–45.

Williams, D. and T. Young, 1994, 'Governance, the World Bank and Liberal Theory', *Political Studies*, Vol.42, pp.84–100.

Wilson, L., 1995, 'Mao's Pleasure', *London Review of Books*, 5 Oct., pp.15–16.

World Bank, 1981, *Accelerated Development in Sub-Saharan Africa*, Washington, DC: World Bank.